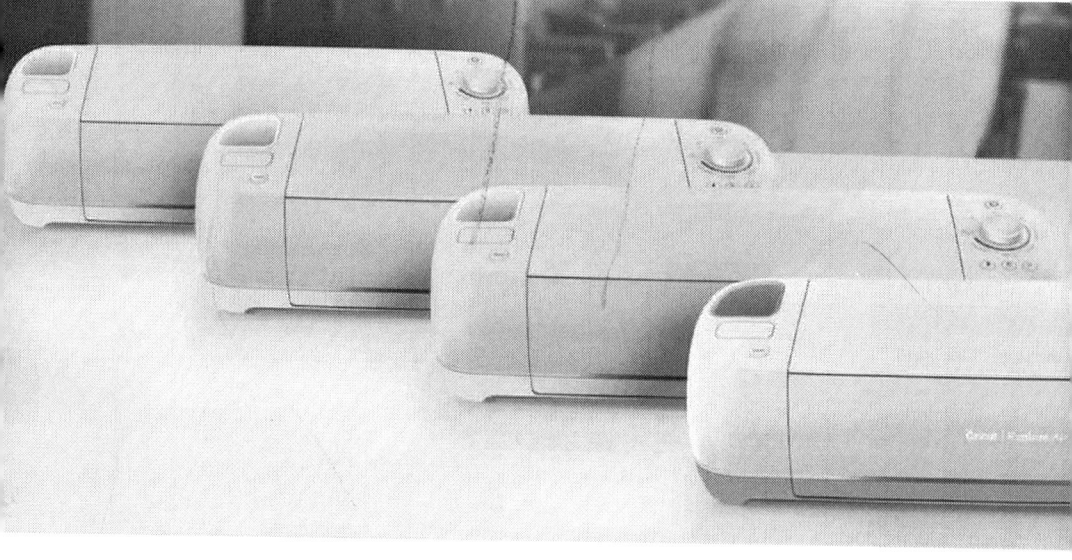

CRICUT

3 BOOKS IN 1:
CRICUT FOR BEGINNERS, DESIGN SPACE, AND PROJECT IDEAS. A STEP-BY-STEP GUIDE TO GET YOU MASTERING ALL THE POTENTIALITIES AND SECRETS OF YOUR MACHINE. INCLUDING PRACTICAL EXAMPLES

Copyright - 2020 -

All rights reserved.

The content contained within this book may not be reproduced, duplicated or transmitted without direct written permission from the author or the publisher.

Under no circumstances will any blame or legal responsibility be held against the publisher, or author, for any damages, reparation, or monetary loss due to the information contained within this book. Either directly or indirectly.

Legal Notice:

This book is copyright protected. This book is only for personal use. You cannot amend, distribute, sell, use, quote or paraphrase any part, or the content within this book, without the consent of the author or publisher.

Disclaimer Notice:

Please note the information contained within this document is for educational and entertainment purposes only. All effort has been executed to present accurate, up to date, and reliable, complete information. No warranties of any kind are declared or implied. Readers acknowledge that the author is not engaging in the rendering of legal, financial, medical or professional advice. The content within this book has been derived from various sources. Please consult a licensed professional before attempting any techniques outlined in this book.

By reading this document, the reader agrees that under no circumstances is the author responsible for any losses, direct or indirect, which are incurred as a result of the use of information contained within this document, including, but not limited to, - errors, omissions, or inaccuracies.

TABLE OF CONTENTS

BOOK 1:
" CRICUT FOR BEGINNERS"

INTRODUCTION 9

CHAPTER - 1
   BASICS OF CRICUT 13

CHAPTER - 2
   UNDERSTANDING THE DESIGN SPACE
   APPLICATION 39

CHAPTER - 3
   CRICUT PROJECTS
   (EASY AND INTERMEDIATE LEVEL) 63

CHAPTER - 4
   CRICUT PROJECTS
   (EXPERT LEVEL) 109

CONCLUSION 167

BOOK 2:
"CRICUT DESIGN SPACE"

INTRODUCTION — 171

CHAPTER - 1
  CHOOSE THE RIGHT MODEL >
  FOR YOU — 183

CHAPTER - 2
  MATERIALS THAT CAN BE
  WORKED ON — 191

USING CRICUT MACHINE — 191

CHAPTER - 3
  TOOL AND ACCESSORIES
  OF CRICUT — 201

CHAPTER - 4
  USE AND CONFIGURATION
  OF CRICUT DESIGN SPACE — 211

CHAPTER - 5
  MACHINE SETUP — 223

CHAPTER - 6
  MAKING YOUR FIRST
  PROJECT IDEAS — 231

CHAPTER - 7
  PDF FILE IN CRICUT DESIGN SPACE — 239

CHAPTER - 8
  TOOLS IN CRICUT DESIGN SPACE — 247

CHAPTER - 9
  HOW TO UPLOAD IMAGE
  WITH A CRICUT MACHINE — 261

CHAPTER - 10
TIPS AND TRICKS TO MAKE
CRICUT EASIER AND EFFICIENT — 267

CHAPTER - 11
BEGINNERS PROJECT TO
START USING CRICUT — 275

CONCLUSION — 283

BOOK 3:
"CRICUT PROJECT IDEAS"

INTRODUCTION — 289

CHAPTER - 1
BEST MATERIALS TO USE WITH <
YOUR CRICUT MACHINE — 299

CHAPTER - 2
WHAT CAN THE CRICUT DO? — 309

CHAPTER - 3
CRICUT PROJECTS — 315

CHAPTER - 4
TIPS AND TECHNIQUES — 323

CHAPTER - 5
TROUBLESHOOTING — 333

CHAPTER - 6
PROJECT AND IDEAS WITH VINYL — 343

CHAPTER - 7
PROJECT AND IDEAS WITH PAPER — 365

CHAPTER - 8
  PROJECT AND IDEAS WITH GLASS   377

CHAPTER - 9
  **CRICUT PROJECTS WITH
  INFUSIBLE INK**   391

CHAPTER - 10
  **UNDERSTANDING CRICUT
  REWARDS**   405

CHAPTER - 11
  CARTRIDGE TECHNIQUES   415

CHAPTER - 12
  **HOW TO MAKE MONEY WITH
  CRICUT**   425

CONCLUSION   435

Pamela Cutter

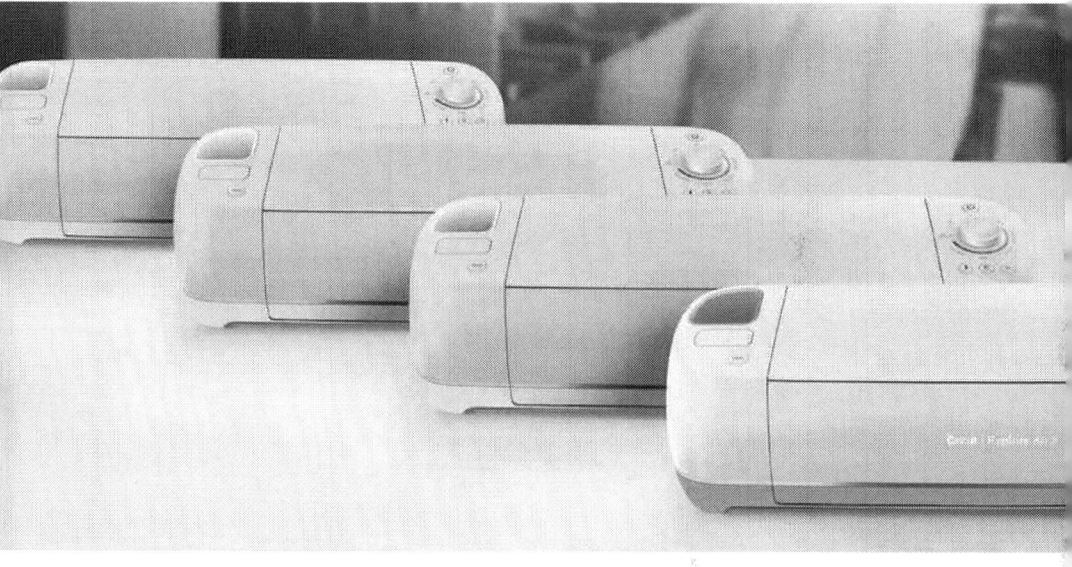

CRICUT FOR BEGINNERS

THE BEST STEP-BY-STEP GUIDE IN 2020 WITH ILLUSTRATED AND DETAILED PRACTICAL EXAMPLES AND PROJECT IDEAS. TIPS AND TRICKS TO DECORATE YOUR SPACES, OBJECTS AND MUCH MORE

Introduction

Congratulations on downloading Cricut for Beginners: The best step-by-step guide in 2020 with illustrated and detailed practical examples and project ideas. Tips and tricks to decorate your spaces, objects and much more and thank you for doing so.

The following chapters will discuss the basic concepts of various "Cricut" machines and how they can be used to create beautiful artwork. In the first chapter of this book, you will learn all about the different kinds of "Cricut" machines that are available in the market today and all their unique features so you can make an informed decision regarding which machine will best meet your craft needs. A detailed explanation of a wide variety of tools and accessories along with their usage will help you decide, whether you need to invest in these tools or not.

In the chapter 2, titled "Understanding the Design Space Application", you will learn all the nuances of the "Design Space" application in a very easy to understand language. The "Design Space" application is an integral part of creating craft projects using the "Cricut" machines and also happens to be the most complicated aspect. The best part of this application is that it is free and easily accessible online. So, you can get started with learning the "Design Space" even before you get your hands on a "Cricut" machine. You will start this chapter with instructions on how to create an account on the official "Cricut" website and get your own "Cricut ID". It will also provide you a detailed overview of the "Design Space" application and all its tools and functionalities. You will learn the how to use the "Edit Bar" to easily make changes to images and texts for your design. The chapter will also help you understand how you can start creating your own projects by making required "Linetype" selection in the "Design Space" application.

In the chapter 3, titled "Cricut Projects (Easy and Intermediate Level)", you will receive step by step instructions on how to create easy and intermediate level projects using paper sheets and for decorating household objects made of glass. You will learn how to create recipe stickers and wedding invitations. The creative use of window cling will completely change how you see out your newly decorated window, be it at your home or inside your car. We all need a pick me up every now and then, so follow the instructions in this book and learn to design your own mirror decoration to help you get out of your morning blues or celebrate a festival. If you are looking to throw a party for your kids or friends, make use of all the party décor projects to create personalized party favor boxes and other memorabilia like treat bags and cake topper.

The final chapter, titled "Cricut Projects (Expert Level), includes a variety of projects that require some enhanced skills and time commitment. You will learn how to use the predefined "Templates" in the "Design Space" application so you can create your design on a background that resembles your actual base material, for example, your own coffee mug. Working with wood can be complicated so we have included intricate details and tips to help you create your wood-based projects with ease and no stress. You will learn how you can use the "Cricut Easy Press" on iron-on vinyl to practically any article of clothing you have. If you are looking to add more personality to your kitchen décor or looking for a gift for a friend, consider creating personalized magnets by uploading pictures of them

Really, you are only limited by your imagination!

As a bonus, more then 20 different tips and tricks have been added to the final chapter under 3 different sections, starting with the "Design Space" application, the "Cricut" device, tools and accessories as well as select cutting material and concluding with how you can clean your device to keep it working like new. So, put on your creative hat and start crafting!

There are plenty of books on this subject on the market, thanks again for choosing this one! Every effort was made to ensure it is full of as much useful information as possible, please enjoy!

Chapter - 1
Basics of Cricut

Are you a passionate crafter searching for an easy to use and highly versatile instrument to seamlessly bring your craft project ideas to life and purchased your first Cricut machine for that purpose? Or perhaps you got a Cricut machine as a gift on your birthday or as a Christmas present, but have been struggling to get started with your brand-new crafting machine? Or perhaps you saw loads of wonderful craft project pictures on "Pinterest" and thought "How are those complex drawings cut with such exquisite details and perfection?" And most importantly you wondered how you could make such beautiful craft projects of your own? Or perhaps you learned about Cricut from a friend or on some social media and you are wondering "What is Cricut and what can it do for me?" In that case, you have got just the right book to help you get started with Cricut machines and master creation of highly artistic craft project ideas right from the inception of

your idea to its actual manifestation into an artwork.

The "Provo Craft & Novelty, Inc." (also referred to as "Provo Craft") headquartered at Spanish Fork, Utah, launched home die-cutting machinery or cutting plotters to simplify the creation of scrapbooks and a variety of craft projects under the brand name "Cricut". The Cricut machines can be used to cut paper, fabric, vinyl, felt and even fondant icing for cakes and baked goods. Cricut is the leading electronic die cutters heavily utilized by paper craftsmen, greeting card manufacturers and scrapbook makers.

The first Cricut machine to hit the market comprised of 6 by 12 inches cutting sheets, while the bigger "Cricut Expression" machine supported cutting sheets of 12 by 12 inches and 12 by 24 inches. The biggest Cricut machine was able to create letters ranging from as small as 0.5 inches to as high as 23.5 inches. To use the "Cricut" and "Cricut Expression" machine you would require matting and blades that could be modified to allow cutting through different kinds of paper, fabric, vinyl, and several other sheet products. The "Cricut personal paper cutter" was designed like a desktop printer and operated as a simple paper cutter on the basis of cutting parameters specified by the user. The "Cricut Cake" could generate cake fondants with desired styles, which could be cut into a variety of shapes using sheets of fondant and were used by chefs and bakers to prepare and adorn cakes for special occasion.

Latest Cricut Machines

The Cricut machines have been upgraded to allow use of a variety of materials and accessories, intended to make "Cricut" as a one stop shop for all your crafting needs and to give life to your artistic ideas. Let's look at the current Cricut models available in the market today and how they can be used to meet your crafting requirements.

Cricut Explore One

The "Cricut Explore One" is a wired model of the Cricut cutting machines with a single tool slot and resembles a printer in appearance. However, rather than printing your patterns on paper, it utilizes an extremely precise blade and a number of rollers arranged in a specific order to cut out almost anything that you can think of. When people hear first about the "Cricut", they assume that it is just a machine targeted toward scrapbook makers. It is capable of cutting beautiful paper shapes and fonts that come loaded on cartridges included with the machine. The "Cricut Explore One" differs from the legacy Cricut machines. You are able to access a huge library of cut files rather than just using the cartridges. It allows you to upload your own images and patterns and edit them to cut desired shapes. Their software can be used on your desktop and tablets in online and offline modes. It is capable of cutting over 100 different types of material. It also enables drawing, scoring and engraving of desired patterns and images.

You can design anything that you would like to cut using their proprietary software called the "Cricut Design Space" (details on how to use this software are provided in the next chapter), put the material on the cutting board, verify your configurations and you are all set.

Cricut Explore Air

The "Cricut Explore Air" is another line of Cricut die-cutting machines and an upgrade to the "Cricut Explore One" machine with a wireless connectivity model. This also has a printer like appearance, which allow you to design your projects on your desktop, and then cut them using high precision blades of the machine. It is capable of cutting through "paper, vinyl, fabric, craft foam, sticker paper, faux leather, among other materials". The "Cricut Explore Air" is capable of cutting up to 12 inches wide using a small precision blade installed in the machine. In reality, you could even use Cricut as a standard printer to print graphics on your chosen material. The device has an accessory slot, which allows you to insert a marker and use the Cricut machine to actually "draw" your design. The "Explore series of Cricut" devices support an enormous digital library of "cartridges" rather than using physical "cartridges". This is ideal to achieve a beautiful handwritten look and perfect for people who are not confident in their artistic handwriting skills. This implies you can add any texts or designs from your personal library using the "Cricut Design Space" and cut them out by simply transferring to the Cricut device.

Cricut Explore Air 2

The "Explore Air 2" was released in early 2017 as an upgrade to the "Explore Air" line, in 3 new exciting colors, namely, "Mint Blue, Rose Anna, Giffin Lilac". The "Explore Air 2" boasts a "fast mode" that is capable of cutting through and writing on card stock, iron-on and vinyl as well as specialty materials such as bonded fabric and cork, at twice the speed as the "Explore Air". However, if you are not under a time constraint you can use the "Precision Mode" to create more intricate cuts with fine details. Needless to say, like all "Cricut" machines this model is super easy to learn even for art beginners and allows you to

Cut, write and score the top 100 materials used in craft projects. You can connect any of your devices like laptop, tablets and phones through Bluetooth, so you don't have to deal with unruly cables. With the "double tool holder", you can easily access your pens and cutting blade. This will allow you to easily switch between cutting the material to quickly decorating it with a written note.

Cricut Maker

On 20 August 2017, the "Cricut Maker" was launched as a brand-new line of products designed for the purpose of cutting thicker materials like "balsa wood, basswood, non-bonded fabric, leather, and felt in just a few clicks. Only "Cricut Maker" offers a distinctive, commercially-developed technology that allows control on the direction of the blade and the cutting pressure that is

best suited for the desired material. Moreover, it has 10 times more cutting energy which will allow you to cut more materials than ever before. "Cricut Maker" has been thoughtfully designed to further simplify and enhance your "DIY" experience and now offers more built-in storage to keep your tools and accessories organized and easily accessible. It is also equipped with a docking port for your mobile devices and tablets, along with a USB port so you can recharge your devices as you use it bring your creativity to life.

The "Cricut Maker" is the first and only device from "Cricut" that can be used with a "Rotary blade" to directly cut fabrics. It is also equipped with a "scoring wheel" that can exert varying pressure to allow scoring of thicker papers. It provides the most diverse variety of tools to cut, score, write and even decorate; so, you can truly bring your dream projects to life. Moreover, the company is looking to add even more tools that can be used with "Cricut Maker" and easily switched to continually support your creative growth. With the versatile housing slot, you can just press the "quick release" button on the device to mount any desired tip and kick start your craft project.

Cricut EasyPress

The "Cricut EasyPress" family is designed to help with your "heat transfer" craft projects, providing even heat distribution from one corner to corner unlike traditional clothing irons. It is also equipped with smart safety functions and easy to control and manage console.

The "dual heating elements and ceramic-coated plate" allow for fast, coherent and ultimate professional dry heat transfer to every corner of the fabric. The "Cricut" website offers an online "Heat Transfer Guide" that allows you to select your "EasyPress" device and then choose the base material or design and type of transfer fabric you are working with to provide you with the "proven time and temperature settings" for all your projects. The "Cricut EasyPress" machines are available in four different dimensions for a broad range of applications – from large and noticeable images to smallest of the text targeted for areas that are hard to reach.

Cricut EasyPress 2

The "Cricut EasyPress 2" is an upgrade to the "Cricut EasyPress" and designed to provide quick, simple and professional quality transfers from baby suits to larger products such as shirts and banners, right from the convenience of your home. ☐

The heat plate design was taken to the next level with a more robust Ceramic-coated surface and two uniquely designed heating elements that are capable of generating heat from border to border for professional looking heat transfers.

With the "Cricut EasyPress 2" you will be able to precisely control the transfer temperature of up to "400°F or 205 °C". You can use their "online heat transfer guide" to simply select the suggested time & temperature settings for your "HTV or Infusible Ink projects". It also boasts advance safety features such as insulated base

which can protect your working surface from heat damage and the auto shut down function that will turn your device off if it is sitting idle for 10 minutes. The "Cricut EasyPress 2" can work in coordination with other "Cricut" cutting devices. So, you can design, cut and transfer desired graphics and pictures using the "Circuit" family devices. ☐

Cricut EasyPress Mini

The "Cricut EasyPress Mini" is another heat press, which is so small that it can easily fit in your pocket but is still packing the power of a regular heat press to allow heat transfer of even the smallest and unique materials. It is only 1.92 inches broad and 3.25 inches high and offers an optimal tip and edge control to position the heat precisely where it is needed. The unique design of the "Cricut EasyPress Mini" with an additional layer of protection on the surface of the plate, which allows you to seamlessly glide on the bases to stick any design. It is also equipped with three different settings for controlled heat transfer. It can easily become your preferred heat press to transfer your creative designed to any base material. As a promise of any "Cricut" device the "EasyPress Mini" also has advance safety features like an insulated safety base which will protect your work area and the auto shut down function that will turn your device off if it is sitting idle for 13 minutes.

Cricut Tools and Accessories

Now that you have learnt about all the "Cricut" machines available in the market today. Let's look at the different tools and accessories that you can use with your machine to turn your creative ideas into reality.

Machine Tools

We will start with the tools that you can mount on your "Cricut" devices to achieve the perfect cut, scoring and writing for a variety of your projects.

1. Deep-Point Blade - The "Cricut Deep-Point Blade" facilitates the effortless cutting of a wider range of products. You can use chipboard to build customized wall calendars, cut personalized stamps using rubber sheets, and even create unique magnets. With this blade, any 1.5mm thick material can be easily cut such as poster boards, heavy cardstock and much more. This blade can be used with the "Cricut Maker" and the "Circuit Explore" line (including the "Explore, Explore One, Explore Air, and Explore Air 2"). It is recommended to be used for these materials:

    "magnet, chipboard, stamp material, thick cardstock, stiffened felt, foam sheets, cardboard". You can buy the "Deep-Point Blade" with the housing for $34.99.

2. Premium Fine-Point Blade - The "Premium Fine-Point Blade" can deliver highly durable precision cutting to ensure your DIY projects are a total win. This high strength blade has been built with German

carbide steel with special design to allow cutting of even the most intricately designed graphics with the "Cricut" machine. It is resistant to regular wear and tear and is capable of cutting through the lightest as well as medium weight materials such as iron-on, vinyl, cardstocks, among others. This blade can also be used with the "Cricut Maker" and the "Circuit Explore" line (including the "Explore, Explore One, Explore Air, and Explore Air 2"). It is recommended to be used for these materials: "faux leather, as iron-on, vinyl, cardstock, poster board". It is also available for purchase with the housing for $34.99.

3. Bonded-Fabric Blade - The "Bonded-Fabric Blade" as the name suggests it is specifically designed to cut through bonded fabric and fabrics with iron-on, by ensuring that the blade is capable of precisely cutting and will stay sharp for long time. It is constructed with premium carbide steel from Germany and is developed to bring your intricately designed graphics to life with the "Cricut Maker". It allows creation of fantastic DIY projects such as personalized applique and sewing projects that will take your fabric crafting skills to the next level. Although this blade can be used with the entire "Circuit Explore" line (including the "Explore, Explore One, Explore Air, and Explore Air 2") and not just the "Cricut Maker". It is also available for purchase with the housing for $34.99.

4. Rotary Blade - The "Rotary Blade" is a uniquely designed sharp blade that can cut exquisite designs from soft textiles for your dream sewing projects much faster and easier than ever before. You will be able to effortlessly cut "silk, cotton, denim, canvas and even burlap". With this blade you will also be able to cut through delicate materials such as crepe paper and create parts to make stunning quilts, plush toys, bags, accessories, decoration, among others. It is recommended that when you start noticing uncut threads or if the material configurations on "Design Space" are not as precise, you should replace your "Rotary Blade" to keep getting high quality results. This blade can only be used with the "Cricut Maker" and doesn't not support the "Circuit Explore" line or any older models. The "Rotary Blade Replacement Kit" is available for purchase at $16.99.

5. Knife Blade - The "Knife Blade" is designed with extra depth to easily and safely cut through thick and dense materials up to "2.4 mm (3/32)". It is good to use, if you are interested in adds dimensions to your project. It can be used for a broad spectrum of practical and artisan materials such as "chipboard, balsa wood, basswood, mat board, craft foam, garment leather and tooled leather". You can easily create "puzzles, models, dinosaur skeletons, dioramas, wood decor, leather goods, toys, and much more". But it is not recommended to cut images or designs that are smaller than 0.75 inches. This blade can only be used with the "Cricut Maker" and doesn't not support the

"Circuit Explore" line or any older models. The "Knife Blade with Drive Housing" is available for purchase at $45.99.

6. Scoring Wheel Tip - The "Scoring Wheel Tip" can be used to transcend creative barriers and create in-depth scoring lines. This tool is designed to help you create professional looking and high finish "tags, cards, and gift boxes" to marvelous" wearable art, 3D home decor and structures" by generating professional level precision on every "crease and fold" project that comes to your mind. You can create crisp creases and perfect folds without struggle, all marked with flawless finish. The patented design of the wheel can effectively work on basic materials while generating 10 times more pressure than the "Scoring Stylus". This blade can only be used with the "Cricut Maker" and doesn't not support the "Circuit Explore" line or any older models. It is available for purchase at $29.99 and "Scoring Wheel Tip with Drive Housing" for $49.99.

Maker Tools

Every craftsman has a distinctive approach to bringing their ideas to life and you may want to supplement your artistic tools by employing one or more of the tools listed below to create stunning projects.

1. Engraving Tip - The "Cricut Engraving Tip" will help you generate customized texts and monograms. You can design ornamental embellishments and flourishes as well as inscribe any famous quote of

your choice on a keepsake. This tip is made with high quality carbide steel that will allow engraving on "Cricut Aluminum Sheets" and anodized aluminum, so you can highlight the silver underneath for a professional looking effect. This tip can be used only with the "Cricut Maker" machine. The "Cricut Engraving Tip" will help you create intricate dog tags with personalized engraving, customized name plates, engraved art and decoration, jewelry, monograms, wood sculptures, and mementos. It is recommended to be used with "aluminum flat, soft metals, leather, acrylic, plastic", among others. You can buy the "Cricut Engraving Tip" for $24.99.

2. Fine Debossing Tip - The "Fine Debossing Tip" (2.0 mm) is the ultimate tool to create elegant paper crafts by incorporating professional finish and elevation to the base material. It will help you achieve crisp debossed designs with fine details. This tip is uniquely designed with a "rolling debossing ball", that will provide you freedom to create customized and personalized designs with exceptional intricacy, unlike standard "embossing folders" available in the market that limit you into a predefined layout. You can easily create dimensional wedding cards, monogrammed thank you notes, or attached flourish to gift box and gift tags, and much more. You can also create an amazing effect on "coated paper, shimmer and glitter paper and foil cardstock". This tip can be used only with the "Cricut Maker" machine. It is recommended to be used with

"cardstock, foil poster board, foil cardstock, foil kraft board, poster board and kraft board". You can buy the "Fine Debossing Tip" for $24.99.

3. Basic Perforation Blade - The "Basic Perforation Blade" is uniquely designed with "2.5 mm teeth and 0.5 mm gaps" to quickly generate smooth tears with accurate and consistent perforation cuts for all your craft projects. For all your perforated design needs this blade will allow you to create models with finely perforated and uniform lines that would eliminate the need for folding the paper prior to tearing it up and is very handy particularly for shapes with curves. You can effortlessly create "tear-out booklet pages, raffle tickets, homemade journals", or any project requiring a tidy tear such as Christmas decorations, paper dolls, tear-away cards or gift coupons, advent calendars, and much more. It is recommended to be used with "fabrics like paper, cardstock, foam, acetate and foil". This blade can be used only with the "Cricut Maker" machine. You can buy the " Basic Perforation Blade " for $29.99, exclusively through "HSN".

4. Wavy Blade - The "Wavy blade" will help you create decorative edges much faster than a drag blade for a broad range of projects with smoothly molded cuts. This uniquely designed blade made from stainless steel is perfect to create "original vinyl decals, iron-on designs, envelopes, cards, gift tags, and collage projects", or when you are looking to add stylish accents with a whimsical wavy edge to your

craft. It is recommended to be used with "iron-on, vinyl, paper, cardstock and fabric". This blade can be used only with the "Cricut Maker" machine. You can buy the "Wavy Blade " for $29.99, exclusively through "HSN".

Pens

"Cricut" offers a range of Pens to help you achieve a flawless and eye-catching handwritten text to create personalized invitations, banners, cards gift tags,

among others. A wide variety of pens are available which can be used with both the "Cricut Maker" and the "Cricut Explore" line, so you can cut and write seamlessly. Most of the pens are "acid free, non-toxic, and permanent" once the text has dried up. Some of the "Cricut Pens" that you can buy are listed below and most of the sets are priced at $12.99.

1. "Cricut Explore Metallic Pen Set" which contains 5 pens, one each in Gold, Silver, Copper, Blue, and Violet.

2. "Fine Point Pen Set, Wisteria" which contains 5 pens of 0.4 tip in Magenta, Tawny, Light Green, Turquoise, and Light Turquoise.

3. "Gel Pen Set, Metallic Dark Petals" which contains 5 medium point (1.0) pens in Dusty Rose, Plum, Green, Black, Silver.

4. "Gel Pen Set, Peacock" which contains 5 fine point (1pt) pens in Aqua, Purple, Dark Gray, Pink, Teal.

5. "Glitter Gel Pen Set, Fiesta" which contains 5 medium point (0.8) pens in Scarlet Red, Dark Brown, Orange, Kelly Green, Tawny.

6. "Glitter Gel Pen Set, Mermaid" which contains 5 medium point (0.8) pens in Plum, Peacock, Dark Rose, Olive, Bordeaux.

7. "Gel Pen Set, Fingerpaint" which contains 5 medium point (1.0) pens in Orange, Lime, Red, Yellow, Blue.

8. "Extra Fine Point Pen Set, Spring Rain" which contains 5 extra-fine point (0.3) pens in Gray, Mint, Raspberry, Peacock, Lilac.

9. "Extra Fine Point Pen Set, Bohemian" which contains 5 extra-fine point (0.3) pens in Raspberry, Teal, Burnt Orange, Plum, Dark Green.

10. "Pen Set, Antiquity" which contains 5 pens in Jade, Wine, Crystal Pink, Gemstone Blue and Midnight.

11. "Variety Pen/Marker Set, Martha Stewart Spring Bouquet" which contains 3 fine point (0.4) pens in Pink Crystal, Cactus Pink, Sage along with 2 medium point (1.0) markers in Gold, Silver.

12. "Extra Fine Point Pen Set, Martha Stewart Gilded Forest" which contains 5 extra fine point (0.3) pens in Dark Green, Black, Dark Blue, Brown, Gray.

13. "Ultimate Fine Point Pen Set" which contains 30 different Fine Point Pens (0.4 tip) in "Black, Red, Blue, Green, Yellow, Sour Apple, Candy Corn, Blueberry, Candy Crystal, Very Berry, Cactus Pink, Bluebonnet,

Lavender, Honeysuckle, Sage, Armadillo, Geode, Indian Red, Adobe Clay, Moccasin, Jade, Gemstone Blue, Wine, Pink Crystal, Coral, Turquoise, Tawny, Light Green, Light Turquoise, and Magenta".

Infusible Ink Pens

The "Infusible Ink Markers" will enable you to create intricate free-hand designs or you can use any of your "Cricut" machines to make customized designs on simple laser copy paper. All the pens are "acid free, water based and ASTM D-4236 compliant". They are available in a multitude of colors and in two-line weights, which upon heat-transfer result into deep, vibrant colors. That will not flake, peel, wrinkle, or crack. These pens can be used with the "Cricut Maker" and the "Cricut Explore" line and require compatible "Infusible Ink blank" and heat press that can reach a temperature of 400°F (205°C). You will be able to draw customized designs and texts for baby bodysuits, T-shirts, bags, coasters, and much more. In contrast to the "iron-on or vinyl" application, in which the drawings need to be plated on a base material with adhesive, the "Infusible Ink" heat transfer is merged into the material itself. Some of the "Infusible Ink" pens available for purchase from "Michaels" for $14.99 include:

1. "Infusible Ink Markers (1.0), Basics" which contains 5 medium point (1.0) markers in Cardinal, Black, Ultraviolet, Tawny, Bright Green.

2. "Infusible Ink Markers (0.4), Basics" which contains 5 fine point (0.4) Infusible Ink™ pens in Cardinal,

Black, Ultraviolet, Tawny, Bright Green.

3. "Infusible Ink Markers (1.0), Neons" which contains 5 medium point (1.0) markers in Neon Pink, Neon Blue, Neon Orange, Neon Yellow, Neon Green.

4. "Infusible Ink Markers (0.4), Neons" which contains 5 fine point (0.4) pens in Neon Pink, Neon Blue, Neon Orange, Neon Yellow, Neon Green.

Craft Tools

"Cricut" also offers a variety of crafting tools such as rulers, fabric shears, seam ripper, thread snips, knives, trimmers, rotary cutter, measuring tape and much more. All the tools are carefully designed to help you take your crafting skills to the next level resulting in professional looking crafts with premium finish. For instance, the "TrueControl Knife Kit" contains five replacement blades along with a storage cartridge to help you monitor and discard the used blades. This knife is designed with razor sharp edge, piercing tip and superior blade lock system" to provide you better control and stunning finishes every time. It can be used to create precision cuts on paper, cardstock, thin plastics, canvas, and various other material. Their "patented hands-free blade changing system" means you can safely change your blades without needing to touch them and accidentally hurting yourself. It also boasts an "anti-roll design" to ensure that the knife will stay in place when not being used along with a padded grip for comfortable handling experience.

Mats

There are 3 different categories of mats offered by "Cricut" that are compatible with different "Cricut" machines and heat presses, as described below:

1. Machine Mats

The "StandardGrip Machine Mat" is 12 x 12 inches and compatible with all the "Circuit" machines". These mats are designed to hold the material firmly in place while you cut through it and then easily remove the material when ready. It is recommended to be used with "cardstock, patterned paper, embossed cardstock, iron-on and vinyl".

They also offer "LightGrip Machine Mat", which is also 12 x 12 inches and specifically designed for adhesion of light weight and delicate materials such as "standard paper, light cardstock and vellum".

Their "StrongGrip Machine Mat" comes in 12 x 24 inches and serves as a sturdy adhesion surface for heavy weight materials including "thick cardstock, glitter cardstock, magnet material, chipboard, poster board and fabric (with stabilizer)". The company claims these mats are their "longest-lasting mat, featuring double-life adhesive technology."

The "FabricGrip Machine Mat" is available in 12 x 12 inches and 12 x 24 inches is designed with high density PVC for extra strength and coated with light adhesive for easy use with various fabrics such as "silk, canvas, burlap, leather and cotton".

2. **Self-Healing Mats** – "Cricut" offers a wide variety of self-healing mats and claims them to be twice more self-healing than their competitors. They are designed with larger numbers on 1" wide border, for easy readability. These mats cannot be used inside the "Cricut" machines. Some of these offerings include, "Decorative Self-Healing Mat, Mint", "Self-Healing Mat, Blue", "Decorative Self-Healing Mat, Lilac" and more.

3. **EasyPress Mats** - The "Cricut EasyPress Mat" is uniquely designed to work with "Cricut EasyPress" for impeccable heat transfer projects. The long-lasting cover offers even thermal conduction and uniform distribution of the heat. The interior liner can easily absorb moisture resulting in clean and dry heat. The foil membrane can reflect heat onto the material, preventing the transfer of moisture vapors while the silicone foam insulates the surface and protects it against heat damage. They come in 3 different sizes, namely, 12 x 12 inches, 20 x 16 inches and 8 x 10 inches and special "Decorative Polka Dot Mats in blue/mint and rose/lilac" in 14 x 14 inches.

Storage

There are 3 different categories of storage bags specifically designed for "Cricut" machines and tools as described below:

1. Machine Totes - These premium storage bags are 26" long, 9.25" wide and 9.25" tall and carefully designed so you can organize and store your "Cricut" machine

at home and easily transport if needed. The bag has side pockets and compartments to allow storage of craft tools and supplies, and comes with a sturdy double-snap handle. These bags have soft padding to provide additional protection and shock absorption. You can buy these bags in different colors (Purple, Navy, Tweed and Raspberry) for $149.99.

2. Rolling Craft Tote – These bags are equipped with rollers for easy portability and storage at home. They are 26" long, 10.25" wide and 14.38" tall but remember these bags are designed to store your craft supplies and will not fit any "Cricut" machines. These bags are also available in different colors (Purple, Navy, Tweed and Raspberry) for $199.99.

3. EasyPress Tote - These bags are specifically designed for storage of "Cricut EasyPress" along with its safety base, mat and other small accessories at home or on the go. They are made from robust and heat-resistant material to protect your device against bumps and scratches while you work through your heat-transfer projects. A convenient shoulder strap and powerful gripped handle will allow for easy carrying around with the Velcro strap to secure your device for travel. A back pocket and front pocket are added to store the mats and iron-on accessories.

Cricut BrightPad

The "Cricut BrightPad" is an electronic crafting pad that looks like a tablet. You can use this to light up your paper designs for easier drawing, tracing, weeding, quilting and lower the strain on your eyes in the process. It is thin, lightweight and sturdy for comfortable use and portability, with 9 x 11.5 inches of uniformly LED lit area and 5 different brightness settings. It is made of "6H Hardness Surface", which makes it highly resistant to scratches. You can use it to weed vinyl or iron-on designs and paper piecing quilt blocks. Bas well as for models, jewelry, needlepoint. You can buy a "Cricut BrightPad" in Rose or Mint color for $79.99.

Cricut Cuttlebug Machine

The "Cricut Cuttlebug" is a machine to cut and emboss a range of different materials. With clean and crisp cuts as well as uniform and deep emboss, for professional quality results. "Criut" also offers an entire line of compatible "Cuttlebug embossing folders and cutting dies", while you can still use other folders and dies that are offered by other leading brands. You can use this machine to not only cut and emboss paper but a variety of other materials including "tissue paper, foils, acetate ribbon and thin leather". You can buy a "Cricut Cuttlebug Machine" in Rose or Mint color for $89.99. A variety of accessories for this material are also offered including cutting spacers and embossing folders.

Materials

There is wide variety of materials that can be used with the "Cricut machines but here is a list of few of them for the "Cricut Explore" line and "Cricut Maker".

Cricut Explore

Paper	Vinyl	Iron – On
Cardstock	Fabric	Poster Board
Adhesive Foil	Aluminum Foil	Birch
Burlap	Canvas	Chalkboard Vinyl
Clear Printable Sticker Paper	Construction Paper	Copy Paper – 20lb
Cork, Adhesive-backed	Corrugated Cardboard	Craft Foam
Cutting Mat Protector	Deluxe Paper	Denim, bonded
Distressed Craft Foam,	Duct Tape	Embossed foil paper
Epoxy Glitter Paper	Faux Leather	Faux Suede
Felt	Foil Acetate	Grocery Bag
Chipboard	Magnetic Sheet	Notebook Paper
Paint Chip	Parchment Paper	Photo Paper
Silk, bonded	Vellum	Washi Sheet
Wax Paper	Wrapping Paper	Glitter Paper

Cricut Maker

Garment Leather	Tooling Leather	Acetate
Adhesive Foil	Adhesive Sheet	Aluminum Foil
Balsa	Bamboo Fabric	Basswood
Bengaline	Birch	Boucle
Broadcloth	Burlap	Burnt-out Velvet
Calico	Cambric	Canvas
Carbon Fiber	Cardstock	Cashmere
Cereal Box	Chalkboard Vinyl	Challis
Chambray	Chantily Lace	Chiffon
Charmeuse Satin	Chintz	Corduroy
Corrugated Paper and Cardboard	Cotton	Crepe Charmeuse
Damask	Tulle	Denim
Duck Cloth	Duct Tape Sheet	Dupiono Silk
EVA Foam	Faille	Faux Fur
Felt	Fleece	Freezer Paper
Gabardine	Gauze	Georgette
Gossamer	Grosgrain	Heather
Jacquard	Jersey	Jute
Khaki	Lame	Linen
Lycra	Magnetic Sheet	Matboard
Matelasse	Matte Vinyl	Melton Wool
Mesh	Microfiber	Moleskin

Monk's Cloth	Mulberry Paper	Muslin
Neoprene	Nylon	Oil Cloth
Organza	Ottoman	Oxford
Paint Chip	Panne Velvet	Pearl Paper
Photo Paper	Plush	Poplin
Quilt Batting	Rayon	Satin silk
Spandex	Tafetta	Tissue Paper
Transfer Sheet	Tulle	Tweed
Velour	Velvet	Viscose
Voile	Waffle Cloth	Washi Sheet
Wax Paper	Window Cling	Wool Crepe
Wrapping Paper	True Brushed Paper	Ziberline

Chapter - 2

Understanding the Design Space Application

Cricut" is poised to become a one stop shop for all your crafting and DIY project ideas. Their "Design Space" application is developed to let the artist inside you flourish into the world of technological advancements. It is a free and easy-to-learn design software that can work with all kinds of "Cricut" devices. It is also a cloud-based application, which allows you to seamlessly access all your design files from any device whenever you need it.

Cricut Design Space" is a companion application that supports designing and cutting with "Cricut Explore" and "Cricut Maker" machines. You will be able to start a project from scratch or choose from a wide variety of images, fonts and ready to print designs of "Make it Now" projects. The software is synchronized across your devices so you can start a project on your mobile phone when the inspiration strikes and pick it right up from your laptop. It also supports the integrated camera on your devices so you can view your designs on real-life backgrounds. You can then wirelessly connect the "Design Space" with your "Cricut Explore" or "Cricut Maker" to easily print and cut your designs.

Here are some of the amazing features offered by "Cricut Design Space":

- Seamlessly design and cut all your crafts with any of the "Cricut Explore" and "Cricut Maker" machines.

- Wide variety of selection from over 50k pictures, fonts and projects through the "Cricut Image Library". And you can also upload your own pictures and fonts absolutely free of any charge to create personalized designs.

- You will also be able to edit and enhance your uploaded pictures to take your projects to the next level.

- This application allows you to download pictures and fonts on your devices so you can continue designing and cutting your project even with no Internet.

- The "Make It Now" projects are carefully crafts so you easily design your ideas and quickly cut the any of the pre-designs, when you are running short on time.

- You can create decorations for holiday and party, cards, wedding invitations, scrapbooks, fashionable accessories and jewelry, personalized crafts for babies and kids, and the list goes on and on.

- By connection with "Cricut" machines, you can easily

cut a range of different materials such as "paper, vinyl, iron-on, cardstock, poster board, fabric and even thicker materials like leather".

- You can create an account on "Cricut" for free and sign in with your "Cricut ID" to work on your fonts, pictures and projects. It would even let's you easily pay for any purchase made on "Cricut.com" or directly within "Design Space".

- The "Cricut" machines and "Design Space" support Bluetooth connectivity so your can wirelessly connect the software with your machines. However, some machine may require "wireless Bluetooth adapter" that you can easily purchase online.

Creating an account on "Cricut.com"

Now that you understand what "Design Space" is and how you can use to create beautiful DIY projects. Let's look at how you can get your own "Cricut ID" to log into the "Design Space" application.

Step #1

On the official "Cricut" site, select "Design" from the top right corner of the screen.

Shop | Design

Step #2

A new window will open, from the bottom of the screen select "Create A Cricut ID".

Step #3

Now, in the window as shown in the picture below, you would need to enter your personal information, such as, first name, last name, email ID and password.

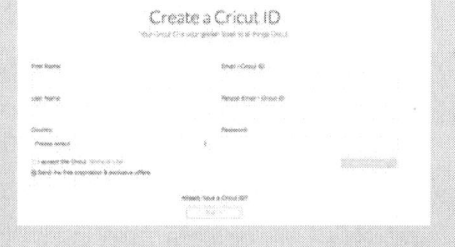

Step #4

You would then need to check the box next to "I accept the Cricut Terms of Use" and click on "Create a Cricut ID".

Step #5

You will be instantly taken to the "Design Space" landing page and a message reading "New! Set your machine mode" will be displayed.

With the steps above you have registered your email address as your new "Cricut ID"!!!!

Now, let's see how you can complete your registration and start using "Design Space".

Step #1

When you log into "Design Space" for the first time, your screen will display the message as shown in the picture below.

> **New! Set your machine mode.**
> This IMPORTANT feature sets up Design Space to match your machine type.
> Let's do it now.

Step #2

Click on "Next" as displayed in the picture above, a blacked-out screen with "Machine" on the top right corner of the screen will be displayed as shown in the picture below.

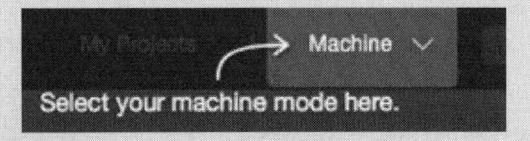

Step #3

Click on "Machine" and the options of the "Cricut" machines will be displayed as shown below.

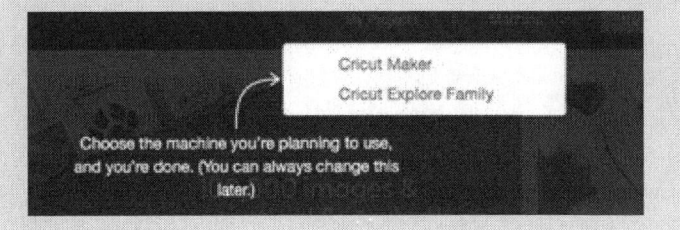

Step #3

You can select your device from the two options. For this example, "Cricut Maker" was selected and upon selection, the next screen will confirm the device you selected, as shown in the picture below.

Remember, if you wish to toggle to the "Cricut Explore", all you have to do is click on the "Maker" and you will see the drop-down option for the two machines again, as shown in the picture below.

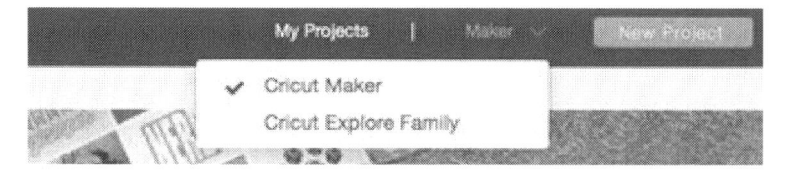

Design Space on Mobile Devices

As mentioned earlier, the "Cricut Design Space" is cloud based and you can pick up your project across various platforms. Here's how you can download the latest version (v 3.18.1) of this application on your mobile devices.

Apple App Store (iOS) – Simply search for "Cricut" on the App store from your iPhone or iPad and select "GET" to begin the download. You can then easily login with your registered "Cricut ID" to continue working on your projects on your phone.

Google Play (Android) – You can search for "Cricut" on the Google Play from your android phone and table. Then select "Install" to begin the download. Once completed use your "Cricut ID" to login and pick up your projects and ideas where you left off.

"Design Space" Canvas

Think on the "Design Space" canvas as your playground where you can turn your ideas into reality. You will be able to create new projects, add images and/or texts to your existing projects and continue editing them until you are happy with the results. So here is an overview of different elements of "Design Space" canvas, as shown in the picture below:

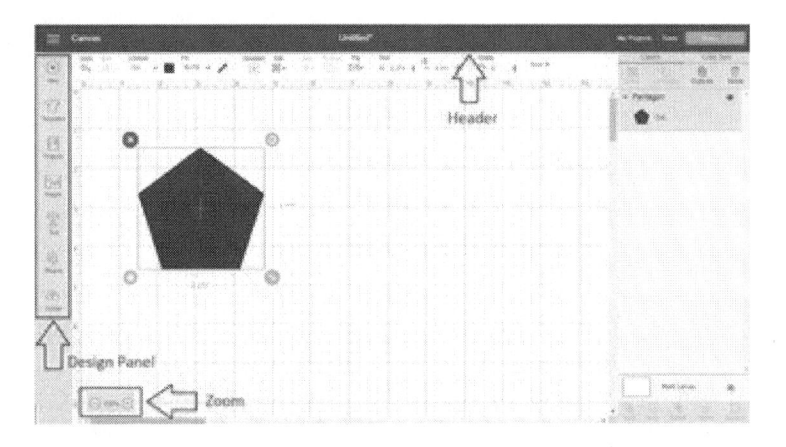

Design Panel

- **New** — To start building a new project you must always click on the "New" tab.

- **Templates** – To view your final design in real-life background, you can use any of the relevant templates by clicking on the "Templates" tab.

- **Projects** – To search, select and cut designs from an already existing project, you can use the "Projects" tab, which will contain a variety of other projects along with your own projects.

- **Images** – The "Cricut Image Library" contains a wide

variety of pictures available at your fingertips for free and to buy. The "Images" tab will also contain any image that you may upload. So, you can click on the images icon to search, select and insert any desired image into the Canvas.

- **Text** – You can use the "Text" tab to add desired phrases or words directly to the Canvas.

- **Shape** – You can use the "Shape" tab to insert simple shapes square, rectangle, triangle, circle and score lines into your Canvas.

- **Upload** – You can use the "Upload" tab to use your own image files including jpg, gif, png, bmp, svg, and dxf at no charge.

Header

- **Menu** – The "hamburger" icon on the top left of the screen will allow you to navigate through "Cricut Design Space". You can directly access "Home", "Canvas" and several other "Design Space" features, such as "New Machine Setup", "Link Cartridges", "Settings", "Help", and "Sign Out".

- **Page Title** – This will help you remember the whether you are on "Home" or "Canvas" page of "Design Space". By clicking on the "Page Title", you will be able to close an open tab.

- **Project Name** – This will show you the name of your project. If you've not already saved your project, then "Untitled" will be displayed as the name of the project.

- **My Projects** – You can open your saved projects by clicking on "My Projects".

- **Save** – In order to access your projects across your devices and multiple platforms, you must save your projects to your account by clicking on the "Save" icon and providing a name for your projects. Note -If you would like to keep your project private and all to yourself then make sure you uncheck the "Public" option while saving your project. Once the project has been saved and you would like to rename your project, just click on "Save As" and enter a new name for your project.

- **Make it** – Click on the "Make It" icon when you have prepped your mats and are ready to transfer your project to your "Cricut" machine.

Zoom

You can "Zoom In" to look at the finer details of your project and "Zoom Out" to see an overview of the same.

"Design Space" – Edit Bar

Let's look closely at the "Edit Bar" so you can better understand how you can edit your projects to perfection.

Editing Images

The blank "Edit Bar" is shown in the picture below. All the functions that can be seen on the "Edit Bar" are explained right after, so we can get you started on creating your first craft project on "Design Space".

- **"Undo/Redo"** – You can use the "Undo" button to revert to your previous state and use the "Redo" button to perform the step that was undone.

- **"Linetype"** – All the way the machine can interact with the design base material on the mat, namely, "Cut, Draw, Score, Engrave, Deboss, Perf, and Wavy" are called as "Linetype".

- **"Linetype Swatch"** – If you would like to choose additional layer attributes for your design, you can select the "Linetype swatch". The alternatives available will be updated on the basis of the "Linetype" you selected. When the "Cut" option is chosen, you will notice a solid line next to the "Linetype" icon, an outline if the "Draw" is chosen and when the "Score" is chosen, a "/" will be visible. Here are some details on the features that will be available for your selected "Linetype".

"Cut" Attributes

1. **Material colors** – You can select desired color the "Material colors palette" to instantly match the colors of your project. A "checkmark" will be displayed in the "color swatch" for the design layer that you are working on.

2. **Basic colors** – You will also be able to select a color

from the "basic color palette".

3. **Advanced** – You can move the slider to choose a color from the "custom color picker" or if you know exact "hex" numbers for your desired color, simply plug those numbers in and you will get that color for your design.

"Draw" Attributes – If you have selected the "Draw" Linetype, you will be given the option to Choose a "Cricut pen type" from the drop-down. The colors available for your selected "pen type" will be displayed in the list accordingly.

- **"Fill"** – You can select from a variety of colors and patterns to fill your image layer. This feature requires you to select the "Cut Linetype" as a prerequisite. There are two options available under "Fill" icon, as mentioned below:

- **No Fill** – This option will be displayed when you have not filled in a color or design in the selected layer of your design and you only want to cut the layer. You could use this option to revert the layer to a "cut-only" state in case you are not happy with the fill in the selected layer.

- **Print** - You can select this option for accessing "Print Then Cut" color and pattern choices.

- **"Fill Swatch"** – If you would like to choose from other "Fill" attributes for a layer, click on the "Fill Swatch" and options below will be displayed.

- **Original Artwork** – If you are not excited about the fill of the design and want to restore to the original image, you can do this by selecting "Original artwork".

- **Color** - You can choose your desired color from the "current material colors, a basic colors palette, the custom color picker, or by entering a hex color code".

- **Pattern** - You could also fill an image or text layer with a pattern. If you filter the pattern selection by color it will be easier to find the right pattern which you can further modify using the "Edit Pattern" tools.

- **"Select All/ Deselect"** – This feature will allow you to simultaneously select and/or deselect the objects on the Canvas.

- **"Edit"** – You will be able to find the standard image and text editing tools, such as, "Cut, Copy and Paste" in this dropdown.

- **"Align"** – You can use this feature to align the margins of different items on the Canvas. You can align the margins "left, right, top, or bottom, or have horizontal or vertical centers". It will also allow you to horizontally or vertically distribute the objects. This feature comes in handy when you are working on designs with multiple layers.

- **"Arrange"** – You will be able to modify the order of appearance of the objects on the Canvas, with options including "Send to Back, Move Backward, Move to Front, and Move Forward". Your modifications will be immediately visible in the Layers panel. This might get little confusing so here's a quick tip on how you can choose the option that meets your need.

- **"Send to Back"** – Use this option when you want to move the selected item to the deep end of your image stack. As a result, that item will be displayed at the bottom of the "Layers panel".

- **"Move Backward"** – Use this option when you want to send the selected item one layer backwards in your image stack.

- **"Move Forward"** – Use this option when you want to move the selected item a layer forward on your image stack.

- **"Send to Front"** – Use this option when you want to move the selected item to the very front of the image stack. As a result, that item will be displayed at the top of the "Layers panel".

- **"Flip"** – With this feature, you will be able to flip the selected item either vertically or horizontally at its center.

- **"Size"** – If you need to alter the height or width of an object then you can simply type in the exact dimensions in the given boxes or click on the "stepper" to increase or decreases the size while looking at the changes on your design. Remember to first lock the image aspect ratio by clicking on the "Lock" icon to ensure that as you modify one dimension the whole image will be modified in the same proportion.

- **"Rotate"** – You will be able to modify the angle of the selected item using the "stepper" or you can type in the exact degree by which you want to modify the image.

- **"More"** – If your screen resolution doesn't allow the complete "Edit" bar to be visible then you would see a "More" drop down containing the features that do not appear on your screen.

- **"Position"** – You can use this option to change the position of your selected item using the "stepper" or you can type in the exact distance by which you want to move the image from the top-left corner of the Canvas.

Editing Fonts

If you decided to add text to your design or select a "text object" on the Canvas or select a "text layer" in the Layers Panel, the "Text Edit Bar" will be displayed directly below the image "Edit Bar" on your screen. All the functions that can be seen on the "Text Edit Bar" are shown in the picture and explained below.

- **"Font"** – This will provide you a list of "Cricut" fonts along with all the fonts available on your computer.

- **"Font Drop Down"** – You will be able to view all the fonts available to you or may choose to view just the "Cricut" fonts, or only fonts installed on your system, or all the fonts at the same time, using the "Font Drop-Down". Font filters may also be searched and applied. Just browse the font list and choose your desired font to be applied to the selected text.

- **"Font Filter"** – You can use this feature for filtering the fonts by category and alter the fonts that are displayed in the "Font Type" menu.

- **"All Fonts"** – To view all available fonts that can be used for your project.

- **"System Fonts"** – To view only the fonts installed on your system.

- **"Cricut Fonts"** – To view just the fonts from "Cricut" library.

- **"Single Layer Fonts"** – To view fonts containing only a single layer.

- **"Writing Style Fonts"** - To view fonts that are designed particularly to be written by hand. These fonts are characterized by letters with single stroke that makes them appear like handwritten letters.

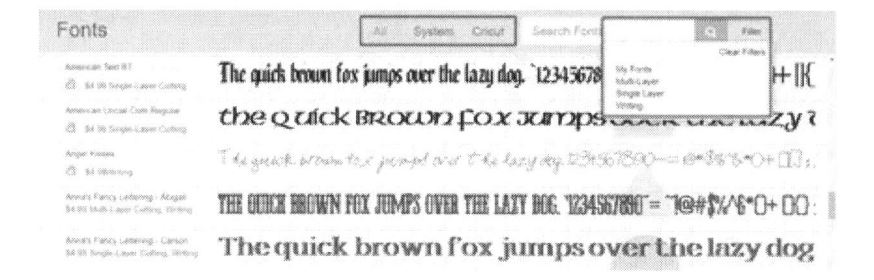

- **"Style"** – This feature will allow you to select the style of your font such as "regular, bold, italic and bold italic". You may also see the option of "writing" when applicable font has been selected. Remember, the style of "Cricut" fonts may differ from your system fonts.

- **"Font Size"** – You can adjust the size of the fonts by typing in the desired point size or using the "stepper" to gradually adjust the font size by 1 point.

- **"Letter Space"** – You may want to adjust the spacing between letters of your text by typing in the desired value or using the "stepper".

- **"Line Space"** – If you need to adjust the spacing between individual rows of text, just type in the desired value or use the "stepper".

- **"Alignment"** – You can also modify the alignment of the entire block of text to one of these options: "left, right, centered, or full justification".

- **"Curve"** – You can enhance your text by bending it into a circular shape using the "Curve" feature and changing the diameter to your desired length.

- **"Advanced"** – The features in the "Advanced" tool

will allow you ungroup text contained within a block of text. This includes grouping of individual letters as well as lines and layers of text.

- **"Ungroup to Letters"** – This feature will enable you to ungroup letters within a text and create individual layers for every letter. These letters will then be displayed in the "Layers panel", where you can modify the size and position of each letter independently while keeping the layers of these letters grouped together.

- **"Ungroup to Lines"** – You will be able to ungroup rows of text within a text box and every line will be in a group of its own layers and will be displayed in the "Layers panel" as an image that can be modified independently.

- **"Ungroup to Layers"** – You can use this feature to "ungroup multilayered text so that each layer group shows in the Layers Panel as an image that can be edited independently".

Activity Selection to start the project on Design Space

"Cricut" cutting machines are capable of doing more than just cut when used in conjunction with "Design Space" and other "Cricut" tools and accessories. As mentioned earlier, within "Design Space", each of these activities namely "Cut, Draw, Score, Engrave, Deboss, Perf, and Wavy" are called "Linetype".

When you are ready to start designing your project, the first step is to identify which "Linetype" is applicable to you and make the appropriate selection as shown in the steps below:

Step #1

Login to "Design Space" and make sure that you machine selection is correct. Then select "New Project", either on the top right corner of the screen or from the landing page, as shown in the picture below.

Note - For the first time users you will be displayed a message to download the "Design Space" plugin for your system. Click on download to download the zip file.

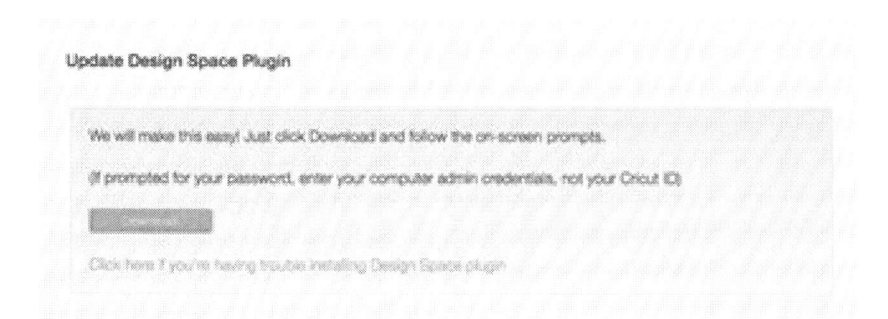

Step #2

Once the download has started you will see the message below on your screen. To install the plugin, enter your computer's administrator ID and password and follow the prompts. Do not confuse this with your "Cricut ID".

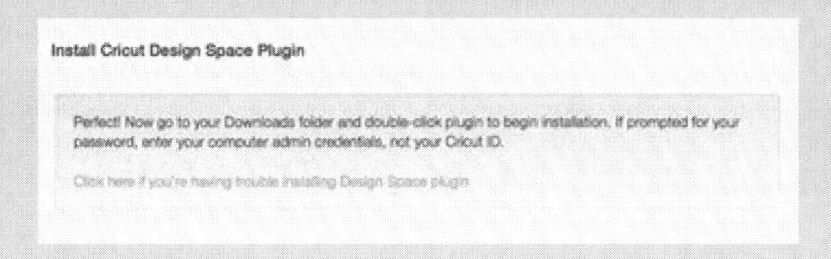

Install Cricut Design Space Plugin

Perfect! Now go to your Downloads folder and double-click plugin to begin installation. If prompted for your password, enter your computer admin credentials, not your Cricut ID.

Click here if you're having trouble installing Design Space plugin.

Once the installation has finished, the message as shown in the picture above will disappear and you will be able to access the blank canvas.

Step #3

On the blank canvas as shown in the picture below, click on the images icon and a list of free and for purchase images available through the "Design Space" image library will open. You can also select text by clicking on the text icon and follow the steps below.

Step #4

Select an image that best meets your need and click on "Insert Images" at the bottom of your screen, as shown in the picture below.

Step #5

Your selected image will be loaded onto the canvas and the tools panel on top of the screen will become active in black fonts. On the top left corner of the screen, click on "Linetype" and select the activity that fits your project.

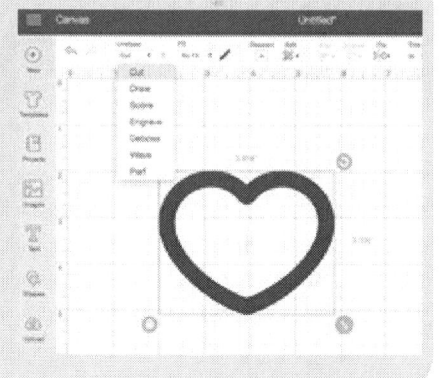

Step #6

Based on your "Linetype" selection, the image will be modified to reflect the change and once you are ready to transfer your project to the machine, "Design Space" will guide you to mount the appropriate tool in the machine.

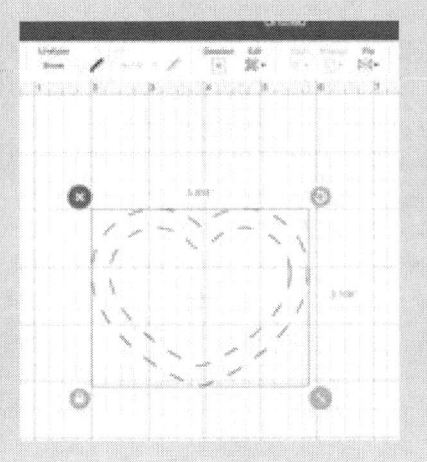

Tip: "You can change the Linetype of multiple layers at once. Just select all the layers you want, followed by the desired Linetype from the dropdown".

Setting up your "Cricut" machine on "Design Space"

To get started with your projects, you must first setup your cutting machine on the "Design Space" using your "Cricut ID" by following the instructions below:

Step #1

Click on the hamburger icon next to the "Canvas" on the top left of the screen.

Step #2

Click on "New Machine Setup" from the available options.

Step #3

You will see the different "Cricut" devices on your screen. Simply select the device you are looking to pair.

Step #4

Follow the instructions on the screen, as shown in the picture below.

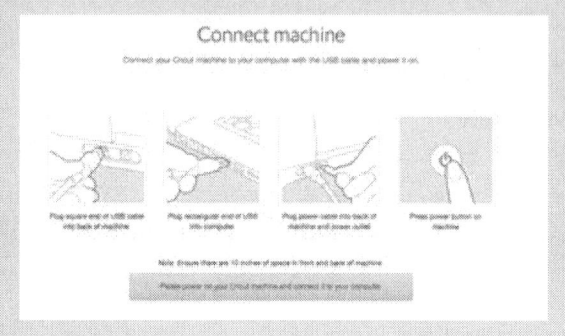

Step #5

Click "Continue" and you are all set!

Note – If you have another device that you have just purchased and need to set up. Follow the instructions above and simply select the other device that you need to set.

Chapter - 3

Cricut Projects

(Easy and Intermediate Level)

You are now ready to get started with developing some projects. In this chapter you will learn a variety of easy and intermediate level projects focusing on paper, glass applications and some projects to host highly personalized party. So, without further adieu lets get you started!

Paper Projects

It is ideal to start your first project using paper-based designs, since these projects are easier to not only design but also to cut. You can get professional looking results with minimum investment. You will learn to create a variety of projects that you can further customize as you follow the instructions below and have unique designs of your own.

I - Recipe Stickers (Easy)

Materials needed – "Cricut Maker" or "Cricut Explore", sticker paper and cutting mat.

Step #1

To start a new project, after you have logged into your "Cricut" account on "Design Space", click on the "New Project" button on the top right corner of the screen and a blank canvas will be displayed.

Step #2

Click on the "Images" icon on the "Design Panel" and type in "stickers" in the search bar. Click on desired image, then click on the "Insert Images" button at the bottom of the screen, per the picture below.

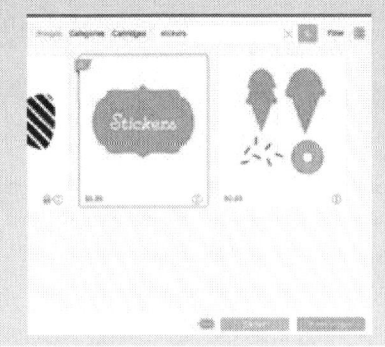

Step #3

The selected image will be displayed on the canvas and is ready to be edited. You can make multiple changes to the image as you need, for example, you could change the color of the image or change its size (sticker should be between 2-4 inches wide). The image selected for this project has words "stickers" inside the design, so let's delete that by first clicking on the "Ungroup" button and selecting the "Stickers" layer and clicking on the red "x" button. Click on the "Text" button and type in the name of your recipe, as shown in the picture below.

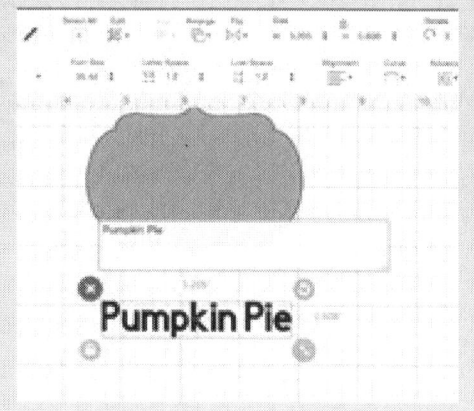

Step #4

Drag and drop the text in the middle of the design and select the entire design. Now, click on "Align" and select "Center Horizontally" and "Center Vertically".

Step #5

Select the entire design and click on "Group" icon on the top top right of the screen under "Layers panel". Now, copy and paste the designs and update the text for all your recipes, as shown in the picture below. (Use your keyboard shortcut "Ctrl + C" and "Ctrl + V" or select the image and click on "Edit" from the "Edit bar" to view the dropdown option for "Copy" and "Paste".)

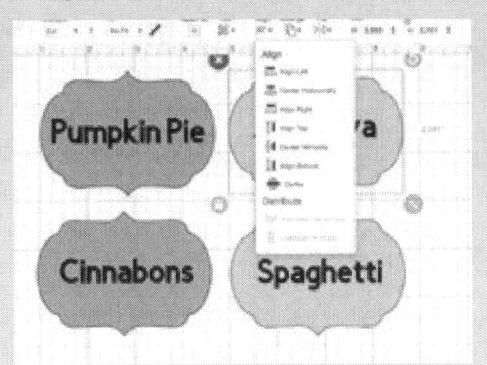

Step #6

Click on "Save" at the top right corner of the screen and enter a name for your project, for example, "Recipe Stickers" then click "Save", as shown in the picture below.

Step #7

The design is ready to be cut. Simply click on the "Make It" button on the top right corner of the screen. You will see the required mats and material displayed on the screen. (Click on 2 to view the mat instructions for the remaining objects of your design, as shown in the pictures below).

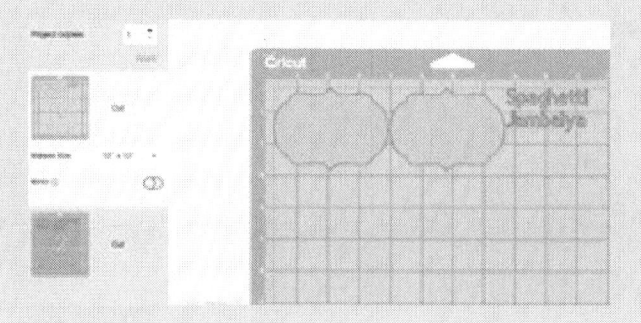

Step #8

Load the sticker paper to your "Cricut" machine and click "Continue" at the bottom right corner of the screen to start cutting your design.

Note – The "Continue" button will not appear if you used images and/or fonts for your design that are not free and available for purchase only. You will instead see a "Purchase" at the bottom right of the screen, so you can buy the image or font first and once the purchase has been made, the "Continue" button will be available to you.

Step #9

Once your "Cricut" device has been connected to your computer, set your cut setting to "Vinyl". It is recommended to use this setting to cut the sticker paper since it tends to be thicker than regular paper. Place the sticker paper on top of the cutting mat and load into the "Cricut" device by pushing against the rollers. The "Load/Unload" button will start flashing so just press it. Then press the "Go" button which would already be flashing. Viola! You have your own customized recipe stickers.

II – Wedding Invitations (Easy)

Materials needed – "Cricut Maker" or "Cricut Explore", cutting mat and Cardstock or your choice of decorative paper/ crepe paper/ fabric, home printer (if not using "Cricut Maker").

Step #1

To start a new project, after you have logged into your "Cricut" account on "Design Space", click on the "New Project" button on the top right corner of the screen and a blank canvas will be displayed.

Step #2

The easiest way to create your own wedding invitation is by customizing an already existing project form the "Design Space" library. Click on the "Projects" icon on the "Design Panel", selected "Cards" from the "All Categories" drop-down then type in "wedding invite" in the search bar, as shown in the picture below.

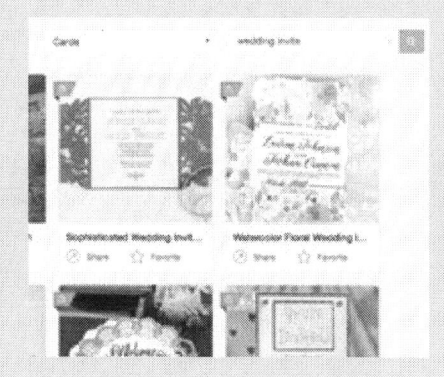

Step #3

The project selected for this example is displayed in the picture below. Click "Customize" at the bottom of the screen so you can edit the text for your invite.

Step #4

The design will be loaded on to the canvas. Click on the "Text" button and type in the details for your invite, as shown in the picture below. You can change the font of the text and the color as well as the alignment from the "Edit Text Bar" on top of the screen and remember to change the "Fill" to "Print". You can even change the size of the design as needed. (An invitation card is recommended to be 6-9 inches wide).

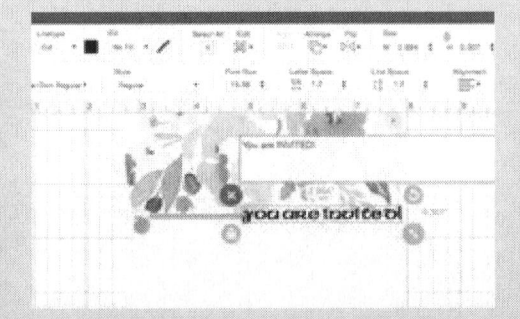

Step #5

Select the entire design and click on "Group" icon on the top right of the screen under "Layers panel". Click on "Save" at the top right corner of the screen and enter a name for your project, for example, "Wedding Invite" then click "Save".

Step #6

The design is ready to be printed and cut. Simply click on the "Make It" button on the top right corner of the screen. You will see the required mats and material displayed on the screen and use your printer to print the design on your chosen material (white cardstock or paper), as shown in the picture below.

Tip – Calibrate your machine first for the "Print then Cut" project by clicking on the hamburger icon next to the "Canvas" on the top left of the screen and follow the prompts on the screen, as shown in the picture below.

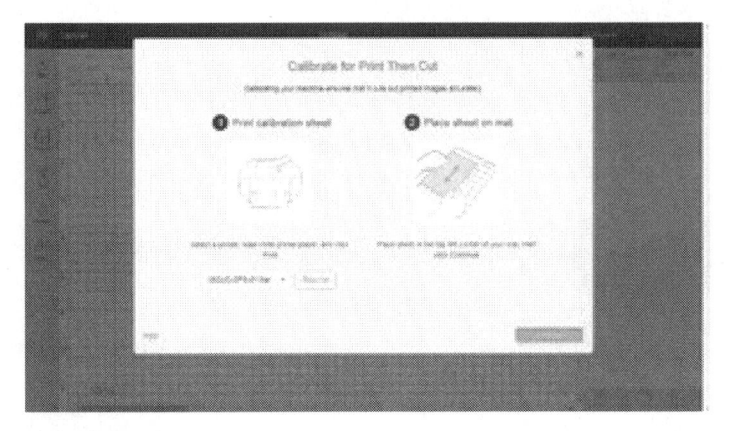

Step #7

Load the material with printed design to your "Cricut" machine and click "Continue" at the bottom right corner of the screen to start cutting your design.

Note – The "Continue" button will not appear if you used images and/or fonts for your design that are not free and available for purchase only. You will instead see a "Purchase" at the bottom right of the screen, so you can buy the image or font first and once the purchase has been made, the "Continue" button will be available to you.

Step #8

Once your "Cricut" device has been connected to your computer, set your cut setting to "Vinyl". It is recommended to use this setting to cut the sticker paper since it tends to be thicker than regular paper. Place the sticker paper on top of the cutting mat and load into the "Cricut" device by pushing against the rollers. The "Load/Unload" button will start flashing so just press it. Then press the "Go" button which would already be flashing. Viola! You have your own customized wedding invitation. Put them in an envelope and send them out to all your guests.

III – Custom Notebooks (Easy)

Materials needed – "Cricut Maker" or "Cricut Explore", cutting mat and washi sheets or your choice of decorative paper/ crepe paper/ fabric.

Step #1

To start a new project, after you have logged into your "Cricut" account on "Design Space", click on the "New Project" button on the top right corner of the screen and a blank canvas will be displayed.

Step #2

In this example, we will use an already existing project from the "Cricut" library and customize it. So click on the "Projects" icon on the "Design Panel" and type in "notebook" in the search bar.

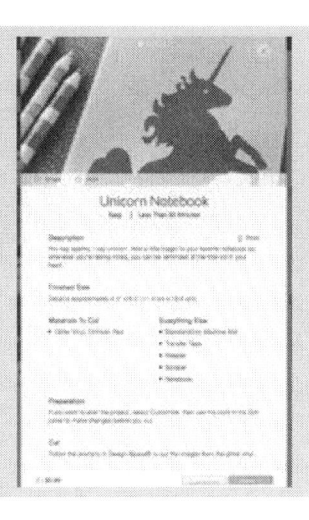

You can view all the projects available by clicking on them and a pop-up window displaying all the details of the project will appear on your screen, as shown in the picture below displaying the details of the project selected for this example.

Step #3

Click on "Customize" so you can further edit this project to your preference.

Step #4

The unicorn design will be displayed on the Canvas. You can see in the "Layers panel" that this is a single layer design so it is very easy to modify. You can change the color of the unicorn or fill in a pattern. Click on the "Linetype Swatch" to view the color palette and select the desired color as shown in the pictures below.

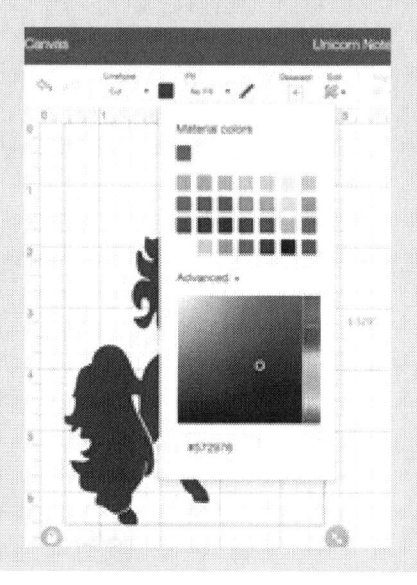

Step #5

The design is ready to be cut. Simply click on the "Make It" button on the top right corner of the screen. You will see the required mats and material displayed on the screen.

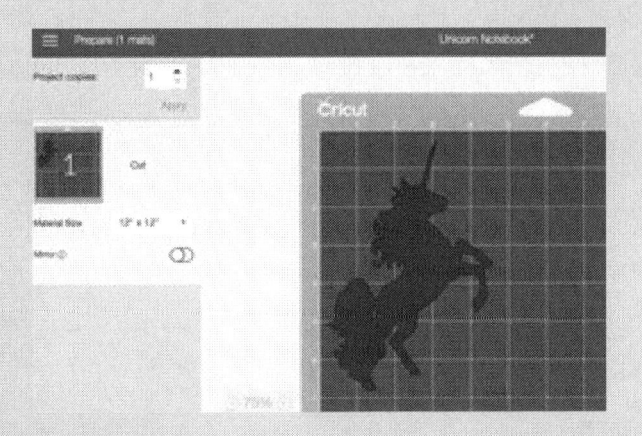

Step #6

Load the washi paper sheet to your "Cricut" machine and click "Continue" at the bottom right corner of the screen to start cutting your design.

Note – The "Continue" button will not appear if you used images and/or fonts for your design that are not free and available for purchase only. You will instead see a "Purchase" at the bottom right of the screen, so you can buy the image or font first and once the purchase has been made, the "Continue" button will be available to you.

Step #7

Connect your "Cricut" device to your computer and place the washi paper or your chosen paper on top of the cutting mat and load into the "Cricut" machine by pushing against the rollers. The "Load/Unload" button will start flashing so just press it. Then press the "Go" button which would already be flashing. Viola! You have your own customized unicorn notebook, resembling the notebook below:

Glass Application Projects

Glass application projects are extremely fun and perfect to add some personality to your house and even your car. You will learn to create a variety of projects that you can further customize as you follow the instructions below and have unique designs of your own.

I – Window Decoration (Easy)

Materials needed – "Cricut Maker" or "Cricut Explore", cutting mat, orange window cling (non adhesive material that has static cling so it can be easily applied on glass; since it does not have sticky cling like vinyl, make sure you put this on the inner side of the window to protect exposure from external weather).

Step #1

To start a new project, after you have logged into your "Cricut" account on "Design Space", click on the "New Project" button on the top right corner of the screen and a blank canvas will be displayed.

Step #2

Let's use an already existing project from the "Cricut" library and customize it. So click on the "Projects" icon on the "Design Panel" and click on the "All Categories" drop-down menu to view all existing projects that you can select from. For this example, we will click on "Home Decor" then type in "window" in the search bar to narrow your search to window cling projects.

You can view all the projects available by clicking on them and a pop-up window displaying all the details of the project will appear on your screen.

Step #3

The project selected for this example is displayed in the picture below. Click "Customize" at the bottom of the screen so you can edit the design as desired.

Step #4

Your selected design will be displayed on the Canvas. You can see in the "Layers panel" that this design contains multiple layers but the two bottom layers are hidden from the canvas and will be excluded from being cut. You can change the color of the design by clicking on the "Linetype Swatch" to view the color palette and select the desired color as shown in the picture below.

Step #5

The design is ready to be printed and cut. Simply click on the "Make It" button on the top right corner of the screen. You will see the required mats and material displayed on the screen.

Step #6

Load the orange window cling to your "Cricut" machine and click "Continue" at the bottom right corner of the screen to start cutting your design.

Note – The "Continue" button will not appear if you used images and/or fonts for your design that are not free and available for purchase only. You will instead see a "Purchase" at the bottom right of the screen, so you can buy the image or font first and once the purchase has been made, the "Continue" button will be available to you.

Step #7

Once your "Cricut" device has been connected to your computer, set your cut setting to "Vinyl". It is recommended to use this setting to cut the sticker paper since it tends to be thicker than regular paper. Place the sticker paper on top of the cutting mat and load into the "Cricut" device by pushing against the rollers. The "Load/Unload" button will start flashing so just press it. Then press the "Go" button which would already be flashing. Viola! You have window decorations ready for Halloween.

II – Car Decal (Intermediate)

Materials needed – "Cricut Maker" or "Cricut Explore", cutting mat, vinyl, transfer tape, scrapper.

Step #1

To start a new project, after you have logged into your "Cricut" account on "Design Space", click on the "New Project" button on the top right corner of the screen and a blank canvas will be displayed.

Step #2

Let's use our own image for this project. Search the web to find the image that you would like and store it on your computer. Now, click on "Upload" icon from the "Designer Panel" on the left of the screen.

Step #3

A screen with "Upload Image" and "Upload Pattern" will be displayed. Click on the "Upload Image" button.

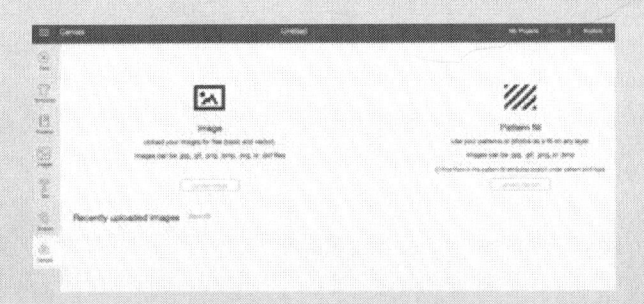

Step #4

Click on "Browse" or simply drag and drop your image on the screen.

Step #5

Your uploaded image will be displayed on the screen and you would be able to select if you would like to upload the image as a simple "single layer" picture or complex "multiple layer" picture. For the decal image below, we will select "simple" and click on "Continue".

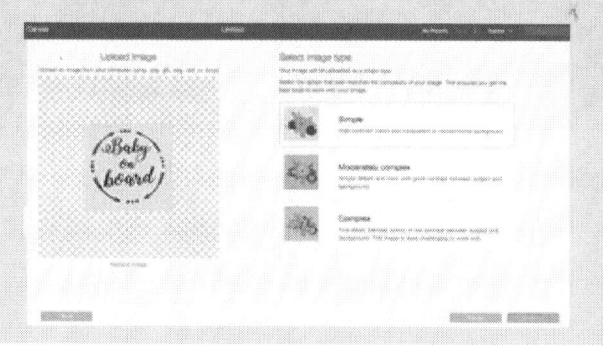

Step #6

You will then be prompted to selectively erase elements of the image if you need to. For this image we will click "Continue" at the bottom right of the screen to proceed without erasing any element of this image.

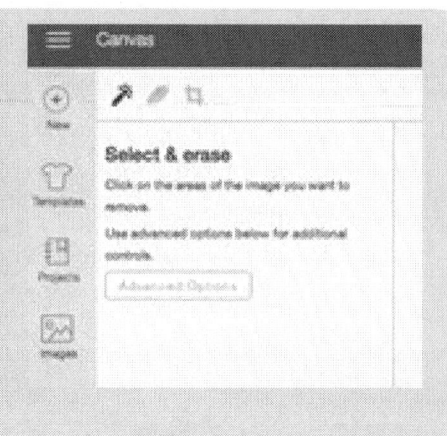

Step #7

On the preceding screen, give a name to your image so you can easily retrieve it in future and it is recommended to add relevant tags for the same. You can then save the image as "Print then Cut image" or "Cut" image. "Saving as a Print Then Cut image will preserve the entire image, including internal colors and patterns, and add it to the design screen as a Print Then Cut image. Saving as a Cut image will save only the outer silhouette as the image cut path". For this example, we will save the image as "Print then Cut" image by clicking on the picture on the left and click "Save" at the bottom right of the screen.

Your uploaded image will now appear in the "Uploaded Images Library" at the bottom of the screen.

Step #8

Select the uploaded image and click on "Insert Images" at the bottom of the screen. Your image will be displayed on the canvas and is now ready to be edited.

Step #9

You can change the size of the image as needed and click on "Make It" button on the top right corner of the screen. You will see the required mats and material displayed on the screen.

Step #10

Load the window cling to your "Cricut" machine and click "Continue" at the bottom right corner of the screen to start cutting your design.

Step #11

Once your "Cricut" device has been connected to your computer, set your cut setting to your chosen material. Place the window cling on top of the cutting mat and load into the "Cricut" machine by pushing against the rollers. The "Load/Unload" button will start flashing so just press it. Then press the "Go" button which would already be flashing. Your car decal is ready to be pasted now.

Step #12

Carefully remove the excess material from the sheet. To easily paste your decal on the car window without stretching the pieces, put the transfer tape on top of the cut design. After you have cleaned the car window, slowly peel the paper backing on the vinyl from one end to the other in a rolling motion to ensure even placement. Now, use the scraper tool on top of the transfer tape to remove any bubbles and then just peel off the transfer tape. And you are all set!

III – Holiday Mirror Decoration (Intermediate)

Materials needed – "Cricut Maker" or "Cricut Explore", cutting mat, vinyl, transfer tape, scrapper.

Step #1

To start a new project, after you have logged into your "Cricut" account on "Design Space", click on the "New Project" button on the top right corner of the screen and a blank canvas will be displayed.

Step #2

Let's leverage the "Cricut Image Library" to create our project design by customizing an image from the library. Click on the "Images" icon on the "Design Panel" and type in "reindeer" in the search bar and select a picture that you like. You might have to scroll down to find the image used in this project. Click on it and a small icon will be added to the "Insert Image" bar at the bottom of the screen. Click on "Insert Images" at the bottom of the screen.

Step #3

Now type in "wreath" in the search bar and scroll down to find the image used in this project. Click on it and a small icon will be added to the "Insert Image" bar at the bottom of the screen. Click on "Insert Images" at the bottom of the screen.

Step #4

Your selected images will appear stacked up on the Canvas, as shown in the picture below.

Step #5

Let's edit this image as needed, for example, you could enlarge the background image and resize the deer image with text. Adjust the size of the image as you wish and change the colors if you desire by selecting the appropriate layer from the "Layers panel". For this example, we change the color of the background wreath to dark green.

Step #6

Now, click on the "Fill" icon from the "Edit Bar" at the top of the screen to select "Print" and then change the color of the deer to red. Click on the lock icon at the bottom left of the deer image so you can adjust the size of the image without locking the aspect ratio to better fit the image inside the wreath.

Step #7

Select the entire design and click on "Group" icon on the top right of the screen under "Layers panel". Click on "Save" at the top right corner of the screen and enter a name for your project, for example, "Wedding Invite" then click "Save".

Note - Depending on the order of the insert you may need to bring the deer image on top. To do this select the image and click on "Arrange" and then select "Move Forward. Your final design will look like the picture below.

Step #8

The design is ready to be cut. Simply click on the "Make It" button on the top right corner of the screen. You will see the required mats and material displayed on the screen.

Step #9

Load the vinyl sheet to your "Cricut" machine and click "Continue" at the bottom right corner of the screen to start cutting your design.

Note – The "Continue" button will not appear if you used images and/or fonts for your design that are not free and available for purchase only. You will instead see a "Purchase" at the bottom right of the screen, so you can buy the image or font first and once the purchase has been made, the "Continue" button will be available to you.

Step #10

Connect your "Cricut" device to your computer and place the vinyl on top of the cutting mat and load into the "Cricut" machine by pushing against the rollers. The "Load/Unload" button will start flashing so just press it. Then press the "Go" button which would already be flashing.

Step #11

Carefully remove the excess vinyl from the sheet. To easily paste your decal on the mirror without stretching the pieces, put the transfer tape on top of the cut design. After you have cleaned the mirror, slowly peel the paper backing on the vinyl from one end to the other in a rolling motion to ensure even placement. Now, use the scraper tool on top of the transfer tape to remove any bubbles and then just peel off the transfer tape. Viola! You have your own customized mirror decal, that may look like the picture below.

IV – Wine Glass Decoration (Easy)

Materials needed – "Cricut Maker" or "Cricut Explore", cutting mat, vinyl (gold), transfer tape, scrapper, wine glasses.

Step #1

To start a new project, after you have logged into your "Cricut" account on "Design Space", click on the "New Project" button on the top right corner of the screen and a blank canvas will be displayed.

Step #2

Let's use text for this project. Click on "Text" from the "Designs Panel" on the left of the screen and type in "WINE O'clock" or any other phrase you may like.

Step #3

For the image below, the font "Anna's Fancy Lettering – Hannah" in purple as shown in the picture below was selected. But you can let your creativity take over this step and choose any color or font that you like. Select and copy-paste your image for the number of times you want to print your design.

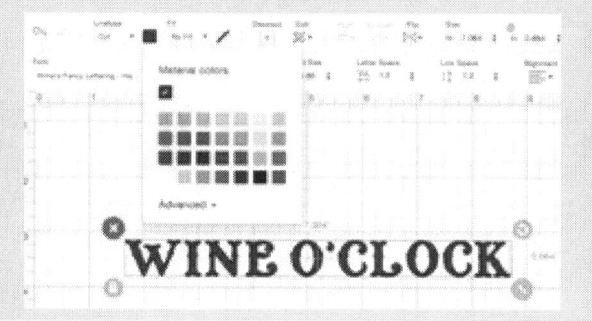

Step #4

Click on "Save" at the top right corner of the screen and give desired name to the project, for example, "Wine Glass Decoration" and click "Save".

Step #5

The design is ready to be cut. Simply click on the "Make It" button on the top right corner of the screen. You will see the required mats and material displayed on the screen, as shown in the picture below.

Step #6

Load the vinyl to your "Cricut" machine and click "Continue" at the bottom right corner of the screen to start cutting your design.

Step #7

Connect your "Cricut" device to your computer and place the washi paper or your chosen paper on top of the cutting mat and load into the "Cricut" machine by pushing against the rollers. The "Load/Unload" button will start flashing so just press it. Then press the "Go" button which would already be flashing.

Step #8

Carefully remove the excess vinyl from the sheet. To easily paste your design on the wine glass without stretching the pieces, put the transfer tape on top of the cut design. After you have cleaned the surface, slowly peel the paper backing on the vinyl from one end to the other in a rolling motion to ensure even placement. Now, use the scraper tool on top of the transfer tape to remove any bubbles and then just peel off the transfer tape. Viola! You have your own customized wine glasses, that may look like the picture below.

Party Projects

Planning a party can be as stressful as exciting. To make your party truly memorable, the easiest approach is to have customized party favor boxes and other return gifts. A lot of such projects are covered in this book, that you can further customize to throw a highly personalized and unforgettable party. Following the instructions below and feel free to further customize your designs with a variety of colors and patterns.

I – Clear Party Favor Boxes (Intermediate)

Materials needed – "Cricut Maker", standard grip mat, scoring wheel, foil acetate.

Step #1

To start a new project, after you have logged into your "Cricut" account on "Design Space", click on the "New Project" button on the top right corner of the screen and a blank canvas will be displayed.

Step #2

We will again use an already existing project from the "Cricut" library and customize it since it's the easiest approach for beginners to get their hands-on experience without having a lot of prior practice. So, click on the "Projects" icon on the "Design Panel" and click on the "All Categories" drop-down menu to view all existing projects that you can select from. For this example, we will click on "Parties & Events" then type in "favor box" in the search bar to narrow your search to party favor box projects.

Step #3

You can view all the projects available by clicking on them and a pop-up window displaying all the details of the project will appear on your screen. The project selected for this example is shown in the picture below.

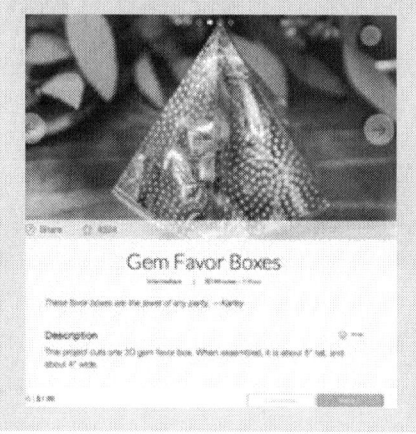

Step #4

The project selected for this project is displayed in the picture below. Click "Customize" at the bottom to edit the project to your preference.

Note - If you change the size of the design i.e. the box, change the grouped design at the same time and do not attempt to resize a particular piece so design will fit together upon folding.

Step #5

Now, your design is ready to be scored and cut. Simply click on the "Make It" button on the top right corner of the screen. You will see the required mats and material displayed on the screen. Set the material to "Foil Acetate" and mount the scoring wheel. Make sure you click on the "Mirror" button under the "Material Size" on the left of the screen.

Step #6

Load the material with printed design to your "Cricut" machine and click "Continue" at the bottom right corner of the screen to start cutting your design.

Note – The "Continue" button will not appear if you used images and/or fonts for your design that are not free and available for purchase only. You will instead see a "Purchase" at the bottom right of the screen, so you can buy the image or font first and once the purchase has been made, the "Continue" button will be available to you.

Step #7

Place the foil acetate on the mat with the shiny or the pretty side down. Calibrate your device and use appropriate setting to cut your chosen material. Place the vinyl on top of the cutting mat and load into the "Cricut" machine by pushing against the rollers. The "Load/Unload" button will start flashing so just press it. Then press the "Go" button which would already be flashing.

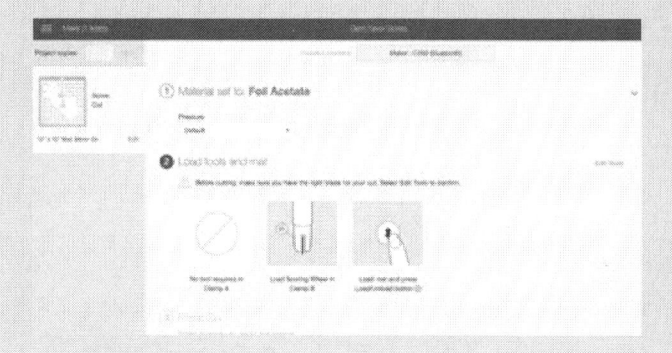

Step #8

Once the scoring has been completed, replace the scoring wheel with the fine point blade to finish the cutting of the design. Press the "Go" button again, which would already be flashing.

Step #9

After you have unloaded the mat, carefully remove the foil from the mat and fold the box along the score lines and push the triangle tabs into the available slots around the whole box. The final product would look as shown in the picture below. Fill your boxes with candy or other goodies and you have your personally designed party favors!

II – Trick or Treat Bag (Easy)

Materials needed – "Cricut Maker" or "Cricut Explorer", standard grip mat, transfer tape, scraper, everyday vinyl, small craft paper bags.

Step #1

To start a new project, after you have logged into your "Cricut" account on "Design Space", click on the "New Project" button on the top right corner of the screen and a blank canvas will be displayed.

Step #2

Click on the "Images" icon on the "Design Panel" and type in "Halloween" in the search bar to use an image from the "Cricut Image Library" for this project and click on "Insert Images" at the bottom of the screen. The image selected are shown in the picture below.

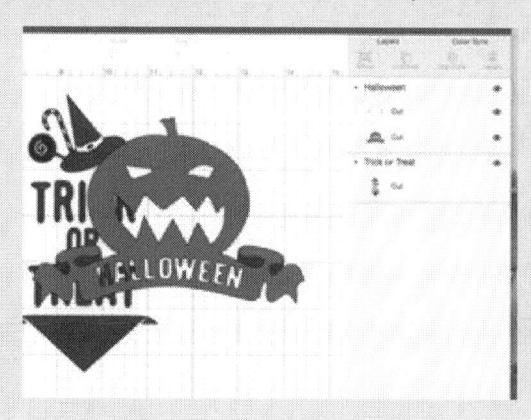

Step #3

Your selected images will appear on the Canvas and you can notice from the "Layers Panel" on the right that one of the images has multiple layers, which can be edited individually. You can edit either or both the image as needed, for example, you could resize the image based on the size of your craft bag and change the color or fill in a pattern in the image by selecting the image and clicking on applicable tool on the "Edit Bar", as shown in the picture below.

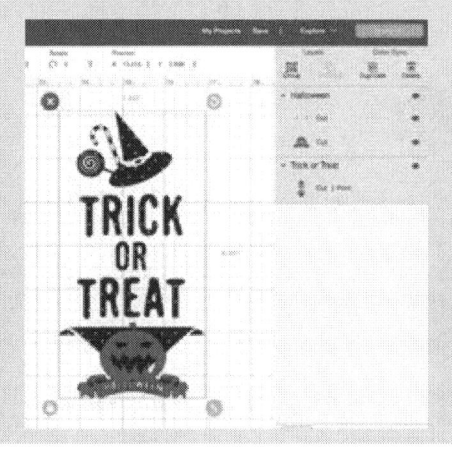

Step #4

Select the entire design and click on "Group" icon on the top right of the screen under "Layers panel". Click on "Save" at the top right corner of the screen and enter a name for your project, for example, "trick or treat bag" and click "Save".

Step #5

Now, your design is ready to be cut (you would need to print the design first, if you selected a fill color or pattern). Simply click on the "Make It" button on the top right corner of the screen. You will see the required mats and material displayed on the screen.

Step #6

Click "Continue" at the bottom right corner of the screen. After you have loaded the vinyl to the "Cricut" machine and print the design onto the paper.

Note – The "Continue" button will not appear if you used images and/or fonts for your design that are not free and available for purchase only. You will instead see a "Purchase" at the bottom right of the screen, so you can buy the image or font first and once the purchase has been made, the "Continue" button will be available to you.

Step #7

Once your "Cricut" device has been connected to your computer, set your cut setting to "Vinyl". Place the vinyl on top of the cutting mat and load into the "Cricut" machine by pushing against the rollers. The "Load/Unload" button will start flashing so just press it. Then press the "Go" button which would already be flashing.

Step #8

Carefully remove the excess vinyl from the sheet. To easily paste your design on the craft bag without stretching the pieces, put the transfer tape on top of the cut design. Now, slowly peel the paper backing on the vinyl from one end to the other in a rolling motion to ensure even placement and use the scraper tool on top of the transfer tape to remove any bubbles and then just peel off the transfer tape. Viola! You have your own customized Halloween trick or treat bags, that may look like the picture below.

III – Cake Topper (Cake)

Materials needed – "Cricut Maker" or "Cricut Explorer", standard grip mat, hot glue gun, bamboo skewer or wooden dowel, cardstock in desired colors (green, yellow, white).

Step #1

To start a new project, after you have logged into your "Cricut" account on "Design Space", click on the "New Project" button on the top right corner of the screen and a blank canvas will be displayed.

Step #2

Let's use text for this project. Click on "Text" from the "Designs Panel" on the left of the screen and type in "Oh" then click on the "Text" button again and type "BOY".

Step #3

Then align the two texts and click on the "Group" icon on the "Layers Panel". For the image below, the font "Close to My Heart - Artbooking" in Regular and color as shown in the picture below were selected. But you can let your creativity take over this step and choose any color or font that you like.

Step #4

Click on "Save" at the top right corner of the screen and give desired name to the project, for example, "Cake Topper – Oh BOY" and click "Save".

Step #5

Your design is ready to be cut now. Simply click on the "Make It" button on the top right corner of the screen. You will see the required mats and material displayed on the screen. Load the material with printed design to your "Cricut" machine and click "Continue" at the bottom right corner of the screen to start cutting your design.

Note – The font used is available for purchase so click on "Purchase" at the bottom right of the screen to buy the images before you can print them. And once you have made the purchase the "Continue" button will be available to you.

Step #6

Once your "Cricut" device has been connected to your computer, set your cut setting to cut your chosen material. Place the cardstock on top of the cutting mat and load into the "Cricut" machine by pushing against the rollers. The "Load/Unload" button will start flashing so just press it. Then press the "Go" button which would already be flashing.

Step #7

Now use the hot glue gun to adhere the design on to a bamboo skewer or wooden dowel and Viola! You have your own customized cake topper that may look like the picture.

Chapter - 4

Cricut Projects
(Expert Level)

In this chapter we will continue looking at more projects you can create using your "Cricut" devices and then learn how you can clean your devices. The projects included in this chapter require more experience working with "Cricut" and "Design Space", but that should not discourage you from pursuing these projects. You can take an inspiration and make it work with your skillset. You would also learn a whole lot of tips and tricks on how to craft your projects using the "Design Space" application.

Ceramic Application Projects

Let's start these projects using ceramic as the base material. You will learn to create a variety of projects that you can further customize as you follow the instructions below and have unique designs of your own.

I – Personalized Mugs (Iron-On Vinyl)

Materials needed – "Cricut Maker" or "Cricut Explore", standard grip mat, printable "Cricut" iron-on or heat transfer vinyl, "Cricut Easy Press Mini", "Easy Press" mat, weeding tool, ceramic mug.

Step #1

To start a new project, after you have logged into your "Cricut" account on "Design Space", click on the "New Project" button on the top right corner of the screen and a blank canvas will be displayed.

Step #2

Click on the "Images" icon on the "Design Panel" and type in "America" in the search bar. Click on the desired image, then click on the "Insert Images" button at the bottom of the screen, per the picture below. Your selected images will then be displayed on the Canvas.

Step #3

Click on "Templates" icon on the "Designs Panel" on the left of the screen. If you type in "mug" in the templates search bar, it will be much faster to find the mug template for your project, as shown in the picture below.

Step #4

Simply click on the mug icon and the mug template will be loaded on the canvas still holding the image you selected for your design, as shown in the picture below.

Step #5

Click on the "mugs" icon at the bottom right of the screen and the options to change the "Type" and "Size" of the template will appear on the screen. To decorate mugs with non-standard sizes, click on the "Size" icon and select "Custom" to update your mug size.

Note – If your mug size needs to be changed further, click on the "Lock" icon to independently adjust the height and width of the mug. You can also select the color of your mug to make your design even more compatible to your actual mug, as shown in the picture below.

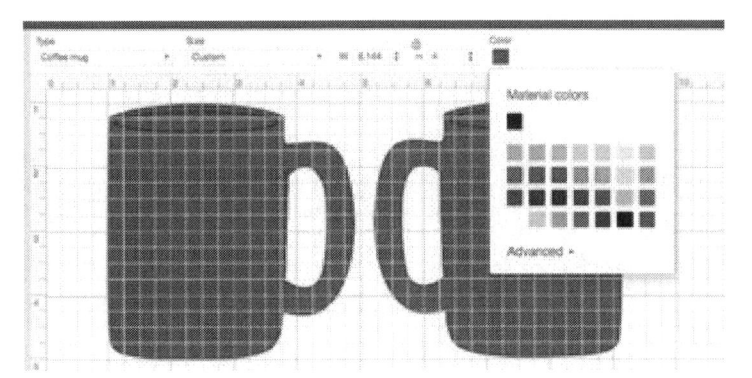

Step #6

Now, you can further edit your design, for example, you could resize the image to fit in on the mug template. Click on "Shapes" icon on the "Designs Panel" if you would like to add hearts, stars or other shapes to your design in desired shape and color, to further customize it as shown in the picture below.

Step #7

Click on "Save" at the top right corner of the screen and give desired name to the project, for example, "Mug Decoration" and click "Save".

Step #8

The design is ready to be printed and cut. Simply click on the "Make It" button on the top right corner of the screen. You will see the required mats and material displayed on the screen and use your ink jet printer to print the design on your printable iron-on vinyl, as shown in the picture below.

Note – "One side of the Printable Iron-on Dark sheet is white with a matte finish; the other side is printed with blue grid lines. Print on the matte side; the side with the blue gridlines is the iron-on backing which will be removed prior to applying your design to your material".

Step #9

Load the material with printed design to your "Cricut" machine and click "Continue" at the bottom right corner of the screen to start cutting your design.

Note – The "Continue" button will not appear if you used images and/or fonts for your design that are not free and available for purchase only. You will instead see a "Purchase" at the bottom right of the screen, so you can buy the image or font first and once the purchase has been made, the "Continue" button will be available to you.

Step #10

Once your "Cricut" device has been connected to your computer, set your cut setting to "Printable Iron-On". Place the iron-on with the printed side up in the top left corner of the cutting mat and press "Go". Load your mat into your "Cricut" machine and "Design Space" will guide you through the cutting of the image. Carefully remove the excess material from the sheet using the "weeder tool", making sure only the design remains on the clear liner.

Step #11

Using the "Cricut Easy Press Mini" and "Easy Press Mat" the iron-on layers can be easily transferred to your mug. Preheat your "Easy Press Mini" and put your design on the desired area and apply pressure for couple of minutes or more (Sample project in the picture below). Wait for few minutes prior to peeling off the design while it is still warm. (Since the design is delicate, use the spatula tool or your fingers to rub the letters down the mug before starting to peel the design). You now have a personalized mug to flaunt your love for America!

II – Personalized Coaster Tiles

Materials needed – "Cricut Maker" or "Cricut Explore", standard grip mat, printable "Cricut" iron-on or heat transfer vinyl, "Cricut Easy Press Mini", "Easy Press" mat, weeding tool, ceramic coaster tiles.

Step #1

To start a new project, after you have logged into your "Cricut" account on "Design Space", click on the "New Project" button on the top right corner of the screen and a blank canvas will be displayed.

Step #2

Let's use our own image for this project. Search the web to find the image that you would like and store it on your computer. Now, click on "Upload" icon from the "Designer Panel" on the left of the screen. For this project, we will select a monogram image.

Step #3

A screen with "Upload Image" and "Upload Pattern" will be displayed. Click on the "Upload Image" button.

Step #4

Click on "Browse" or simply drag and drop your image on the screen.

Step #5

The uploaded image will be displayed next to the "Select Image Type" option. You can choose from "Simple", "Moderately Complex" and "Complex" to store your images. For the monogram image we have uploaded, the image type "Simple" was selected.

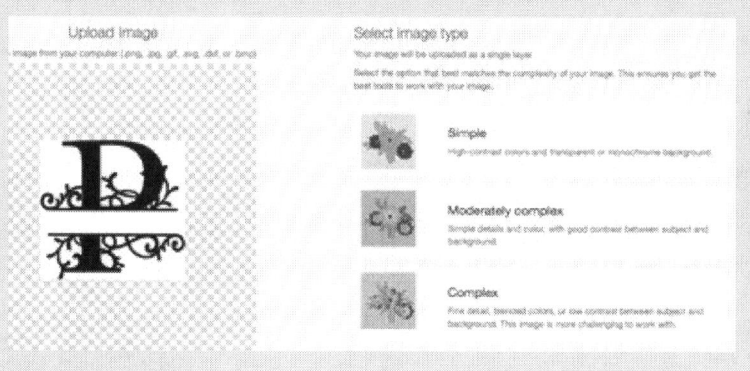

Step #6

The option to selectively erase elements of the image will be displayed on the screen. No updates are needed for this monogram so just click "Continue" at the bottom right of the screen.

Step #7

On the next screen, enter a name for the monogram, which will help you retrieve the image easily when needed and add some relevant tags for your image. Now you can save this image either as "Print then Cut image" or "Cut" image. "Saving as a Print Then Cut image will preserve the entire image, including internal colors and patterns, and add it to the design screen as a Print Then Cut image. Saving as a Cut image will save only the outer silhouette as the image cut path". For this project, the uploaded image will be saved as "Print then Cut" image by clicking on the picture on the left, then clicking on the "Save" button at the bottom right of the screen.

Step #8

Your uploaded image is not a part of the "Uploaded Images Library", that can be accessed at the bottom of the screen. You can choose the uploaded image for your design by clicking on the "Insert Images" button at the bottom of the screen. Your image will be displayed on the canvas and can be edited as needed.

Step #9

Now, to personalize this monogram design for the coasters you can add text to it by clicking on the "Text" icon from the "Designs Panel" on the left of the screen and typing in "Your Name" or any other phrases of your choice.

Step #10

For the image below, the font "American Uncial Corn Regular" in Regular and color (green) as shown in the picture below were selected. But you can let your creativity take over this step and choose any color or font that you like. Now, select the text and the image and click on "Group". Select and copy-paste your design for the number of times you want to print your design.

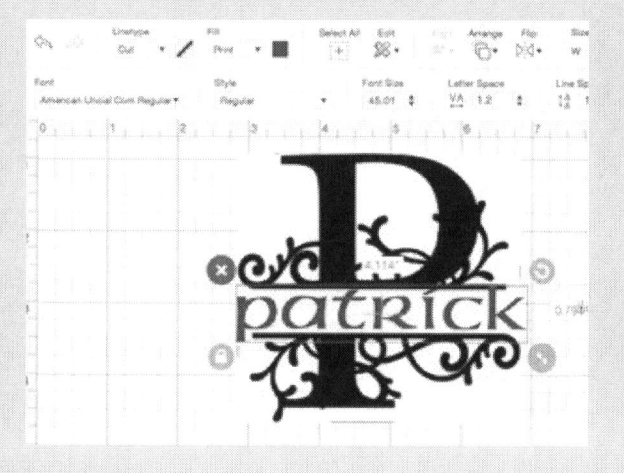

Step #11

Click "Save" at the top right corner of the screen and provide name to your project, for example, "Monogram Ceramic Coasters" then click "Save" again.

Step #12

You can resize the design as needed to match the size of your coaster, although the recommended size is 4 x 4 inches for most common tile coasters. The design can be printed and cut at this stage. The design is ready to be printed and cut. Simply click on the "Make It" button on the top right corner of the screen. You will see the required mats and material displayed on the screen and use your ink jet printer to print the design on your printable iron-on vinyl.

Step #13

Load the material with printed design to your "Cricut" machine and click "Continue" at the bottom right corner of the screen to start cutting your design.

Note – The "Continue" button will not appear if you used images and/or fonts for your design that are not free and available for purchase only. You will instead see a "Purchase" at the bottom right of the screen, so you can buy the image or font first and once the purchase has been made, the "Continue" button will be available to you.

Step #14

Once your "Cricut" device has been connected to your computer, set your cut setting to "Printable Iron-On". Place the iron-on with the printed side up in the top left corner of the cutting mat and press "Go". Load your mat into your "Cricut" machine and "Design Space" will guide you through the cutting of the image. Carefully remove the excess material from the sheet using the "weeder tool", making sure only the design remains on the clear liner.

Step #15

Using the "Cricut Easy Press Mini" and "Easy Press Mat" the iron-on layers can be easily transferred to your mug. Preheat your "Easy Press Mini" and put your design on the desired area and apply pressure for couple of minutes or more (Sample project in the picture below). Wait for few minutes prior to peeling off the design while it is still warm. (Since the design is delicate, use the spatula tool or your fingers to rub the letters down the mug before starting to peel the design). You now have personalized coasters that you can gift to your friends and family or enhance the charm of your home!

Wood Application Projects

Creating wood application projects is particularly tricky since it involves significant investment in terms of time and money and one wrong execution can lead to unsatisfactory results. Therefore, at the conclusion of this chapter a number of tips and tricks on working with wood has been provided for you. Now, let's look at a some of the wood-based projects that you can further customize while following the instructions below and create unique designs of your own.

I – Decorated Wooden Plaque (Salute to our soldiers)

Materials needed – "Cricut Maker" or "Cricut Explore", "Cricut Easy Press", standard grip mat, light grip mat, "Cricut Easy Press" mat, everyday Iron-On (black or desired color), color laser printer, printer paper, "Mod Podge Photo Transfer Medium", "Mod Podge Antique Matte", paintbrush, weeding tool, sponge, foam bush, variety of embellishments, wooden plaque or slice (min 6 x 5 inches).

Note - This is an expert level project, so we will be using an image from the

"Cricut Image Library" as well as uploaded image of our own and edit the design using the "Slice" tool on "Design Space".

Step #1

To start a new project, after you have logged into your "Cricut" account on "Design Space", click on the "New Project" button on the top right corner of the screen and a blank canvas will be displayed.

Step #2

Let's add an image of our own (if you have any family member or friend in the service, you can use their picture or find a picture on the internet). Click on "Upload" icon from the "Designer Panel" on the left of the screen, then click on the "Upload Image" button and select "Browse" to select your image on your computer. Save your uploaded image as "Complex". The image used for this project is available on the internet and shown in the picture below. Click "Continue" and select "Save as a Print then Cut image" and click on "Save" at the bottom of the screen. The uploaded image will be displayed under the "Recently uploaded Images" section, so simply select the image and click on "Insert Images" to retrieve the image on the canvas.

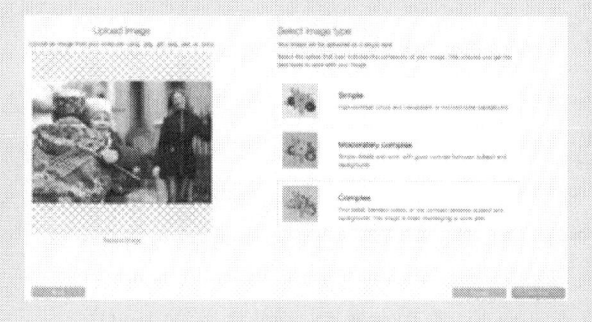

Step #3

Click on the "Images" icon on the "Design Panel" and select the "Categories" tab. Scroll down to find "Patriotic" and click on it. Then type in "home of the brave" in the search bar so you can easily fin the other image used in this project, as shown in the picture below. (Feel free to choose any other image that may caught your eye). Click on "Insert Images" at the bottom of the screen.

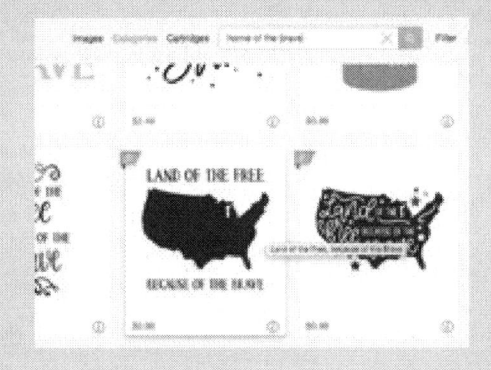

Step #4

Your selected images will appear on the Canvas and you can notice from the "Layers Panel" on the right that our selected images are single layer. Let's edit the design now! First, resize the uploaded image and move it on top of the USA shape image. Then, click on "Arrange" from the "Edit Bar" on top of the screen and select "Send to Back", as shown in the picture below.

Step #5

Now, select the entire design and click on "Slice" at the at the bottom left of the screen. You will see additional layers under the "Layers Panel". Select layers that do not need to be cut or printed as part of the design by and click on the "Delete" button to remove them, as shown in the picture below. Only the layer containing the uploaded image in the shape of USA should be left on the canvas.

Note – In this example, we only deleted the 2nd layer from the picture below.

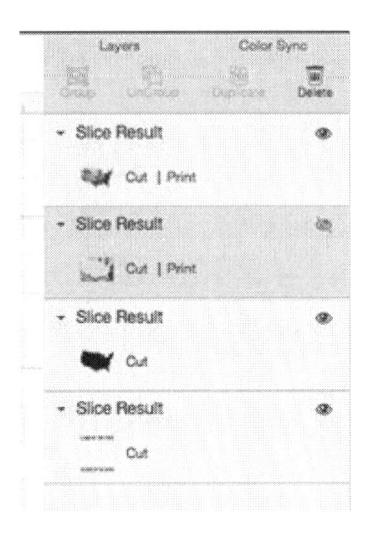

Step #6

Click on "Save" at the top right corner of the screen and give desired name to the project, for example, "Patriotic Plaque - 1" and click "Save".

Step #7

Now, your design is ready to be printed. Simply click on the "Make It" button on the top right corner of the screen. You will see the required mats and material displayed on the screen. Make sure you click on the "Mirror" button under the "Material Size" on the left of the screen and as shown in the picture below.

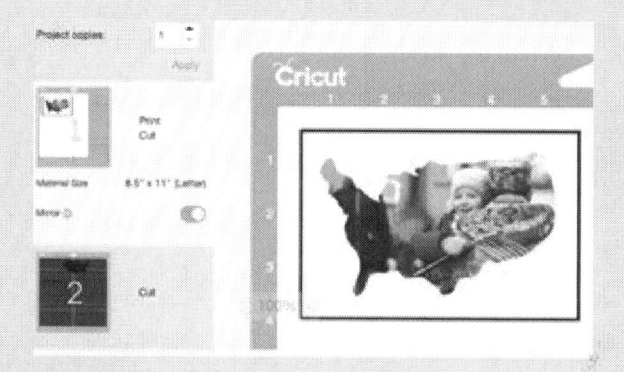

Step #8

After you have loaded the printer paper to the "Cricut" machine, click "Continue" at the bottom right corner of the screen to print the design.

Note – The USA image used is available for purchase so click on "Purchase" at the bottom right of the screen to buy the images before you can print the design. And once you have made the purchase the "Continue" button will be available to you.

Step #9

Once your "Cricut" device has been connected to your computer, set your cut setting to "Vinyl". Place the black vinyl on top of the cutting mat with the shiny side or clear liner facing down on the mat and load the mat into the "Cricut" device by pushing against the rollers. The "Load/Unload" button will start flashing so just press it. Then press the "Go" button which would already be flashing.

Step #10

Carefully remove the excess vinyl from the sheet using the weeder tool, so only the design is left on the clear liner. Now use the "Cricut Easy Press" and "Easy Press Mat" to transfer the iron-on layers to the wooden plaque. The recommended temperature for everyday iron-on material and wood base material is 3o0 °F to be applied for 40 seconds with firm pressure and preheating your "Easy Press" for 5 seconds. Then slowly remove the liner while it is still warm.

Note – To find the recommended temperature and time of application with "Cricut Easy Press", you can use the "Interactive Quick Reference Guide" available on the official "Cricut" website.

Step #11

Now, using a foam brush dipped in the "Mod Podge Photo Transfer Medium" saturate the printed side of the image. Now, put the paper containing the printed image on the wood with the printed side facing down then position at the center of the iron-on vinyl and smooth it out with your hands.

Step #12

Allow to dry for at least 24 hours then use a moist sponge to gently rub off the printer paper from the wood and let the wood dry out completely.

Step #13

Now, to seal the entire wooden plaque use the "Mod Podge Antique Matte" and let the wood dry and Viola! You have your own customized wooden plaques, that may look like the picture below.

II – Wooden Craft Supplies Box

Materials needed – "Cricut Maker" or "Cricut Explore", standard grip mat (12 x 24 inches), purple spray paint (or color of your choice), white spray paint (or color of your choice), stencil vinyl, wooden box.

Step #1

To start a new project, after you have logged into your "Cricut" account on "Design Space", click on the "New Project" button on the top right corner of the screen and a blank canvas will be displayed.

Step #2

Click on the "Images" icon on the "Design Panel" and type in "pattern" in the search bar. Click on desired image, then click on the "Insert Images" button at the bottom of the screen. The image (Aztec Pattern) selected for this project is shown in the picture below.

Step #3

Your selected image will be loaded on the canvas and can be edited now. You can resize the image to meet the dimensions of your wooden box (click on the lock at the left bottom of the image, so you can change the width of the image in rectangular manner if needed). You can also change the color of the image to your preference by clicking on the "Linetype Swatch" and choosing your color of choice.

Step #4

Click on "Save" at the top right corner of the screen and enter a name for your project, for example, "Wooden Craft Box" then click "Save".

Step #5

The design is ready to be cut. Simply click on the "Make It" button on the top right corner of the screen. You will see the required mats and material displayed on the screen.

Step #6

Load the stencil vinyl to your "Cricut" machine and click "Continue" at the bottom right corner of the screen to start cutting your design.

Note – The "Continue" button will not appear if you used images and/or fonts for your design that are not free and available for purchase only. You will instead see a "Purchase" at the bottom right of the screen, so you can buy the image or font first and once the purchase has been made, the "Continue" button will be available to you.

Step #7

Once your "Cricut" device has been connected to your computer, set your cut setting to "Vinyl". Place the stencil vinyl on top of the cutting mat and load into the "Cricut" device by pushing against the rollers. The "Load/Unload" button will start flashing so just press it. Then press the "Go" button which would already be flashing.

Step #8

Use the weeding tool to remove the positive pieces of the design leaving any of the negative pieces of the design behind. Use the white spray paint or the paint color you would like to serve as the background of the design to paint the wooden box.

Step #9

Transfer the vinyl stencil to the wooden box using the transfer tape and smooth it out for even application, making sure all the edges are sticking securely on the box.

Step #10

Now, use the purple spray paint or the paint of your chosen color to paint over the stencil on the box and let the pain dry completely before removing the stencil. Your completed project may look like the picture below.

Clothing Application Projects

Personalized clothing is the new talk of the town with the advent of the social media. It has evolved as a way of expression of not only our individual personality but also exhibit unity of a team or organization. Therefore, a variety of clothing objects that are most commonly personalized are included in this section. Feel free to further customize these projects as you follow the given instructions to create unique designs of your own.

I – Personalized T-Shirt

Materials needed – "Cricut Maker" or "Cricut Explore", standard grip mat (12 x 24 inches), printable iron-on, t-shirt, "Cricut Easy Press", "Easy Press" mat, weeding tool.

Step #1

To start a new project, after you have logged into your "Cricut" account on "Design Space", click on the "New Project" button on the top right corner of the screen and a blank canvas will be displayed.

Step #2

Let's use an image of our own for this project. Click on "Upload" icon from the "Designer Panel" on the left of the screen, then click on the "Upload Image" button and select "Browse" to select your image on your computer. Save your uploaded image as "Complex" and click "Continue". Then select "Save as a Print then Cut image" and click on "Save" at the bottom of the screen. The uploaded image will be displayed under the "Recently uploaded Images" section, so simply select the image and click on "Insert Images" to retrieve the image on the canvas.

Step #3

Your selected images will appear on the Canvas, as shown in the picture below. You can resize the image to make sure it fits nicely on your t-shirt.

Step #4

Click on "Save" at the top right corner of the screen and give desired name to the project, for example, "Personalized T-shirt" and click "Save".

Step #5

The design is ready to be printed and cut. Simply click on the "Make It" button on the top right corner of the screen. You will see the required mats and material displayed on the screen. Make sure you click on the "Mirror" button under the "Material Size" on the left of the screen.

Step #6

Load the iron-on with printed design to your "Cricut" machine and click "Continue" at the bottom right corner of the screen to start cutting your design.

Step #7

Once your "Cricut" device has been connected to your computer, set your cut setting to "Iron-On". Place the iron-on with its shiny side (clear liner) down on the cutting mat. Load your mat into your "Cricut" machine and "Design Space" will guide you through the cutting of the image. Carefully remove the excess material from the sheet using the "weeder tool", making sure only the design remains on the clear liner.

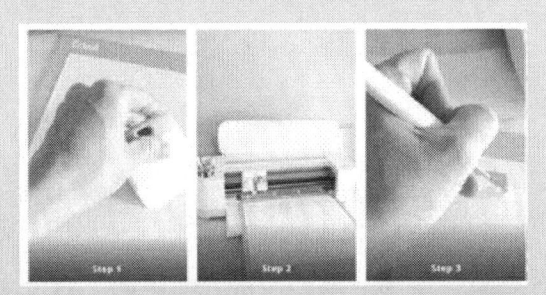

Step #8

Using the "Cricut Easy Press" and "Easy Press Mat" the iron-on layers can be easily transferred to your t-shirt. The recommended temperature for everyday iron-on material and cotton base material is 330 °F. So, preheat your "Easy Press".

Step #9

Use the "Easy Press" to get rid of any wrinkles from your transfer target area by pressing on it for 5 seconds. Then put your design on the area and heat the area while applying pressure for 30 seconds and flip your t-shirt to apply the heat and pressure for another 15 seconds. (Note – If your design is larger than the size of your "Easy Press", then apply pressure for 30 seconds on each side of the design and a little bit of overlap would not cause any damage to the design). Wait for couple of minutes prior to peeling off the design while it is still warm and has not cooled off completely. You now have your own personalized.

II – Customized Socks

Materials needed – "Cricut Maker" or "Cricut Explore", standard grip mat, Everyday iron-on (recommended "Sportflex Iron-On") or heat transfer vinyl, socks, "Cricut Easy Press", "Easy Press" mat, weeding tool.

Step #1

To start a new project, after you have logged into your "Cricut" account on "Design Space", click on the "New Project" button on the top right corner of the screen and a blank canvas will be displayed.

Step #2

Let's use text for this project. Click on "Text" from the "Designs Panel" on the left of the screen and type in "IF YOU CAN READ THIS" and "BRING ME PIZZA" or any other phrases you may like. Now, for the sock we want the text to be horizontal so just press enter after each word to move it down to the next line. Click on "Alignment" then "Center" to align the text as shown in the picture below.

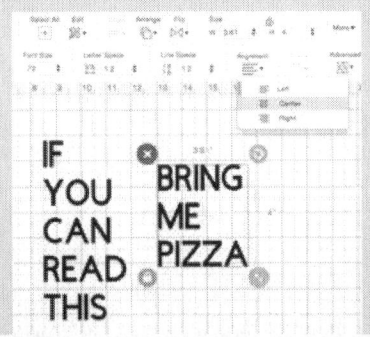

Step #3

For the image below, the font "Alleycat ICG" in Regular and color as shown in the picture below were selected. But you can let your creativity take over this step and choose any color or font that you like. Select and copy-paste your image for the number of times you want to print your design.

Step #4

Click on "Save" at the top right corner of the screen and give desired name to the project, for example, "Sock Project" and click "Save".

Step #5

Simply click on the "Make It" button on the top right corner of the screen. You will see the required mats and material displayed on the screen. Make sure you click on the "Mirror" button under the "Material Size" on the left of the screen.

Step #6

Load the iron-on in your desired color to your "Cricut" machine and click "Continue" at the bottom right corner of the screen to start cutting your design.

Step #7

Once your "Cricut" device has been connected to your computer, set your cut setting to "Iron-On". Place the iron-on with its shiny side (clear liner) down on the cutting mat. Load your mat into your "Cricut" machine and "Design Space" will guide you through the cutting of the image. Carefully remove the excess material from the sheet using the "weeder tool", making sure only the design remains on the clear liner.

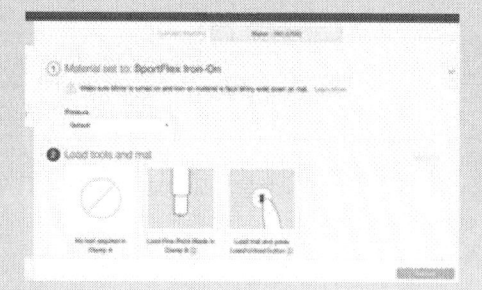

Step #8

Using the "Cricut Easy Press" and "Easy Press Mat" the iron-on layers can be easily transferred to your sock. The recommended temperature for "Sportflex Iron-On" material and cotton base material is 305 °F. So, preheat your "Easy Press".

Step #9

Put your design on the desired area and apply pressure for 30 seconds. Then flip your sock to apply the heat and pressure for another 15 seconds on the other side. Wait for couple of minutes prior to peeling off the design while it is still warm. (Since the design is delicate, use the spatula tool or your fingers to rub the letters down the sock before starting to peel the design). You now have a cool pair of socks that might look like the picture below!

Home Decor Projects

The passion for decorating a house has always been at the heart of the crafting and rightly so since we spent most of our time at home making memories for a lifetime. There are so many aspects to decorating a house to make it into a home that reflects your style and values. We will be going through a couple of projects that can be customized to have unique and highly personalized decoration for your house. Following the instructions below and feel free to further customize your designs with a variety of colors and patterns.

I – Motivational Poster

Materials needed – "Cricut Maker" or "Cricut Explorer", lightgrip mat, adhesive for paper, adhesive foam dots, cardstock in desired colors, picture frame.

Step #1

To start a new project, after you have logged into your "Cricut" account on "Design Space", click on the "New Project" button on the top right corner of the screen and a blank canvas will be displayed.

Step #2

Let's create our own design for this project using basic shapes and text. click on the "Text" icon and type in "IF YOU CAN DREAM IT, YOU CAN DO IT!".

Step #3

For the image below, the font "Linotype Aperto Corn Semi Bold" in Regular. Click on the "Linetype Swatch" to change the color of text then copy the text twice. Change the colors of the copies and arrange them over the original text, adjusting the position so you get a dramatic layered effect, as shown in the picture below was selected. But you can let your creativity take over this step and choose any color or font that you like.

Step #4

Click on "Shapes" and add a "hexagon" to serve as the background. Click on "star" to add some stars to your design. Simply click on the "Linetype Swatch" to change the colors of the shapes. Then select the "Hexagon" layer from the "Layers panel" and click on "Arrange" on the top of the screen from the "Edit Bar" and select "Send To Back".

Step #5

Select the "star" layers from the "Layers panel" and click on "Arrange" on the top of the screen from the "Edit Bar" and select "Move Backward" so you get the text layer on the top. Remember to group the images together by clicking on "Group" on the right of the screen under "Layers panel". You can now edit your image as needed, for example, you could resize and arrange the images as shown in the picture below. (A good size for a poster is 11 x 11 inches but may vary depending on the size of your picture frame.)

Step #6

Click on "Save" at the top right corner of the screen and give desired name to the project, for example, "Motivational Poster - 1" and click "Save".

Step #7

The design is ready to be cut now. Simply click on the "Make It" button on the top right corner of the screen. You will see the required mats and material displayed on the screen.

Step #8

Click "Continue" at the bottom right corner of the screen. Load the cardstock material to the "Cricut" machine following the instructions on the "Design Space".

Step #9

Once your "Cricut" device has been connected to your computer, set your cut setting to "Carstock". Place the cardstock on top of the cutting mat and load into the "Cricut" machine by pushing against the rollers. The "Load/Unload" button will start flashing so just press it. Then press the "Go" button which would already be flashing.

Step #10

Use the adhesive and adhesive foam squares to assemble the layers of the design on the frame and work your way up. So, paste the hexagon at the bottom, following by placing the stars on top of the base. Then paste the three layers of the text on top of one another and Viola! You will have your own motivational poster to keep your spirits up, that may look like the picture below.

II – Personalized Fridge Magnets

Materials needed – "Cricut Maker" or "Cricut Explorer", standard grip mat, printer, "Cricut" magnet sheets.

Step #1

To start a new project, after you have logged into your "Cricut" account on "Design Space", click on the "New Project" button on the top right corner of the screen and a blank canvas will be displayed.

Step #2

For your personalized magnets, upload a picture of yourself or your family to the "Design Space" application as a pattern. Click on the "Upload" icon from the "Designer Panel" on the left of the screen.

Step #3

A screen with "Upload Image" and "Upload Pattern" will be displayed. Click on the "Upload Pattern" button.

Step #4

Click on "Browse" or simply drag and drop your image on the screen.

Step #5

Your uploaded image will be displayed on the screen and you would be able to change the name of the pattern and select any of the recommended themes, styles, or colors tags then click on "Save".

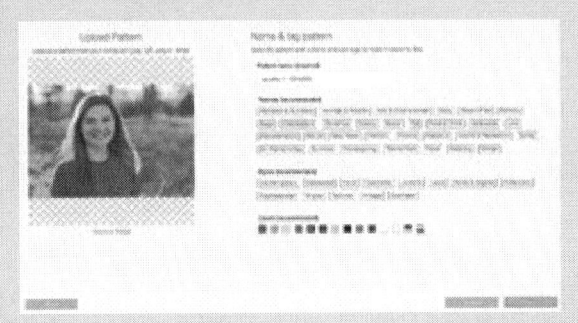

Once the picture has been uploaded, you will briefly see a notification on the top of the screen stating the same.

Step #6

Click on "Shapes" and select "Octagon" or "Hexagon" or your desired shape. Change the size to 3.5 inches wide and copy the shape then change the size to 3 inches, as shown in the picture below.

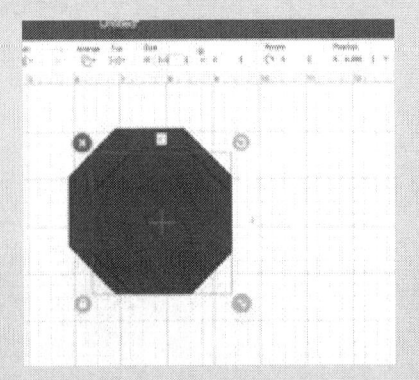

Step #7

Now select both the shapes and click on "Align" on the top of the screen and select "Center Horizontally" and then select "Center Vertically" so the inner layer will fit perfectly inside the outer layer, as shown in the picture below.

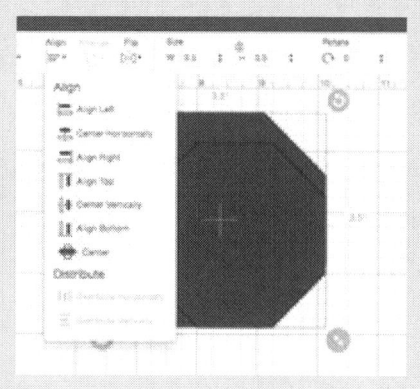

Step #8

Click on "Group" on the "Layers Panel" on the left of the screen, so you wouldn't accidentally disturb the arrangement of the layers.

Step #9

Select the inner layer by clicking on the first layer on the "Layers Panel" and click on "Fill" and select Print.

Step #10

Now, click on the "Fill Swatch" and under "Print Type" select "Pattern". Your uploaded image will be displayed on the top. Simply click on it and your image will be filled inside the shape.

Step #11

You may want to edit the pattern to make it fit better inside the shape. To do this, click on "Edit Pattern" at the bottom of the "Print Type" pop-up, as shown in the picture below.

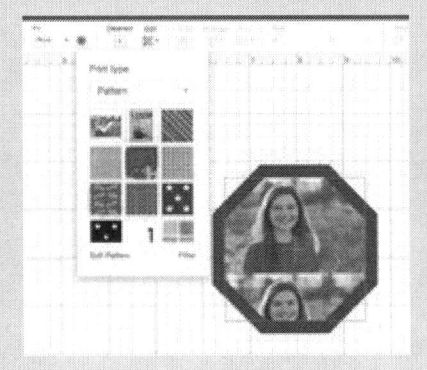

Step #12

The "Edit Pattern" window will be displayed. Use the "Scale" function to resize the image and use the "Horizontal" and "Vertical" options to align the position of the image. You can even rotate the image if you want to give it a more dramatic look using the "Rotate" function. Once you are happy with the modifications, simply close the box and your changes will be applied to the design.

Step #13

Now, select the outer layer from "Layers Panel" and click on the "Fill Swatch" and under "Print Type" select "Pattern". Select a pattern to be used as the background for your magnet, as shown in the picture below. (You can also just use a different color for the background, if desired, by clicking on the "Linetype Swatch" and choosing the color of your choice).

Step #14

Click on "Save" at the top right corner of the screen and give desired name to the project, for example, "Magnet -Kate" and click "Save".

Step #15

Simply click on the "Make It" button on the top right corner of the screen. You will see the required mats and material displayed on the screen.

Step #16

Make sure your printer is connected and click "Continue" at the bottom right corner of the screen. Load the "Cricut" magnet sheet to the printer and follow the instructions on the screen as shown in the picture below.

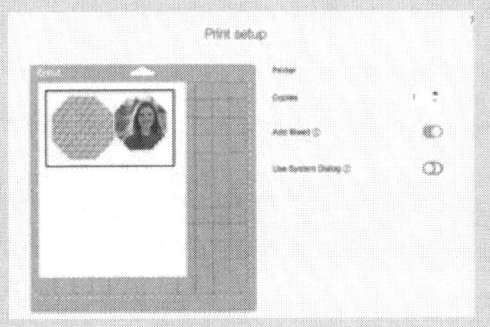

Step #17

Once your "Cricut" device has been connected to your computer, set your cut setting to "Vinyl". Place the printed magnet sheet on top of the cutting mat and load into the "Cricut" machine by pushing against the rollers. The "Load/Unload" button will start flashing so just press it. Then press the "Go" button which would already be flashing. Once the sheets have finished cutting, you will have your own personalized refrigerator magnets!

TIPS and TRICKS!!!

Learning to use the "Cricut" machine definitely involves a steep learning curve. The more complicated aspect of it all is using the "Design Space" software to hone down a variety of features and tools to help you craft your designs and turn your "inspiration into creation". There are multiple shortcuts on the "Design Space" application to make your designing not only easy but more efficient. Let's look at some of the tips and tricks that will make your creative self-stronger and happier! We will cover these in 3 different sections, starting with the "Design Space" application, the "Cricut" device, tools and accessories as well as select cutting material and concluding with how you can clean your device to keep it working like new.

"Design Space" application

- The "Weld", "Contour" and "Slice" functionalities to customize your designs. These 3 tools will be activated at the bottom of the screen for designs that allow for these changes.

- The "Weld" tool will allow you to merge two different designs to obtain one composite design, without any leftover seams and cut lines that might be present on the individual designs. This helps you in obtaining single continuous cut for your design so you do not need to glue and assemble multiple pieces to obtain the final design, for example, creation of cake toppers, gift tags and other decorations.

- The "Contour" tool can be used to activate or deactivate any cut lines in any cut files and thereby allowing you to customize the image in various ways. So imagine you have an image of a flower and you want to remove the details of the design and obtain more of an outline of the flower, you can do so by clicking on the "Contour" button at the bottom of the screen and selecting the different elements of the image that you want to turn on or off from the contour pop-up window.

- The "Slice" tool can be used to slice a design from an image by cutting out or removing elements of the image, as shown in the picture below. (This feature has been used in one of the expert level projects mentioned earlier in this chapter)

- Use your search keywords wisely. The search functionality within the "Design Space" is not very dynamic so your choice of keywords will make a big difference on the designs and projects that will be displayed to you. For example, if you search for images containing dotted designs and search with keyword "Dots", you would be given around 120 images but if you search with the term "Dot" you would see almost twice as many images. You should also search with synonyms and closely related terms of your target project idea. For instance, if you wanted to create a

Halloween project, you can search with terms like pumpkin, costumes and trick or treat among others. This will ensure you are viewing any and all images pertaining to your project.

- The "Cartridge" image sets. It is likely that during your search, you like a design more than any other made available to you but it is not exactly how you want it to be. Well, simply click on the small information circle (i) at the bottom of the image and you will be able to view the entire image set or "cartridge" of images similar to your selected image within the "Design Space Image Library".

- A treasure trove of free fonts and images. As a beginner you would want to utilize a large number of free fonts and images to get your hands-on experience with your "Cricut" device. This is a great way to spend less money and still be able to create stunning craft projects. Within the "Design Space" application, you can click on the "Filter" icon next to the search bar (available within the images, fonts and projects tabs) and select "Free" to only view free resources within each category.

- Use synchronized colors to save time and money. This is a great tool when you have designs that are either a composite of multiple images or inherently contains different hues of the same color. Instead of using 5 different shades of the same color, you can synchronize the colors so you need to use only one colored sheet. To do this, simply click on the "Color

Sync" tab on the "Layers Panel" on the top right corner of the screen. Then drag and drop desired layer(s) of the design to your target color layer and the moved layer will immediately be modified to have the same color as the target color.

- Use the "Hide" tool to selectively cut images from the Canvas. When you are looking to turn your imagination into a work of art, you may want to view and take inspirations from multiple images while you work on your design. But once you obtain your desired design you would not want to cut every other image on your canvas. This is where the "Hide" tool comes in handy, so you do not need to delete the images on the Canvas to avoid cutting them along with your project design. To hide the image, you just need to click on the "eye" symbol next to those specific image layers on the "Layers Panel". The hidden images will not be deleted from the Canvas but would not appear on the cutting mat when you click the "Make It" button to cut your project.

- Ability to change the design lines to be cut, scored or drawn. With the latest version of the "Design Space" application, you have the ability to simply change the "Linetype" of a design from it's predefined type to your desired action, instead of looking for designs that have predefined line type meeting your project need. For example, if your selected design is set at "Linetype" Cut but you want the design to be "Linetype" Score, you can easily change the "Linetype" by clicking on the "Linetype" drop-down and making your selection.

- The power of the "Pattern" tool. As you have learnt from the last project of this book, "Personalized Fridge Magnets", you can use your own uploaded images to be used as pattern fill for your designs. Moreover, you will also be able to edit the image pattern and the patterns that already exit within the "Design Space" application to create your own unique and customized patterns. The "Edit Pattern" window allows you to adjust the resolution and positioning of the pattern on your design and much more. (Remember, to use the "Pattern" feature you must use the "Print then Cut" approach for your project, with access to a printer).

- Utilize the standard "keyboard shortcuts". The "Design Space" application does have all the required tools and buttons (refer to chapter 2 for the list of all the buttons and their use) to allow you to edit the images and fonts but if you prefer to use your keyboard shortcuts to quickly edit the image, the "Design Space" application will support that. Some of the keyboard shortcuts you can use include: "Copy (Control + C)"; "Paste (Control + V)"; "Delete (Delete key)"; "Copy (Control + Z)".

- You can utilize the "Slice" tool to crop the image. The "Design Space" application still lacks the "Crop" functionality, so if you need to crop an image, you will need to get creative. A good tip is to use the "Slice" tool along with the "Shapes" to get your desired image.

- Change the position of the design on the cutting Mat. When you are ready to cut your design and click on the "Make It" button, you will notice that your design will be aligned on the top left corner of the mat. Now, if you are using material that was previously cut at it's top left corner, you can simply drag and move the image on the "Design Space" mat to meet the positioning of your cutting material. You will be able to cut the image anywhere on the mat by moving the design on that specific position on the mat.

- Moving design from one mat to the another. Yes! You can not only move the design over the mat itself, you can also move the design from one mat to another by simply clicking on the three dots (...) on top of the mat and select "Move to another mat". You will then view a pop-up window where you can select from the existing mats for your project to be used as the new mat for your selected design.

- Save cut materials as Favorites for quick access. Instead of spending time filtering and searching for your cut material on the "Design Space" application over and over, just save your frequently used material by clicking on the star next to the "Cricut" logo on the "Design Space" application to save them under the "Favorites" tab next to the default "All Materials" tab. When you are getting ready to cut your project, under the "Set Material" tab, your

"Favorites" material will be displayed on the screen, as shown in the picture below.

- You can store the most frequently used cut materials on the "Cricut Maker". Unlike the "Cricut Explore" series which has dial settings for a variety of commonly used cut materials, the "Cricut Maker" requires you to use a "Custom Materials" menu within the "Design Space" application that can be accessed using the button on the machine bearing "Cricut" logo, since there is no dial to choose the material you want to cut.

- Choose to repeat the cut of the same mat or skip a mat from being cut altogether. By following the instructions on the "Design Space" and feeding the right color and size of the material to the machine, you will be able to get your design perfectly cut. You can change the order in which the mats are cut, repeat the cut of your desired mat and even skip cutting a mat, if needed. You can do this easily by simply clicking on and selecting the mat you would like to cut.

- You can edit the cut settings your materials. You might notice that even when you have selected the default settings to cut the desired material, the material may not cut as desired. To help with this, "Design Space" allows you to adjust the cut settings for all the materials such as the depth of the cut, the cutting blade and the number of the passes to be made by the "Cricut" device. Since this may not be as intuitive to most beginners, here's a step by step walkthrough of this process:

1. When using the "Cricut Maker", select "Materials" on the cut screen and if using the "Cricut Explore" series, set the dial to "Custom".

2. Click on "Browse All Materials" from the top of the menu.

3. From the bottom of the screen, select "Material Settings".

4. The pop-up window for the "Custom Materials" will be displayed as shown in the picture below, where you can make the required adjustments.

- Adjust the pressure with which the material can be cut. You may want to just adjust the pressure with which the cut is made to obtain clean and neat cut of the material, without needing to going through the process described above to adjust the cut setting of the material. On the cut screen, once you have selected the cut material, a drop-down option with "Default" setting will be displayed. Simply click on the drop-down button, and adjust pressure to "More" or "Less".

- "Cricut Access Membership" – At a monthly fee of around $8 or an annual membership fee, you will be able to use a larger variety of fonts and imaged for free. You will be able to freely use more than 30K images, over 370 fonts and thousands of projects saving a lot of money in the long run, depending on your usage.

"Cricut" devices, tools and accessories

- How to clean your cutting mat - If you would like to prolong the life of your cutting mats, it is important to clean them every now and then (if not after each use). You can just wipe the mat with baby wipes or use other wet wipes that do not contain any alcohol and are fragrance free. This will ensure that there is not residual build up from cardstock and vinyl and other such materials and from accumulating dust and lint.

- Carry out a sample cut prior to cutting your design – To make sure that you do not end up with a cut that does not meet your expectations it is recommended to do a test cut first. This will help you check the sharpness of the blade as well as the cut setting for your material and make the required adjustments to get clean cut projects.

- Carefully remove the materials off the cutting mat – It is highly recommended to use appropriate tools to remove the material from the mat. But it is equally important to pay attention to how you are peeling the design from the mat. To prevent the material from getting damaged, it is better to peel the mat away from the design by turning the mat upside down and bending a corner of the material. Then you can slip in the spatula to remove the project easily and with no damage.

- Use "Non-Cricut" craft pen(s) – If you have Sharpie pens or other craft pens, don't be afraid to use them with your "Cricut" device to save some money from buying new pen.

- Dedicated blades to increase the shelf life – If you are able to use dedicated bladed for your frequently used cutting material, your blades will last longer. For instance, you can have one blade for vinyl only and another just to cut cardstock. Since both the materials, in this case, have different strength, the pressure and sharpness required to produce clean cut will also vary. Therefore, dedicated blades will maintain it's sharpness much longer.

- Storage of mats and vinyl rolls – Using standard hooks, you can easily hang your mats as a display on the wall. This will make the mats more accessible and you would not need to spend time searching for the required mats. Similarly, you can utilize trash bag holders to store and organize your vinyl or paper rolls and easily retrieve the desired material when needed.

- No "BrightPad"! No Problem! – It is definitely ideal to weed your vinyl and other delicate designs by placing the design on top of the "BrightPad. The light from the "BrightPad" peeks through the cut lines so you can easily weed the design without damaging it. But if you do not want to invest in a "BrightPad", try hanging the vinyl on a window for similar light effect to carefully weed your design.

- Convenient Charging Port – The "Cricut Maker" device is equipped with USB port on the side that will allow you to power your electronic devices, so you can charge your phone or tablet while you work to get your craft projects completed.

- Tips when working with wood – The wood projects tend to be time consuming and labor intensive and of course, long lasting. So you want to get it right the first time. Below are some tips to help you get the best wood projects with no stress.

- Ensure that your projects are carried out using a sealer so that the wood does not get damaged unexpectedly.

- When using vinyl or iron-on designs, use sanding paper to sand the wood and obtain a flat surface prior to application of the design. Wooden plaques are not always flat, as it's a natural product. The surface may need to be sand so that all sections of the design material will stick evenly on the surface.

- Consider using a stamping effect for your paper design, when using wood and paper designs to produce a rustic feel for your project.

- When choosing a stain color for the wooden plaque, make sure that your project color aligns with that color and other project that you already have in your house. Don't be scared to combine different wood stain colors and use your own customized stain!

- For easy and effective application of wood glue, it is recommended to wet the wood with a damp cloth first. After the wood glue has been applied to the plaque, clamp it and allow it to set for at least 24 hours.

- If you are planning to use pallet wood make sure to clean the pallet plaque using a wire brush.

Cleaning the "Cricut" device

With extended period of use, it is likely that your machine would have collected dirt and grime. So, here are some tips on how you can clean your machine and keep it looking and working as new.

- Prior to cleaning the machine, make sure that it has been powered off and disconnected from the power source.

- Use microfiber cloth or a piece of soft clean cloth sprayed with a glass cleaning solution to clean the machine.

- In case of static electricity build up on the machine due to dust or paper particles, use the same cloth to wipe off the residues and get rid of the static from the machine.

- For grease build up on the bar that allows the carriage travels, use a soft cloth or tissue or cotton swab and gently remove the grease from the machine.

- Do not use nail polish remover or any other acetone containing solution to clean the machine, as it may permanently damage the plastic shell of the machine.

To keep the machine running smoothly you may want to grease it, following the instructions below:

1. Power off your machine and carefully push the "Cut Smart" carriage to the left of the machine.

2. Use a tissue to wipe the carriage bar (located in front of the belt).

3. Now, carefully move the bar to the right and clean again with the tissue.

4. Carefully move the bar to the center and use a cotton swab to lubricate both the sides of the carriage by "applying a light coating of grease around the bar to form a 1/4-inch ring on each side of the carriage".

5. In order to evenly distribute the grease on the carriage, slowly move the carriage from one end to another a couple of times and wipe off any excessive grease.

(Note – It is recommended to use grease packet supplied by "Cricut" only and no other grease from a third party should be used)

Conclusion

Thank you for making it through to the end of Cricut for Beginners: The best step-by-step guide in 2020 with illustrated and detailed practical examples and project ideas. Tips and tricks to decorate your spaces, objects and much more, let's hope it was informative and able to provide you with all of the tools you need to achieve your goals whatever they may be.

The next step is to use the detailed instructions provided in this book to create your own unique craft projects that reflect your personality and will serve as a testament of your creativity. The detail explanation of all the ways you can use and leverage different "Cricut" devices will help you turn even the most unimaginable ideas into beautiful craft projects in no time. All the nuances of the "Design Space" application have also been explained in exquisite detail. You have learnt all about the free resources including images, fonts and projects that are available through the "Cricut" library so you can save money as you learn and sharpen your craft skills.

The detailed instructions with step by step process including pictures are written in an easy to understand language so you can have this book with you as you work to design your projects using the "Design Space" application, cut them using the "Cricut" cutting machine and subsequently use the "Cricut Easy Press" for expert level projects. You can use this book as your graduating scale and start by crafting the projects marked as easy, then progress to the intermediate level projects. I would recommend to sharpen your skills by exploring and playing with the "Design Space" application in your spare time before you start creating expert level projects. Art has a long history of speaking without any language and transcending barriers. You now have your own way of expressing your ideas and turning your inspiration into creation.

Finally, if you found this book useful in any way, a review on Amazon is always appreciated!

Pamela Cutter

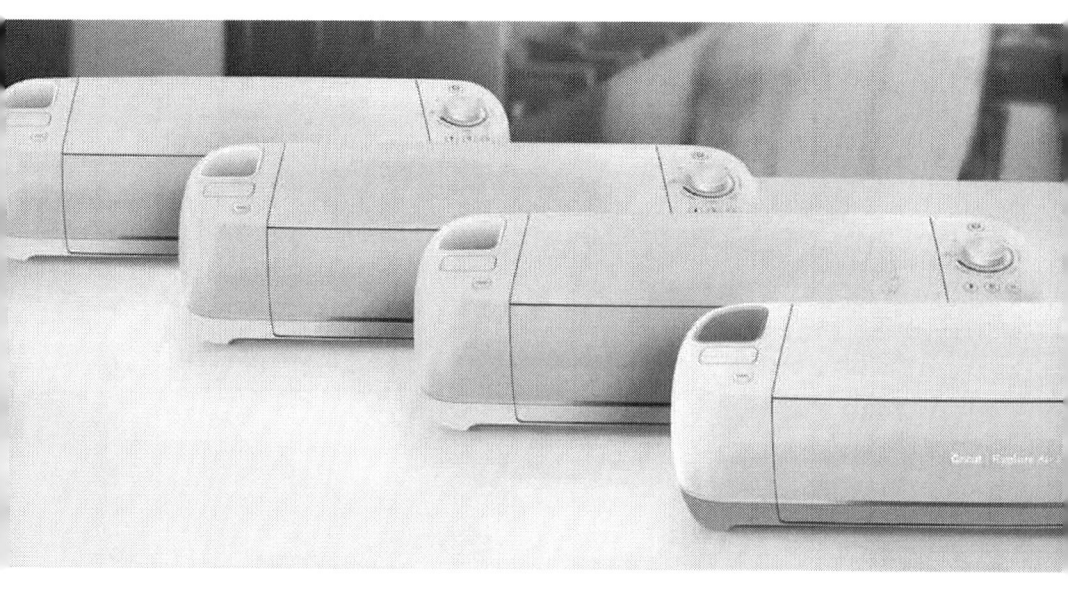

CRICUT DESIGN SPACE

A STEP BY STEP GUIDE TO DESIGN SPACE WITH ILLUSTRATIONS AND SCREENSHOTS

Introduction

Cricut Design Space is special software created for crafting with Cricut machines, and it represents open-source software where you can create your designs or use Cricut designs that can be unlocked for access via Design Space. Everything you need for your crafting with the Cricut machine is available with Design Space features and commands. This software will be the starting point of your projects and this is also where all the magic happens. Design Space is completely free to use and it comes with purchasing a Cricut machine. There are already ready-to-make designs available in the software while you can access Design Space via multiple devices, including your laptop and your smartphone. Once you get familiar with all commands you can use with your designs as you are starting from scratch on your projects. You will soon learn that Cricut and Design Space has everything a crafter needs for a project well done. The software needs to be set up when using it for the first time; however, the process is made easy with step-by-step guidance. Once you set up your Design Space, you are ready to go and try out commands and functions the software has to offer. At first, you may find it a bit difficult to get around all the functions and commands; however, we are making sure that you can get familiar with all crucial operations on Design Software.

What is the Cricut Design Canvas Space Area?

Canvas Space Area is the part of the software where all the magic of creating projects for Cricut begins. Here is where you will be able to make edits and design your projects before you start cutting towards making your final product. Once you set up your Design Space software, in case you wish to gain access to the library of designs you will need to subscribe to Cricut Access, which provides you with exclusive and premium fonts and designs. You can always make your designs and patterns once you get familiar with the software. When you start working on Design Space, all your designs and edits will be done in the Canvas window. Canvas has multiple icons and commands, which is why we will go through each of the available buttons. By getting familiar with commands, you will soon be able to make your designs and start working on your projects. Canvas is comprised out of four basic sections, editing area, layers panels, canvas area and insert area.

Cricut Design Space Canvas – What to Do and How to Do Canvassing?

We will get into the details on how to work in Canvas and how to insert your images and patterns, edit your designs and perform other actions that can be done in Design Space. Let's see how you can start working in Canvas, step-by-step.

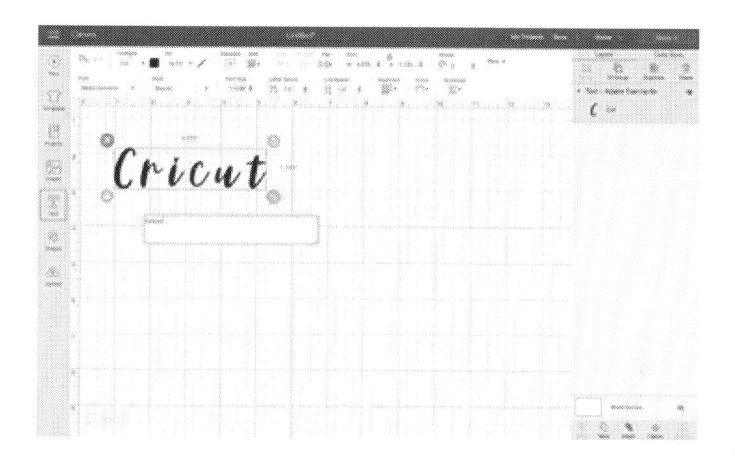

This is how the Canvas window looks like when active, while you can also notice that you have numerous options and commands within the software.

Canvas Editing Area

Canvas editing area is the section where you will do all your edits, which includes arranging project elements in the canvas area and editing your designs. Editing area is located on the top of the Canvas and also allows changing fonts, size of fonts and designs as well as enables alignment of design pieces. This is where you are preparing your project from scratch. The editing area/panel can be divided into two sub areas or subpanels. The top panel of the Canvas editing area serves the purpose of holding the main functions for creating new projects, save your projects once your design is ready and send your designs to the machine to start making projects. The second sub panel found at the bottom of the Canvas editing panel holds commands for designing and editing your projects.

Top Editing Subpanel

The top editing subpanel is comprised of several important functions. If you click on "Canvas" you will gain access to the Toggle menu – more details on what you can do with the Toggle menu will be disclosed further. You can also see the next command shown as "Untitled" – This is where you name your projects, following the list of your saved projects under "My project", "Save" button, and "Maker" (Machine button) and the execution button "Make it" colored in green.

Canvas - Toggle menu

Although you can gain access to the Toggle menu through the "Canvas" menu and Canvas window, the Toggle menu is not directly related to editing functions and commands crucial for working in the editing area of Canvas. Still, it would be handy for you to find your way around the Toggle menu, which is why we are also addressing these commands as well. You will find all commands regarding the software right here in this dropping menu. You can view your profile from the Toggle menu, update your firmware and software, perform setup for your new machine, check your account details, link cartridges, manage your subscription through Cricut Access, access settings, features and find Help button for support from Cricut. You can also sign out from your account through the Toggle menu. Settings option will allow adjusting the visibility and measurements for your Canvas area.

Project Name (Untitled*)

All new projects start with "Untitled" tags, while this is the area where you can name your projects that can be later viewed and accessed under the "My projects" section. You won't be able to name your project until you start working in the sense of adding at least one element to the Canvas area.

My projects

Every project you save and name can be found under "My projects", you can save as many projects as you like and reuse them by redesigning, re-cutting and editing. This is where you will find an entire list of all the saved projects, which is handy since you might want to work on a project similar to what you have already done. That way you don't always need to start from scratch.

Save button

Save option won't be available until you start working in the Canvas area and have at least placed one element or pattern on the Canvas. Once you start working, the Save button will become active and you can click on it to save your projects. All projects are saved on the Cricut cloud storage space, while you can also save your project as you are working on it to prevent losing your work in case of a potential crash of the cloud system. This is less likely to happen, but if you want to be on the safe side, you can save your project as you are working on it, saving your project every time you make some progress.

Maker (Machine)

You can click on this button to access your machine options. This button represents your Cricut machine and depending on which machine you have and use for crafting; you will have different options available.

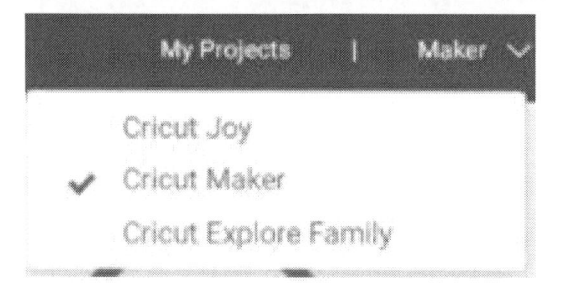

Once you click on the Maker option, (machine), you will access all your machines that have been already set up in case you are using more than one Cricut model. Model Maker has different options than other machines

Make it button

Once you have finished with editing and designing, you can save your project in case you wish to keep it in the library my projects, then click on Make it button to prepare for cutting. You can prepare several mats at the time, preparing more cuts and placing them in the queue. You can choose which design should be cut first as you will have all your prepared mats categorized by color on the left side of the window.

Bottom Editing Subpanel

The second subpanel of the editing menu has multiple controls for designing and editing your projects. In case you have already worked with software such as Illustrator, Photoshop, or similar software, you will find most commands familiar. Even if you have never worked on similar software, you will find most of the commands and options to be logical and self-explanatory.

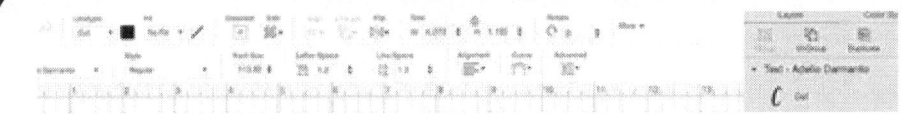

Nevertheless, to help you find your way around the editing panel, we will go through each command available in the second subpanel. You will use these functions to edit your materials and create your designs.

Undo/Redo

This is probably a familiar function as you can use these buttons (arrows) to correct your mistakes and get back to the previous version of your design in a click. Making mistakes and changing your mind on shapes and colors is a natural thing when during the creative process, which is how these buttons become more than handy.

Linotype

Linotype and fill are options related to the type of blade you wish to use on a given project. Depending on which Cricut machine model you are using, you will have different options for cutting. Once you choose the machine you want to cut with, you will be presented with different types of blades and cutting available for that machine. Based on which material you are using for your project you can choose the type of blade. As far as options for cutting style concerned, you have more than several options to choose from – Wave, Perforation, Deboss, Score, Engrave, Cut and Draw. All of these options are available with Cricut Maker. In case you are using other machines, there will be fewer options to choose from, making the cutting styles more basic when compared to options available with Maker.

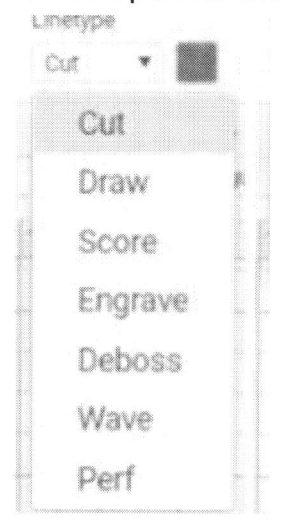

This is how the dropdown menu will look like if you are using Maker once you click on the Linotype option.

As you may notice, in case you are using Explore instead of Maker, there will be only three options to choose from.

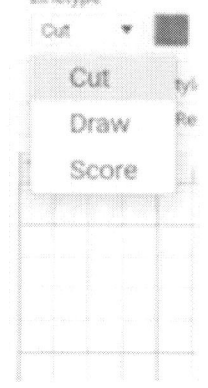

" Cut" option will be your default line type until you have uploaded your design file, which is when you can choose other options as well. The machine won't cut your design until you choose the "Make it" command.

Fill

This option is made for printing, which is how you can choose the filling for your patterns. In case you choose No Fill that means that you won't be printing anything on your design.

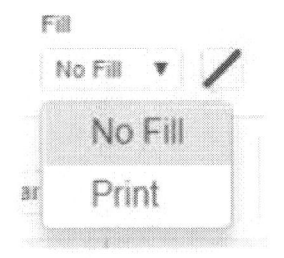

The second option you will get is "Print", which is a great addition to the Cricut machine as you can print anything on your design, including letters and patterns to make your projects complete.

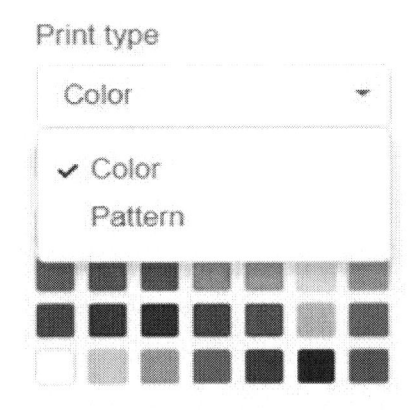

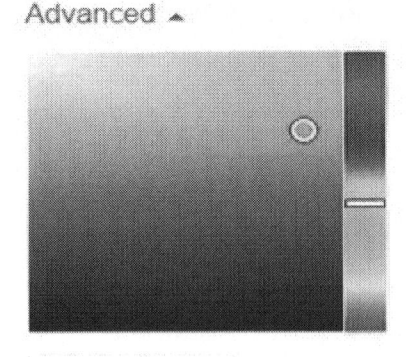

The printing will start from your printer once you click "Make it", after which your Cricut machine will do the remaining part – cutting.

Draw

" Draw" is one of the available options you can choose within "Linotype". This option won't allow you to color your patterns and designs but enables you to use your pens for cutting and drawing. Once the pen is selected, you can select the color of your pen while the available layers will be shown in the Canvas area.

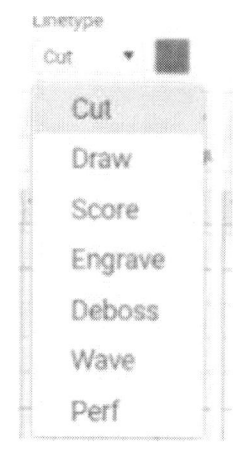

Cut

Cut is the default line type for Cricut Canvas, except in the case when JPEG or PNG is uploaded to your design on Canvas. Once you click "Make it", the machine will cut your designs.

Chapter - 1

Choose the Right Model for You

The Cricut machine isn't actually the least expensive. One unit is about on the $300 value run, and what precisely isn't the friendliest cost. To get the best on estimating, you can generally do brisk hunts on the web, for example, eBay and other related destinations. You can likewise however at shopping center deals if web based purchasing alarms you somewhat. Keep in mind, it about looking and being tolerant simultaneously. Upbeat scrapbook making!

This is a small, portable hand-crank machine that has a maximum cutting width of six inches. It only works with dies and embossing folders; however, it's perfect for those who are looking for a machine they can use for scrapbooking and card making.

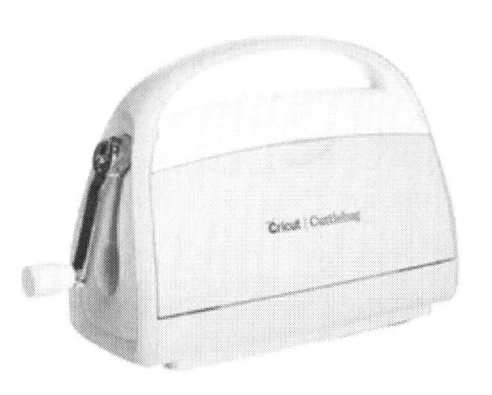

The hand-crank machine has been a staple in the Cricut family and you can usually find a new one for under $100. A used hand-crank can be far less money. If it's in good condition and that's what you want, you can sometimes find them for as low as $25 at garage sales and garage sale sites.

Cricut maker

This year, a new model was released called The Cricut Maker. It has the capability of cutting more materials than any previous models and the company boasts its fast, precise cutting.

The Cricut Maker is considered to be Cricut's flagship model. This is the one that can do just about anything under the sun on just about any material you can fit into the mat guides of your machine. The one drawback of this powerhouse model is the price point. This does make this model more prohibitive, unless you plan to make crafts that you can sell with this model. If this is your intention, you can rest assured that whatever you turn out with this machine will be the best of the best, every single time. If you're selling your crafts, this baby will pay for itself in little to no time at all.

That in mind, the Cricut Maker costs $399.99. That is a large sum of money for someone who doesn't have it and even to someone who does have it. My advice would be to save until you can afford it or put it on your wish list in the meantime and subtly hint to your loved ones that you'll absolutely love to have one of these bad boys. Hopefully, someone will catch on and not balk at the huge amount of dollars that it will eat up.

The Cricut Maker can be used with your own images, which is a plus for those who prefer to use their own or don't want to buy a subscription or pay for individual images. It allows you to personalize your items and make your own statement. You can make personalized cards, signs, and anything your heart desires. The ability to personalize your items with multiple lines and fonts broadens your horizon, and if you make products to sell, you can offer personalization.

Cricut Cake

If you do manage to find either one of these machines, you can expect the price to amount to nothing less than $142.99 for the Cricut Cake Mini and $199.99 for the Cricut Cake Personal Electronic Cutter.

All in all, I think that if you can get your hands on the Cricut Cake that will be incredible. It's not without its faults, but for a cake decorator and simple crafter, the Cricut Cake is perfect. The materials above can be cut just as good as with any other machine if you switch out the blade and use the right pressure, speed, and mat. You might struggle with slicing items that the machine was not designed to cut, though, so keep that in mind. There will be a limit when it comes to the variety of materials that you will be able to craft with, but it does work just fine with the things listed above.

The Cricut Cake is perfect for cutting unique details for any cake that you are decorating, especially for lettering and making silhouettes that are difficult to free-hand. The fondant cutouts can also be used to dress up cupcakes. Whatever the occasion may be, the Cricut Cake machine can cut your decorative fondant or gum paste perfectly.

Cricut Explore

With all the capabilities of the Cricut Explore One and more, the Cricut Explore Air model comes equipped with Bluetooth capability, has a built-in storage cup to keep your tools in one place while you're working, so they won't roll away or get lost in the shuffle.

This model does have two on-board accessory clamps, which allow for simultaneous marking and cutting or scoring. These clamps are marked with an A and a B so you can be sure your tools are going in the right places, every time you load them in.

This model is equipped to handle the same 100 materials as the Cricut Explore One, and operates at the same speed, so the price difference reflects those differences and the similarities! This is a great value for the powerhouse that you're getting.

At the time of writing this, the cost for the Cricut Explore Air is $249.99

Cricut Explore One

In terms of what is currently available from Cricut, this is the most basic machine they offer. This machine boasts being able to cut 100 of the most popular materials that are currently available to use with your Cricut machine, as well as being perfectly user friendly.

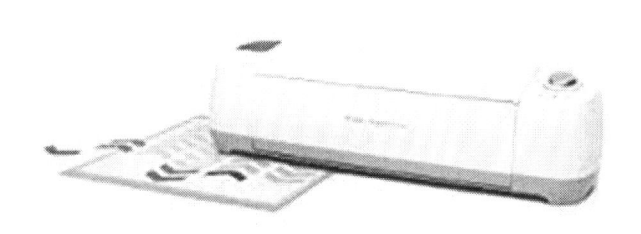

The Cricut Explore One is considered to be the no-frills beginner model of Cricut craft plotters and operates at a lower speed than the other models available. Unlike the others available in the current product line, the Cricut Explore One has only one accessory clamp inside, so cutting or scoring, and drawing cannot be done simultaneously. They can, however, be done in rapid succession, one right after the other.

While this is a great tool for a wide range of crafts on 100 different materials, and which can get you well on your way to designing breathtaking crafts that are always a cut above others, the cost is not as high as you might imagine, if you intend to use your craft plotter mainly for those special occasions where something handcrafted would be perfect, then this a great machine to have on hand. The cost for the Cricut Explore One is $179.99

Cricut Explore Air 2

This model cuts materials at twice the speed of the previous two models, has Bluetooth capability, and has the two on-board accessory clamps.

The storage cup on the top of the machine features a secondary, shallow cut to store your replacement blade housings when they're not in use, so that if you happen to be swapping between several different tips for a project, they're all readily available to you throughout your project. Both of the cups have a soft silicone bottom, so you won't have to worry about the blades on your machine becoming dull or scratched!

For someone who finds themselves using their Cricut with any regularity, this is the best machine for the job. You will be able to do your crafts twice as fast, and you will get a satisfactory result every time, even at that speed!

At the time of writing, the Cricut Explore Air 2 is priced exactly the same as the Cricut Explore One, at $249.99. If you're looking to jump on this, now is the time to get the best deal.

Whatever you can afford, there is really no wrong way you can go. It all depends on what you want to do with the machine and how much money you are willing to spend.

Choose wisely

It takes structures that you make or transfer (like those you get free from us) into their Design Space programming and removes them.

Would you be able to transfer my pictures to use with Cricut?

Indeed! You can transfer your pictures, or any of our free SVG and me cut records that are as of now arranged to be perfect with Cricut Design Space.

What various materials would i be able to cut with Cricut?

Everybody will in general consider Cricut machines as cutting paper or vinyl, yet the fact of the matter is there are a LOT more things that a Cricut can cut. The Cricut Explore Air 2 can cut more than 60 sorts of materials!

Will it be simple for me to figure out how to utilize Cricut Design Space to make my custom ventures?

That's right, and I'm here to help! Look at our Cricut instructional exercises page here, which is a great spot for learners to begin! We include new recordings every week and even give accommodating free assets and agendas, so ensure you return frequently.

With the current line of available models, the Cricut Design Space allows you to be an innovative as you can possibly be with the design process, so none of your creative flow is eaten up by operations that should be taken care of by your machine.

Chapter - 2

Materials That Can Be Worked On Using Cricut Machine

Cricut jobs are something that you can do with your Cricut cutting machine. It might be anything from simple activities that could provide you with private pleasure to people that may allow you to make revenue. Earlier, this system has been considered nothing but a scrap booker's tool. But with the expanding imagination of humanity, ideas are growing and growing like angry.

People want to realize that the Cricut cutting machine is merely a die cutting tool also it is not the one that is directly accountable for the creation of those designs. The designs can be found via applications cartridges and resources. That entire Cricut machine does is that it dismisses the designs that the user chooses in the capsules or applications and not anything more.

The software that is responsible for producing layouts for your many Cricut tasks is the Cricut design studio. This bad boy has hundreds and hundreds of designs that you are able to select from. Furthermore, you might even create your own design and edit those that are within their library. When you have decided on your layout, have the Cricut machine trimming out it and you are good to go for prime time.

Greeting cards is 1 task that the Cricut machine could possibly be used for. Lots of individuals have their own layout they've conceptualized and imprinted unto their own heads. Nearly all the time, the mall that you see will not have the design that you're looking for. Sometimes they may but that's a leap of faith. Along with the Cricut system, you might create your own design and be delighted with that.

In addition, you're in a position to market these cards that you create and generate income. Today that's company man's mindset for you! This motion will help alleviate frustration and tension and permit you to accomplish a level of calmness or comfort.

Calendars may also be a consideration. Calendars have 12 months annually and each of those months have their own identity. With assistance from a Cricut cutting edge system, you're in a position to help give life to those months. Make sure you produce or chosen designs which might help paint the mood of the month or whatever's linked with that.

Invitations are also exceptional Cricut jobs. You pick a design that's acceptable for the occasion and after that you have made it cut through the Cricut cutting machine. The trick is never to allow you imagination relax. Make sure you keep it going and you'll have more jobs function on.

The Cricut machine has been known as a "scrap booker's best friend". When that was completed, people had to cut the design in order that they could place it to the scrapbook.

The cutting-edge part was the toughest and most compulsory hands which weren't capable of making any mistakes. That point from the scrapbooking world is history on account of this Cricut cutting machine. With this excellent instrument, you may surely do a lot of things like Cricut tasks that could be for your own personal gratification or for company related purposes.

One of the very usual Cricut tasks is clearly scrapbooks. At any time you've got a pair of pictures that share a universal and ordinary motif such as birthdays, weddings, birthdays and so many more, you will turn into scrapbooks to guarantee those moments are relived.

You have to produce designs which may assist the audience feel the atmosphere that is being portrayed. You conceptualize, pick the program in the cartridge or applications and have it trimmed via a Cricut machine. In the event you have people who have to have layouts cut to get their scrapbook, then they can always turn for one to have it done. That is a wonderful potential for some money.

Greeting and greeting cards are also excellent jobs for your Cricut cutting machine. Whenever you take a look at a calendar, then it is 12 weeks indoors. It's possible to utilize the Cricut cutting machine to cut designs from your software that might help portray the whole month which you select. Let's consider for example the month of February. February is connected with love since Valentine's Day happens on the 14th.

You can choose designs that are filled with hearts and anything has to do with love. In the event of greeting cards, you might use the Cricut system to cut back designs that you pick. Sometimes the design that you look for in a greeting might just be discovered in your system so that you're so much better off doing so via Cricut machine.

All these are Cricut tasks which will be able to enable you to exude satisfaction and gain at the specific same instant. Do not stop with these ideas. The vital issue is to innovate.

First, how do you have to get your words in your page?

The easiest is to find a kind of writing you like and practice until you are happy with that. Otherwise it's a trip to the regional scrapbook shop to commit your hard earned money on alphabets - again!

Having loaded the dishwasher, the washing machine in addition to the drier, got the kids to school, made appointments into your dentist and the hair dresser for everyone, attended the pta meeting and obtained the supermarket for dinner, you merely have time between your lunch date with hubby and amassing the dry cleaning to run to the scrapbook store before it's time to collect the kids from school, provide them a snack cook dinner so it's ready once you return from soccer practice, then home again to eat dinner, help with homework, and get the kids to bed, and research some family problems with hubby before you hit the sack... Incidentally, if do you have sufficient time to document?

Anyhow, at any time you do get it in the scrapbook store what exactly are you going to locate there?

You should encounter a humungous option of

- lettering stickers
- Rub-ons
- die cuts
- Stamps
- Duration and duration embellishments

Any of them can create excellent titles, journaling and ideas on your layouts.

Let us take a peek at some of them...

Alphabet decals

The drawback is they never seem to include adequate letters and you might just produce a few words in the specific same fashion. You can get off with different unique fashions such a fashion. And also a couple of layouts permit you to mix and match specific fashions inside the title or bullets for example. It's interesting to add random fashion characters at the center of the journaling, too.

Rub-ons

All these were known as transports when I was a kid, and only came as letters. They come as words or letters and phrases in a range of colors, and many beautiful layouts, too.

Since the name suggests, you simply rub them onto your own page with the very small rod supplied. (It's possible to use a bone folder or perhaps a coin if you eliminate the pole.) It's an excellent idea to lower across the words which you would love to use and put them carefully or you may find stray pieces from the word next door you had not meant to move.

Rub-ons look excellent, and offer a professional finish.

Alphabet stamps

All these are a wonderful buy as you're in a position to steer clear of this 'never-have-all-the-letters-i-need' syndrome that happens with various sites - plus they are re-useable!

It is easy to pin phrases together with replicate letters should you opt for stamps. Simply line up the letters onto a translucent acrylic block to form your expression, leaving the proper size place to the replicate letters which you put in on the following pass.

To rescue the ideal gap, put postage in the place where the letter belongs, and the moment you have completed the word remove it and you're left with a space where you pinpoint the letter afterwards. It's likely to pinpoint the letters properly since it's possible to determine where you are stamping. After use, just wipe clean, replace the sheet and they're ready for next time!

Additional decoration antiques

You will encounter a great deal of fascinating accents to check in your scrap booking pages.

Mechanical and electronic systems

The various die cutting system apps have some excellent alphabets, but if you are new to scrapbooking they might appear a costly technique to create your titles. You will get outstanding use from them particularly in case you produce your own greetings cards, too.

Some titles to watch out for are sizzix, big shot, quickutz, Cricut and xyron, to mention but some.

You can even buy a set of ribbon punches.

What is left?

But, before making the trip to the regional scrapbooking store contemplate utilizing your pc. You now have many fonts onto it and you will find a lot more available to download free from the internet.

Your computer is one of the most flexible practices to earn a journaling or name. With the massive selection of fonts you will find one that suits your design layout, but far more useful is the flexibility with regard to dimensions. It's possible to find the font as large as you want to acquire a title, or small enough to obtain all your journaling onto a tag.

How can you get titles from the pc to your design?

It is very uncomplicated and quick to execute.

- choose a font and size it appropriately to your project.
- type your phrases, and then print using the inverse image setting on your printer options.
- Transfer to the wrong side of your chosen pattern or color paper or cardstock,
- remove and follow your scrap book card or job.

If you don't have, or can't track down the contrary image setting, then:

- Carefully follow on your phrases - a light box will help you to the perfect side of the paper,
- cut within your lines

And there you have it.

It is fantastic to have hundreds of choices of alphabets for our layouts. However, do try to avoid having one fashion too often, as it is likely to be boring to make and also to observe a record full of the exact same designs.

Now you see how easy it is to make excellent names and journaling, there's nothing stopping you. Have fun creating your memories and will you have enough time to save them on amazing scrapbook designs.

Scrap-booking is the latest crafty phenomenon. With the coming of digital cameras, the traditional photo albums have gone by the wayside along with the better way to keep substantial photos and the memories linked. There are numerous programs for avid scrap-bookers from several papers, ribbons, stickers and shapes; can it not be great to have these goods in one central location and at the touch of a button? Cricut expression is your answer. This personal digital cutter enables you to produce a few of the very beautiful and customized shapes to add flare to a most basic of paper crafts.

Chapter - 3

Tool and Accessories of Cricut

When you have a Cricut machine, there are a few tools that you would need which would make your crafting project easier and manageable. All these different tools help with cutting materials. The tools that you would need are:

Cricut Cutting Mat

For every Cricut Machine you have, the must-have item all crafters need is a cutting mat. This cutting mat enables you to hold any material you use while the machine goes through cutting it. These mats come in different grip strength and also varying sizes. You can differentiate it by the colors it comes in based on the grip, so you do not confuse them. Some projects would require you to use the StrongGrip mat, whereas some projects work better using a mat suitable based on the materials you are using, such as fabric.

The outcome of your project depends on the kind of mat you use so choosing the right mat is imperative. The different types of mats available are the LightGrip Mat, StandardGrip Mat, StrongGrip Mat, and the FabricGrip Mat.

Cricut Bright Pad

This Bright Pad includes a five-brightness setting adjustable LED light. It makes your crafting easier, and it aids in illuminating extremely fine lines for tracing. It is extremely useful when you are weeding so if you do find that weeding is a challenge, then the Cricut Bright Pad will solve this issue for you as it makes this process easier.

Cricut Pens

Cricut Pens come in different colors and a variety of sets that make DIY projects such as gift tags, cards, invitations, and banners so much more creative and beautiful. Crafters usually use these pens when they need to Write and Cut. You can get the Metallic pens, Candy Shop pens, the Classic set, Gold set, and even one called the Seaside set.

Lint Roller

It is useful for removing any unwanted pet hairs, dust or excess materials from your mats. Animal hairs are big problems as they stick to the adhesive mats like there is no tomorrow, but a lint roller works great if you want to get rid of them.

Scoring Stylus

Add a scoring stylus to your cart as soon as possible if you are a paper crafter. The tool is excellent for making paper baskets and boxes. It gives the products the professional, store-bought finish and makes them so easy to fold as the stylus already creates the grooves for folding your paper projects.

EasyPress

Invest in an EasyPress. This is perfect if you are interested in printing T-shirts or customizing pillowcases. Basically, anything you want to have printed; you are going to need one of these bad boys to do it. There are lots of bundles available on the Cricut website, and they can range from $119.99 (only the EasyPress) to $389.99 for a large bundle with everything you need to get started on your printing journey and so much more. The prices change depending on the size of the EasyPress, as well as the size of the bundle you wish to take.

Complete Starter Kit

The Complete Starter Kit is great if you don't feel like purchasing tools individually or if you'd rather follow protocol and purchase exactly what you need. The kit comes with all the essential items; that are why it is a great purchase. However, if you're tight on cash, buying the bare necessities will be best. This includes the materials you may require starting crafting, so you don't have to worry about any list of items that need to be bought.

Cartridge

Cartridges are designed to help with the keyboard overlay that is needed for designs. The DesignStudio that is downloadable on the computer will help with developing the design that you are looking for. Each cartridge is designed to have a booklet to help you with how to use it. Each cartridge will only work for that specific overlay; however, a company called Provo Craft designed a universal overlay cartridge that will help with this single use overlay issue. Each Cricut, whether a cake version or a paper version, has a specific set of parameters that will be set to use for cutting. This makes each one of the Cricut machines specific to their use and a unique tool to have.

Buy a cartridge or several. Please do invest in these. They are amazing, and they aren't that expensive if you look around for clearance sales or marked-down prices on Amazon. The selection ranges from themed cartridges to ones that only have fonts. It's great for any project, and it saves you the trouble of struggling with Design Space and creating your own designs. They also come in neat little boxes that are so easy to store and always looks uniform.

Sharpies

Sharpies - you will not be sorry that you have them. Yes, the Cricut pens are cool, but they are overpriced. Purchasing some extra Sharpies – or any form of pens that can be manipulated into fitting into the pen holder – will work perfectly. You will have a variety of colors and save a couple of bucks in the process.

Doors

The door on your Cricut Cutter machine protects the machine when not in use. On many Cricut Cutter machines in various models, there is a compartment on the inside of the door to place any needed tools for crafting. If the doors on your Cricut cutter machine are not staying shut, make sure that you have taken out or unloaded any accessories in the machine's accessory clamp which can cause the doors to remain open. If this is not the case or the doors of the machine will not open or stay open take a picture or video and send it to the Help Center at cricut.com.

Spatula

For lifting cut peace of papers from the cutting mat spatula is used. Other related things like some stuffed card can be used. But, as spatula is not expensive and specially designed tool, so its use is recommended. It does not harm your cutting mat. Removing gross and sticky material from spatula is easy.

Adhesives

Glue, gums are adhesives, choose adhesive of your choice from any well-known brand. Sticky material like adhesives should not be ordinary; purpose of sticking two things together must be fulfilled through your selected adhesive. Different sizes of glue coffee cups are available. Select any jumbo pack or coffee cup or according to your requirement. The drying time of glue also matters, so go for some very good adhesive.

Tapes

Without tape completing task is almost impossible. Consideration Points for selecting tape are: it should be chemical or acid free and it should be very sticky. Glue is alternate for tape but sometime glue also does not work like tape.

Scissors

Keep a pair of sharp scissors with you. Enough sharp to cut cards, ribbons and papers. Must buy a cover for scissors. Place it above the reach of children and in a place where humidity does not affect it. Neat paper or card cutting really affect your decorative work.

Tweezers

Sometimes you need to deal with very tiny papers. Tweezers work efficiently in holding that small piece of papers which usually turns, curves and torn during use. Sometime additional use of glue sticks two papers which are difficult to get separate tweezers are perfect helper at that time. Keep it while doing crafting you will need it.

Trimmers

Blades and trimmers are essential thing it helps in cutting papers very neatly and in desired shape without putting additional effort to create neat effect.

Stock of paper and cards Card are comparatively thicker than paper. They are different things. Buying a stock makes you tension free; either you do test cuttings or throw it in making unusual shapes for trail. They should be sufficient for, until your whole tasks get complete.

Blades

The blades are designed to cut specific textiles when using the Cricut. Every single Cricut machine that you can buy comes with your own specific blade for that machine. You can purchase other blades that would be even more useful for specific textiles. Many of them come with a German fine point carbide blade. This is a useful blade for all projects. This one provides an effortless cutting of a much thicker textile such as leather and wood. There is an individual housing that will be used for this specific blade that is different from the one that comes with your machine, so keep that in mind. There is also an option or a fabric blade that is bonded. This is used to cut fabrics that are already stabilized with some sort of heat-pressed bonding. In the Cricut Maker, you will get a knife blade and a rotary as well. These do not work in other Cricut machines though.

Keypad

The Cricut cartridge contains fonts and images often in a specific theme. The keypad allows you to input phrases and words to tell the Cricut what to cut out using the font in the cartridge.

Buttons

For the most part, all buttons are self-explanatory the on button turns the machine on, the Cut button tells the machine to Cut once the design is already in place, and the Stop button tells the Cricut machine to stop cutting once the design has been fully cut. It is important not to try to Cut or press the Cut button without a cutting mat in place and without a design and cartridge ready to go. Select the STOP button if you've made a mistake during the cutting process, the blade will stop cutting and from there you can correct your mistake. The Off button turns the machine off.

Roller Bar

The roller bar piece of the Cricut Cutter machine has wheels called star wheels. Star wheels allow materials not to shift when cutting. However, when cutting thick materials like felt and foam the star wheels can leave marks and indents in the material. To avoid this marking from the star wheels moves the star wheels all the way to the right side of the rubber bar one by one. If the cartridge is in the way of this maneuver turn your Cricut Cutter Machine off by selecting the OFF button and gently move the cartridge over to either side. To make sure that the material still is not passed over by the star wheels make sure the material has at least one inch away from the right side of the rubber bar where the star wheels are now located.

Display Screen

The display screen on your Cricut Cutter machine shows the design in which the machine will be cutting. The design can be edited on the display screen. Settings for your Cricut machine are also accessible through the display screen, such as: calibrating the screen and resetting the machine. A few common problems with the Display Screen include the LCD being unresponsive, the screen stuck on the End User License Agreement, the display screen being pixelated, and the screen stuck on the Tap to zoom message. If you have any of these issues turn your machine off, then perform a hard reset. If the issue persists, contact Member Care at cricut.com where you can find phone numbers and emails to contact.

Chapter - 4

Use and Configuration of Cricut Design Space

How to Install/Uninstall Design Space

Install on Windows/Mac:

- Click on your browser and navigate to www.design.cricut.com
- Create a Cricut ID if it is your first time or sign in with your Cricut ID. Note this should be done when the page is fully loaded.
- Select New Project tile.
- From the prompt, select Download Plugin.
- Click next when the Cricut installer opens.
- Read the Terms of Use and accept the agreement.
- Select Install.
- Click done when the installation has finished.

- Uninstall on Windows
- Click on the Start button.
- Select Settings Apps.
- Look for Cricut Design Space and choose Uninstall.
- Uninstall on Mac
- Go to Finder and open the Applications folder.
- Search for Cricut Design Space.
- Drag it to trash.
- Right click on the Trashcan and select Empty Trash.
- It is recommended that you restart your computer after uninstalling any program from it before reinstalling any other program.

Install App on iOS

- Search for Cricut Design Space.
- Tap the Get button to download. Verify the download using your iTunes password if prompted. The app will launch and display options for completing the process if not you can start designing immediately.

Uninstall the Cricut Design Space

- Press and hold the Design Space icon until it vibrates.
- Press the X button to delete it from your device.
- Note that if you have saved projects on your device and not on the cloud, uninstalling will delete those

projects. The recommended thing to do is to offload the app instead to save your projects on your device.

Install App on Android

- Open Google Play Store on your device.
- Search for Cricut Design Space.
- Tap on the Install button.

Uninstall App on Android

- Go to Settings app.
- Tap "Apps" or "Applications".
- Swipe to the "Download" tab or "Application Manager".
- Navigate to the App you intend to uninstall.
- Tap the "Uninstall" button.

Connecting the Cricut to Your Computer

- Now, you can turn on your machine.
- To connect the unit that requires the cable to your laptop, you simply have to put the square end in its designated place at the back of your Cricut and attach the rectangular end to the USB port on your desktop or Laptop.
- If you have a wireless device, enable your Bluetooth on whichever device you wish to connect your Cricut to, open the Bluetooth settings, and pair with the machine. You will instantly recognize the name of

your machine.

Working with Fonts in Design Space

One of the unique features in Cricut Maker machine is the ability to personalize your project. This creative ability, innate in us, gives us maximum satisfaction and a great sense of accomplishment.

Working with texts and fonts shows the unique freedom that the user of this machine has; the ability to show the power of creativity. As stated earlier, you can use the Cricut fonts or the one installed on your computer or device. So, how can you add text, select font, install/uninstall font in Windows/Mac? Let us take it one by one.

Add Text to Design Space

If you want to add text to canvas you have to use text tool on the left hand side of the canvas. If you will locate the text at the bottom-left of the screen if you are using IOS or android app. The text bar and text box will appear if you select the text tool in windows or Mac. If you are using IOS or Androids, the font list will open.

After that choose the font you intend to use and then type in your text. Note that you can type the text before selecting the font on a Windows/Mac computer. Select any area outside the text box to close it

Double tap or double click on the text To edit the text, you can choose the action you want including font style, font size, change the font, letter spacing and line spacing from the options available.

Writing with Fonts

A number of Cricut fonts are offered by Cricut Design Space and are specifically designed to be drawn using a pen. In order to use a Cricut pen to write any font you have to change the line type of your text from cut to write. You can choose the font as well as a "Writing style" after you select a font you intend to use.

The Writing style fonts are similar to text written by hand but most fonts will trace the outside of the letters.

System Fonts

These are fonts installed on your computer or mobile device and every time you sign in, the Cricut Design Space will automatically access your system fonts and allow you to use them for free in the Design Space projects.

Note that the system fonts may vary between devices because system fonts are installed on a particular device.

Do not be surprise when you encounter failure to import some system fonts into the Design Space or they behave in an unusual manner when using them in the Design Space, this happens because some of them have design components that are not compatible with Cricut Design space.

When downloading fonts to your device or computer use the instructions on the font site or app to ensure that the installation is done successfully on your device or computer, the instructions are different depending on your platform. The instructions for Windows/Mac, Ios AND Android are given below:

For Windows/Mac:

Choose 'Text' in the design panel which is at the left hand side of the canvas.

Input the text or select the font before inputting the text to form the Text Edit bar.

Click the Font drop-down menu to select the "System" index which will display only the font installed on the computer.

For Android:

Choose 'Text' on the bottom of the screen

Search through the list of the displayed font list, to find your desired System font from the available fonts. The system fonts will have the label 'System'. Choose your desired font and then type in your text.

For iOS:

Choose 'Text' from the bottom of the Canvass screen

From the font list that appear on your device, choose the "System" index

Choose the font you like and type in your text.

Step by Step Guide to Write, Score, Cut and Print with Cricut Maker

Before going into the step by step guide, let us define some important terminologies for proper understanding:

Cut- Refers to cutting layer from your material.

Draw- Refers to drawing on the layer using a Cricut pen.

Score- Refers to scoring the layer using a Scoring Stylus or Scoring Wheel.

Print- Refers to printing the layer using your home printer.

Linetype - Refers to cut, draw and score.

How to Perform Linetype from Windows/Mac

- Place your text or images onto the design screen.

- From the Edit bar, select the Linetype drop-down. Note that the current Linetype is highlighted. Of course, you can change at once Linetype of multiple layers by selecting the layers to be changed and then choose the desired Linetype from the drop-down. The image of the canvas will change to reflect your selection once this is done.

- From there select print. To add color, or pattern fill to the layer, select 'Color' or 'Pattern' from the Fill swatch drop-down.

- This is done by selecting both layers in the Layers panel and clicking the Attach button.

How to Perform Linetype from Android/iOS

- Place your text or images onto the design screen.

- At the bottom of the screen, tap on the "Layers" to access the Layers panel.

- Click on the arrow that is next to the layer to obtain the Layer Attributes Panel. The current Linetype will always be highlighted.

- Tap on the desired Linetype which will change to reflect your selection.

- If you are done with your selection, tap on the 'Layers' to close it.

Cutting Instructions for Materials

Now that you have organized your Linetype, it is time to prepare the material for cutting using the Cricut Maker machine. The instructions for preparing the material are stated in simplified and easy-to-understand way for the user.

- The first thing is to place the craft foam on the mat with the smooth side down.

- All the four edges of the material should be taped to the mat about 1" from each corner.

- Move the White Star Wheels on the Cricut Maker machine to the right. This is to ensure that the Star Wheel will not leave any imprint on the material.

- Ensure that you clean the front metal bar if you

- intend to cut thicker craft foam and also ensure that no part of the material go under the rubber rollers because it can cause the machine to jam.

- Test a cut to ensure that the edges come out fine else replaces the blade before cutting the original material for the project.

- After loading your mat for a Knife Blade project and selecting the cut setting of your choice, the Design Space of the machine will inform you of the expected cut time.

- Note that thicker materials will take more time to cut than thinner materials for obvious reasons. First, thicker materials will require multiple cut-passes; secondly, the cut pressure will be increasing gradually.

Cutting Instructions for Cricut Craft Foam

Place the material, in this case Craft Foam, onto Cricut StrongGrip Machine Mat and ensure that the grain run vertically.

- Select the sizes and images and then load the mat into Cricut Maker.

- Select browse all materials.

- From the list of materials, select Craft Foam.

- Press the Go button.

- It is recommended that you avoid cutting intricate images that are smaller than 2" x 2" in order to get a good job delivery.

How to Prepare Balsa Wood Material for Knife Blade?

- Cut the size of the material that is needed for the project and protect your work surface.

- Clean the surfaces of the wood by removing any stickers or package that can cause obstruction of work. Then, wipe the surface with cloth or spray with compressed air to remove dust and other particles on the surfaces.

- Mirror the images in Design space.

- Create firm bond between your material and the mat's adhesive surface with a brayer.

- Use tape to hold all the edges of the wood.

- Move the White Star Wheels on the Cricut Maker to the right.

- Before you start cutting, ensure that:

- No part of the material goes under the rubber rollers. It can cause jam.

- You test a cut before cutting your main project.

- All cuts are within ¼" from the edge of the wood.

Moving on to Creating Your Project Template

On the home page, select "New Project", which will be followed by a page with a blank canvas that looks like the grid on your Cricut mats? To any artist, the words "empty canvas" is a nightmare in itself so please just bear with me since we will fill that bad boy up in a second. But first, let's go through the menu options.

New

New means that you will start a new project and clicking the tab will redirect you to a blank canvas. Be sure to save all changes on your current project before you go to the new canvas. Otherwise, you will lose all of the progress you have already made on that design.

Chapter - 5

Machine Setup

I am going to help you set up your machine and we will make it as easy as possible so that this will not only go smoothly but so that you can enjoy your machine without frustrating yourself. If you are working with a Mac or a Windows you need to set it up one way, and if you are running on an Android or an iOS you will have to do it another way. Many people think that this process is hard but it's actually quite simple and takes ten steps or less which is great right? How easy is that?

However, in case the door does not open automatically, put mild pressure on it to completely open the door. Then, place the keyboard overlay on the top of the keypad of the machine. At this point, the cartridge of the machine should be inserted into the cartridge slot.

The cartridge slot can be found in the front of the Cricut machine. However, you must ensure the title on the cartridge is in consonance with the one on the keypad overlay. The first way we will show you how to how to set up your machine if you're working with an Android or an iOS, we will go step by step so that the process is able to go smoothly and without repeating steps.

You will need to pair your device (either Android or iOS) with your machine. You are going to need to utilize your Bluetooth to do this.

Download the Design Space App. You will need to install it into your machine as well.

Hit the button that says menu.

Select the button that says machine setup and app overview. Now, you are going to select the button that says new machine setup. There are going to be on-screen promptings that will help you to complete the setup. Just be sure that you are following them accurately and if you can't go quickly that's fine. Go at the pace that you're comfortable with so that you can make sure that you understand what it is they are wanting from you. Going slower will help eliminate mistakes but if you do make mistakes don't feel bad. This happens to people every day and it's easily fixable. You will know that you've done everything right and correctly when it is telling you that it's time to make your first project. Once this happens, you know that your setup is complete. Once you've done this it's time to get crafting!

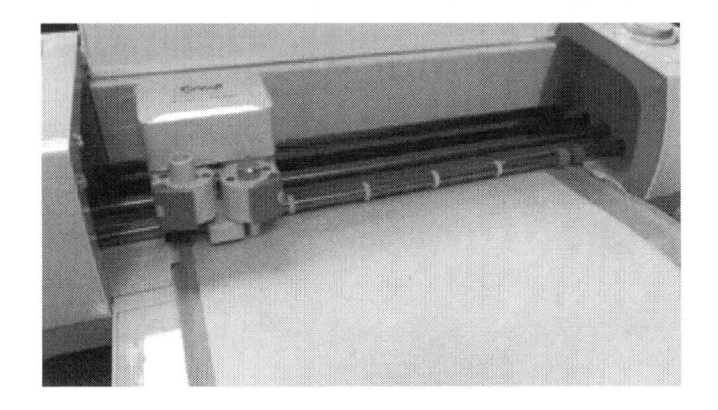

An additional tip for you is that your machine is already automatically registered during the setup. If you don't complete the setup when you connect your machine you need to reconnect it. Because the machine has to be registered this is something that you can't miss.

If you're working with a Windows or a Mac you will need to follow these following instructions to make your machine work. This setup is easy as well and offers one less step than the instructions above and since Macs are considered to be newer this will be a little bit different than the instructions above.

Plugin your machine. Don't turn your machine on or try to without plugging it in first.

Power the machine on

Connect your machine to your computer. You are going to do this in two different fashions. This is a great option because you can choose which option is the best for you. Either of these ways will work well it's just whatever you would like it to be.

Go to the website design.cricut.com/setup in your browser because this is going to be how you are going to finish your set up. From this step, you will be able to complete your setup by making sure you are watching the instructions carefully.

You need to be able to follow the on-screen prompts and instructions to sign in and create your ID. This will be your Cricut ID for the future.

Download the Design Space app and install it to the device. This is going to have so much benefit for you later as this is where you are going to gain a lot of benefits.

Don't forget that you will need to plugin when it prompts you to do so.

You will be able to see that you did everything right and correctly when it wants you to make your first project. Once you reach this step your machine is ready to go, and you can make the practice project so that you can get used to your machine and how it works without wasting materials.

The same tip above about the registration applies here too and if you have a problem setting up on any of the systems you can come back to this site so that you can be able to set it up without trouble or issues. Having the website tell you what you need to do and having the prompts is a great helper to new users or older users of the machine as they offer help pages as well. With simple steps and back up help however starting your machine is easy as can be which is a great benefit to the user. These models are made to be as user-friendly as possible to eliminate the issues that other companies have when their items are being set up.

By now you should have the app installed on your phone or the software already running on your laptop or desktop computer. If you have not yet, you better do so now because things are about to get a lot more serious, and it would help if you have Cricut Design Space in front of you to experiment what we will be discussing.

What's more, you should do this, especially if you are a beginner. Perhaps intermediaries or fairly experienced users can afford not to have the app or software in front of them right now.

Downloading/Installing

Do you actually know where to get the Cricut Design Space? Well, if you are on a desktop or Personal Computer, navigate to https://design.cricut.com.

If your smartphone runs on Android OS, enter the Play Store and use the same search term. Remember that downloading or installing this is completely free of charge. Also, bear in mind that you will need a Cricut ID to sign in. This you can also get for free, even if you do not have a Cricut. Simply follow the prompts provided.

Once you have entered your email and gotten your ID, you will at once be taken into the main domain of the Cricut Design Space, the place where all of the magic happens. Quick tip: bookmark this page to your web toolbar so you can find it easily whenever you want to.

The Canvas you will be shown after - similar to a painter's whiteboard - is the big space where all your designs and progress will reflect - this space has a full grid by default to allow you see everything about a single work without having to pinch-zoom and un-pinch. Nevertheless, you can choose the appearance and measurements of the grid.

Smart guides And Shortcuts

So you want to try out your first design, and you happen to be stuck while trying to position something on your canvas perfectly? In Cricut Design Space, this could happen because the Smart Guides are just too smart for their own good. Want to know what the guides are about?

Quick one: Smart Guides are a feature of the Android and iOS app version of the product. They are designed to help you when you want to position things in relation to other things. But that could not turn out or position the way you want it to. If you want to turn this off on the app version, go to Settings - at the bottom areas of the toolbar - and toggle the Smart Guides off.

Meanwhile, there's something about the desktop version of Cricut Design Space that makes it somewhat cool - it has some keyboard shortcuts that will definitely come in handy. If you want to see them at any point of use, tap on the question mark key on your keyboard -

Shift +. Shortcuts that will prove useful to you include the showhide menu, toggle grid, and select all options.

Other shortcuts also allow you to save and "save project as", undo - this is something you will be thankful for - redo, cut, copy, and paste. What's more, bring forward, send back, bring to front, send to back, and of course, delete.

If you are the kind of technophile who's more used to the keyboard than clicking on a mouse, you will find these shortcuts super useful.

How to Position Items on the CricutCanvas

Not to discourage anyone, but it can take you several months of using the Cricut Design Space almost every day before you will find this useful, and probably a little more time before you can get used to it.

Well, this little nugget actually informs you on how to move and rotate your items on the mat preview. This is done in order to position your cuts and pen write when you want or feel the need to.

You know when you are working on a project and just want to flip things up fast? This feature lets you do so quickly and effortlessly - well, almost (insert smirk emoticon here).

This comes significantly handy when you want to use up scraps and just spread them all over your canvas. If you are working on an address envelope, for instance, you can use this tool so that your letters reflect on the "write" side on the envelope. You may also want to reposition - do so by tapping and dragging an item on your canvas to a new location. Simple enough, isn't it?

On the desktop version, move the objects to another mat and conceal them altogether - just click on the three dots, they are not hard to find since they are virtually in your face. So, now you know how to best position those items to make your design all the more easier.

Do You Want To Sync Your Colors?

Even newbie designer knows the essence and impact of colors. In Cricut Design Space, you need to make sure your colors are happy and in harmony, just like every other artwork.

If you have ever worked on a design that had up to five different shades of pink that all needed to be cut out on separate pieces of paper or vinyl, you would understand what we are talking about. If not, you will understand soon too.

Well, in case you do not know or probably forgot how it feels, it can be very frustrating. It becomes ironic when you develop a red face that terribly matches with the moment.

Chapter - 6

Making your First Project Ideas

Starting your first project does not have to be complicated, and here, we will show you how to start your first project effectively and quickly while making sure that you are not getting overwhelmed or frustrated. As such, we will be explaining how to do this correctly.

The first thing that you need to do is go to Cricut.com. Then click Design found at the top right corner. Once you have the right screen, you will be told that you need to sign in. Plugin the needed information and you will see that the email that you entered is going to be your identification so you will need to remember which one you used. The next step that you will need to complete is when you hit the green button you will be taken inside the app. This is where you begin making your projects. Make sure to add this page to your toolbar by bookmarking it so that you can always find it when you need it.

Everyone's home screen on this looks a little different so keep that in mind. My projects for some people will come up first so keep this in mind as well. Now, you have signed in and you are ready to get started, so the first thing that you will do to start a new project is to click on the window that says Canvas. This is where you are going to do everything that you need for editing before you cut your projects.

The top panel of the app is for editing and arranging what you want in the canvas are. From here, you can choose the fonts you want, the size of the design, and more. The panel is divided into sub-panels and there are two of them that you will see. The first allows the user to name, save and cut your projects while the second will enable you to control and edit things in the canvas area.

The first subpanel will allow you to navigate your canvas to your profile that you have created or add it to the projects. It can also send the completed projects to cut. When you look at the toggle menu, you will see another menu that will slide open. This menu will come in handy, but that is not apart of the canvas which is why it does not need too much detail--we will explain it anyway just so that you will know what it is and how it works. The toggle menu lets you go to your profile and change the photo that you have chosen. There are other technical things that you can do from here as well, including the ability to calibrate your machine and its blade while also having the ability to update the Firmware software of your device.

You should explore the Design Space and look around so that you know everything and get comfortable with the app.

When you look at the settings option that this offers, you will be able to change the measurements and the visibility of the canvas, and this is something that you will be able to use for a great benefit for your projects.

If you need to re-cut a project, you have previously created which makes this a great benefit. This is perfect if you do not want to have to recreate the same project repeatedly. From there, you will be able to have the save option and it is recommended that you save your project as you go. This will help against your browser crashing.

Here's where you need to be specific. Different options are specific to the machine that you have. If you have for example a Maker, but you are designing with the options for Explore, you will realize that there is a multitude of things that you will not be able to do. There are also different options for the line type.

When you are done uploading your files, you are ready to cut on your canvas. Your projects will be divided by mats according to color.

The editing menu is extremely useful as it will help arrange or organize the fonts and images on the canvas. It will also help you edit it to make sure that it is exactly the way you want. You are going to make mistakes, and there are little buttons that can correct that for you in the form of two buttons: the undo or redo button. If you have created something you do not like, you can click the Undo button.

You also have the option of line type and fill. With these options, you will be able to tell your machine what tools and blades to use. A great example is to remember that the Explore only cuts with three blades and the Maker have six. The line type option tells your machine when you are going to cut and what tool to use as well as giving you seven options.

If you have a Maker, every option will be available, but if you have an Explore you only have three options available instead of seven. The first option that you will have is the Cut. This is the default, and it makes every element on your canvas have this option. When you have selected Cut, you can change the fill of the elements and it will translate into different colors of materials that you are going to use.

If you want to draw your designs, you can also do this when you assign this. Instead of cutting, when you choose Make It, this will draw instead. This option does not color your designs.

The next option that you have is Score. When you assign this, all of their designs will appear scored or they will appear dashed. When you click Make It with this option, your cut will score whatever material you are using for these types of projects. You will need the scoring wheel or the scoring stylus for this. Keep in mind that the wheel only works if you have the Maker;

it does not work with the Explore.

The last options are the perforation, the wavy, debossing, and engraving. They work with the quick swap adaptive also. If you already have one, you can just buy the tips. If you do not have one then you can get them as well. They are relatively inexpensive, depending on how you purchase them.

The fill option is mainly used for printing and patterns. It will only be activated if you have cut a line type. No fill means that you will not be printing anything. Print is one of the advantageous features that this machine offers because it allows you to print your designs and then cut them. It is what motivates a lot of people to get a Cricut in the first place because they love the look.

You have another option that says Select All. It can be very frustrating and cause you to become extremely irritated. Instead, click Select All. When you click Select All, you will be able to move them all at once.

The edit icon has a dropdown menu and it gives you options to do the following options:

Align - Aligning will obviously tell you where you are going and it will tell you if you are going to go left, right and things of that nature.

Distribute - Distributing is for spacing between the elements. This is something that is very time consuming and it is not always right if you are doing it on your own. The distribute button is going to help you do this and make sure that it is right.

Arrange - Arranging just means where you are going to be putting the elements on the canvas.

- Flip - Flipping is going to reflect your image.

- Size - Sizing is pretty self-explanatory. It just means modifying the size of your project.

- Rotate - Rotating means that you are turning your project on a specific angle.

- Position - Positioning means where you are putting your project.

- Font - The font option means which font you are using and what style lettering you are doing.

- Style - The style of what you can have means bold, italics, and things of that nature.

- Curve - The curving means that you can curve your text.

- Advance - The advanced options allow you to ungroup letters and grouping your letters as well as other options.

All of these have different options for what you can do with your projects, so it is a great idea to explore them and understand what it is that they can do for you. Which is why we have listed them for you?

Your left panel is for inserting shapes, images, and other items. This panel has seven options which mean that you can create and replace new project templates. This means that you will have a guide on the type of things that you are going to be using for your projects. This is where you can add ready-to-cut projects from the Access. You can see images, and this is where you can select images, text, shapes, and uploads. If you have Cricut Access, the images and ready-to-cut projects and other options like fonts are available to you and it will not cost you. However, if you do not have access to the Cricut Access because they all cost money, you will have to pay for them. This adds up extremely quickly.

The right panel is all about layering. Layers represent every element or design on your canvas. So think of it like putting on your clothes when you get dressed. So, let us imagine that you live somewhere that is very cold. If you live somewhere that is cold, you are going to have an inner layer of underthings, but then you are also going to have pants, socks, a shirt, and the basics. You will also have a hat, gloves, boots, and other items to fight off the cold. The same will happen on your design depending on how complex your project is. You will have different types of layers that you need to make up your project on.

When you Group or ungroup, you are grouping layers or ungrouping layers which is very simple. Delete just means that you are deleting any elements that you have decided that you do not want.

You have Layer Visibility and Line Type Fill which we have already gone over. The Layer Visibility simply means that you are looking at the visibility of your design. The icon should look like a little eyeball.

You will also have Wheel, Attach, Flatten, Contour, or Slice. These tools are especially important because they will let you change your project and take it to the next level. The Slicing tool is perfect for cutting out shapes or other elements from different designs.

Attaching works like grouping the layers, but it is more powerful by offering the ability to remain in place.

The Flatten option means that you are selecting the layers you want to print together as a whole and then you can click Flatten. In this case, the element will become a print and then cut design.

Chapter - 7

PDF File in Cricut Design Space

I'm infatuated with my new Cricut Maker! It's fast and simple to change over your PDF examples to be removed on this stunning new machine. Regardless of whether you don't have the Cricut Maker, you can utilize your other Cricut machines (Explore Air, and Explore Air2) to remove your paper example pieces as well! I utilize mine everything an opportunity to make my doll garments sewing quicker and increasingly exact. As a designer of doll garments PDF designs, this machine has made my activity speedier and simpler after a little set up regardless.

I got my Cricut Maker for Christmas. I've been utilizing Cricut machines since they originally turned out and have possessed every single one that they have made. I think this Maker machine is a distinct advantage for the doll garments network, particularly if you sew for specialty fairs. I have a feeling that I've been hanging tight for it the majority of my "sewing" life. You would now be able to cut texture by essentially laying it on the tangle. There is no compelling reason to apply any stiffener so as to cut it with this phenomenal, new machine. The Cricut Maker is the main machine that has another rotational cutting sharp edge that was specifically made for texture. See progressively about this astounding machine here!

The Cricut Design Space library has many sewing designs for dolls. They cost about equivalent to the PDF designs you purchase from Oh Sew Kat! However, consider the possibility that don't care for those styles, r you need to make something other than what's expected. There are numerous approaches to do this, however, this is the strategy I have utilized, and once you do it more than once, it's extremely quite speedy!

If you don't mind NOTE: Sharing a SVG records (on the web or face to face) you make from a PDF Pattern you acquired is equivalent to sharing the example document, and it is illicit. If you have companions that you need to impart to, it would be ideal if you respect the designer's diligent work and direct them to buy their own duplicate The Design Space programming does not peruse PDF documents. You should change over the example piece pages to .SVG documents so as to bring them into Design Space. There are various approaches to do this. Despite the fact that bringing in the example pieces in pages or gatherings may appear to be enticing, I don't suggest it. Over the long haul, it will be simpler to work with your records if you spare each example piece as a different document. (This will give you a chance to orchestrate the pieces on the slicing mat to lessen the texture utilized, and will be certainly justified regardless of the additional exertion in advance.)

I use Adobe Illustrator to change over my documents. There are other realistic projects accessible on the web. You need one that will peruse a PDF record, and furthermore spare as a SVG document. When you open the PDF document in another program, spare it as another record with another name, so you don't lose your unique, printable example and directions. It's an extraordinary asset to give a shot too.

You just need the diagrams of the example pieces and each piece ought to be spared as an individual SVG record. Utilize the "utilization artboard" check box to keep the measuring right. If an example piece should be cut on a crease, you have to copy that piece, and after that flip it, and join the lines to make one piece. You need to ensure the lines are covered only a hair! Line the two up precisely, so you have the full piece (the Maker will cut a solitary layer of texture there are no folds.) Delete the covering lines and weld the sort out into one shape. Contingent upon how the example piece is arranged on the page, you may need to change or turn a piece or two to get it precisely right. Guarantee each example piece is arranged here and there as per the grain line and you additionally need to ensure they are that way when you cut them.

Open Cricut Design Space and make another task. From the left menu, click UPLOAD. Discover your svg records you made on your PC, and transfer them every individually. When they are altogether stacked, add them to your canvas. They will import in dark. I change the shade of the pieces to enable me to keep them all straight. I utilize different shading for each size doll, and afterward, guarantee that the pieces that would be cut from different textures are additionally spared in different hues so they will cut on different mats. (For instance, an example that has a top and jeans would have two hues.) Once you have imported your SVGs, set aside the effort to stack a bit of duplicate paper in your Cricut machine. Cut out the pieces and contrast them with your printed PDF duplicate to guarantee they are actually the equivalent.

Copy any pieces you have to cut more than one of. One of those should be reflected if they are not the equivalent. For instance, sleeves generally simply should be copied. A bodice back is that as it may, should be copied with one reflected, so you have a privilege and left back bodice. Rather than bringing in a belt or lash, I just make a square shape in Design Space, giving it different shading if important to keep it on a different tangle. Some shorts with a front and a back that are different example pieces will have four different example pieces in your Design Space record. Spare your record so you can utilize it again later!

IT'S EASY TO CUT FABRIC ON THE CRICUT MAKER TO MAKE DOLL CLOTHES.

Lay your texture on your tangle. I like to utilize this device to smooth it out. There are two different ways you can preserve your texture when cutting doll garments on the Cricut Maker. When you hit MAKE IT, you can without much of a stretch move the pieces around and between the mats, yet make certain to keep the pieces arranged accurately for the grain and for directional prints. You can likewise mastermind the pieces before you hit MAKE IT, on your canvas, and then ATTACH them to keep their dividing. If you are utilizing the Cricut application, attempt the snap tangle where you can put your example pieces straightforwardly on to your formed or pre-cut pieces!

Cut out your example pieces, and sew your doll garments together as indicated by the guidelines. The biggest Cricut tangle is 12×24 inches. Here are two Cricut packs that will make your tasks somewhat simpler: Cricut Sewing Kit and the Cricut Brayer and Mat Remover Set.

You're in the correct spot because prepare to be blown away. The vast majority (myself included) had precisely the same inquiries when beginning. In this way, don't get disappointed and how about we handle the Cricut Beginner FAQ now:

It sounds straightforward, yet I ensure that you will be astonished at the quantity of ventures you can make in a small amount of the time you would almost certainly do them by hand. I'm talking sewing designs, organizer stickers, and wooden signs for your home, monogrammed mugs thus considerably more!

This machine is ideal for the imaginative individual who consistently needs to do DIY extends however is lacking in time, so they sit on your Pinterest load up rather. Also if you have a hand crafted business or Etsy shop, I can practically promise you will get a huge amount of incentive out of this machine.

2. Would I be able to transfer my very own pictures to use with Cricut?

Indeed! You can transfer your very own pictures or any of our free SVG and I cut records that are now arranged to be absolutely good with Cricut Design Space.

There are a wide range of picture document types out there. Fundamentally, it utilizes math equations to make the picture dependent on focuses between lines. Try not to stress I can see your eyes staring off into the great unknown and won't go in more profundity than that.

The advantage of this is the SVG designs can be broadened without getting that hazy pixelated look you see with other document types, making them totally wonderful for making undertakings of any size!

If you haven't as of now ensure you look at our Free SVG Library which has huge amounts of designs that you can transfer to Design Space today to get making in minutes.

3. What different materials would I be able to cut with Cricut?

Everybody will, in general, consider Cricut machines as cutting paper or vinyl, yet the fact of the matter is there are a LOT more things that a Cricut can cut. Truth be told, the Cricut Explore Air 2 can cut more than 60 sorts of materials!

For example, it can cut chipboard, balsa (very flimsy) wood, magnet material, aluminum (otherwise known as soft drink jars), thus considerably more! For thicker materials, you will need to move up to the profound cut cutting edge for the best cut quality.

Its strength you inquire? Texture! It has a fresh out of the box new revolving sharp edge which makes it an unquestionable requirement for sewers that can now prepare an undertaking in minutes rather than hours.

Need to see a full rundown of materials and the cutting settings for each? Look at this.

4. What sorts of DIY ventures would i be able to make with a Cricut?

Truly, maybe the best AND most overpowering piece of purchasing a Cricut is that it is SO flexible that you don't have the foggiest idea where to start. In this way, oppose the data over-burden and attempt to concentrate on one anticipate at once.

The amusing thing about Cricut ventures is that, when I was beginning, I will think about a zillion undertakings or see some on Pinterest and think "hello, I want to make that!" Then, I plunk down to make a task, and my brain would go absolutely clear!

Indeed, to help with this, I thought of a HUGE rundown of Cricut ventures (that will keep on developing so continue returning for updates). You can peruse through, pick one from the rundown, and get creating in a matter of moments! Also, it presently accompanies a FREE printable adaptation you can allude to for motivation. Along these lines, ensure you head over and download that if you don't have it.

5. Will it be simple for me to figure out how to utilize Cricut Design Space to make my very own custom activities?

That's right, and I'm here to help! Look at our Cricut instructional exercises page here, which is a great spot for amateurs to begin! We include new recordings every week and even give accommodating free assets and agendas so ensure you return frequently.

You don't have to claim a Cricut to begin rehearsing with Design Space. When you get your machine, you'll be a stage ahead!

Chapter - 8

Tools in Cricut Design Space

Mastering the different panels and their icons

The editing panel

The editing panel is at the top of your Canvas Area. It harbors the controls that make it easier for you to work around a project.

The editing panel is divided into two subpanels.

- Subpanel One
- Subpanel Two.

Subpanel one allows you to create, name, save, and cut a project.

Subpanel two gives you all the editing tools.

Subpanel one.

The Subpanel one has few icons on it. Let's get the icons explained.

- Canvas: I refer to this as the main button on the design space area. A click on the icon/button and a drop down menu will appear with a range of options. From the drop down menu you can do a lot of settings.

From this drop down menu you can manage your profile. Also, you can calibrate your machine; update firmware, link cartridges, etc. If you have a premium access to Cricut design space, you can manage your subscription from the drop down menu.

- Project Name: In Cricut design space, all new projects are by default 'Untitled.' You can only give a project a name when you have started working on it either by placing an element or a text on it.

- My Projects: A click on this icon will lead you to all your prior designs if you have any.

- Save: This icon becomes functional when you have started working on a project. It is always advisable that you save your project as you design should in case of anything going wrong. I learnt this the hard way. During my early days with Cricut, I'd only save when I was done with a project until one day, I was about done with a particular project when my browser crashed and that was it with my project. I couldn't recover it because I never saved.

- Maker (Machine): This icon has two sub-options when you click on it. The two sub-options include, Cricut Maker and Cricut Explore Family. These two options have different tools.

- Make It: When you are done designing and uploading your projects, this is the final icon you click on to have your project cut.

When you click on Make It, there will be a display on your screen which shows the different colors of your project. From the displayed window you can perform other functions like increasing the number of projects to cut, etc. When you are done with your selection, you can click on Continue to proceed.

Subpanel Two (Editing Menu)

The image above represents the editing panel of the Cricut design space. I will take the icons one after another and explain their functions and usefulness. I lettered the different icons to make it easier for better understanding.

The Undo and Redo: This is a very important icon in your design canvas. This icon helps you make corrections either by taking you back or forward a bit.

Whenever you are designing, there is every possibility that you will make mistakes. With the undo and redo option, when you delete something by mistake, clicking redo will bring it back. When you make a mistake in your design space, clicking undo will get out.

Linetype and Fill: The linetype and Fill icon tells your machine the tools, and blades you are going to use for cutting your project.

There are seven options on the Maker Linetype, these includes Cut, Draw, Score,

Engrave, Deboss, Wave, and Perf.

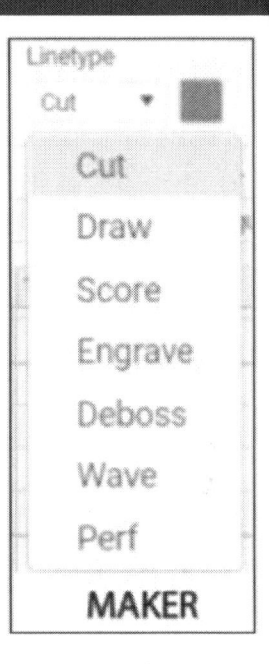

On the Cricut Explore Family linetype, there are just three options.

Explaining the Linetype options tools

- Cut: This is the default linetype of all elements on your canvas, except you upload a PNG or JPEG image. When you press Make It at the end of your design, this prompts your machine to CUT those designs.

The cut option also helps you change the fill of elements in your project. These elements translate into colors of materials which you will use when cutting your project.

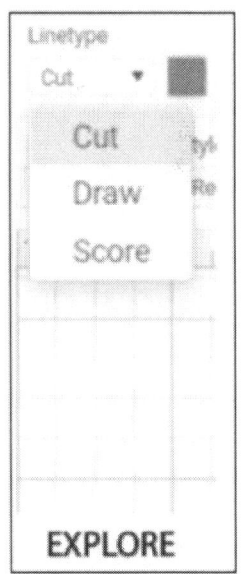

- Draw: This tool on the linetype helps you write on your design. Upon selection of a particular pen, the layers on your canvas area will be listed with the color of the pen you picked.

When the DRAW tool is selected and you click on MAKE IT, your Cricut will either write or draw instead of cutting. Also, this option doesn't color your designs at all.

- Score: The Score tool is an important version of the scoring line which is located on the left panel of your canvas space. When this tool is selected and assigned to a layer, all the designs will appear dashed or scored

At the end of your project when you click on MAKE IT, your Cricut will score the materials instead of cutting them.

- Engrave, Deboss, Wave, and Perf: These are new tools added by Cricut to the Cricut Maker Machine. They are still pretty new, so try them out when you can.

One thing I know for sure about these tools is that they work with the Quick Swap Adaptive Tool.

The FILL tool

This option/tool is used mainly for patterns and printing. The Fill option gets activated only when you are using CUT as a linetype. When you have 'No Fill' it means that you won't be printing any project.

The Print tool is about the most important tool on your design canvas because it makes it possible for you to print your projects and cut them.

When the Fill tool is active, when you click MAKE IT, firstly, the files will be sent to your printer while your Cricut do all the cutting.

The Print has two sub-options that allows you to perform magic on your canvas. These options include the 'Color, and Pattern.' When you explore these options you will be amazed at the project you will create.

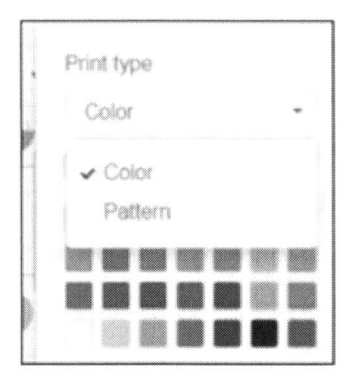

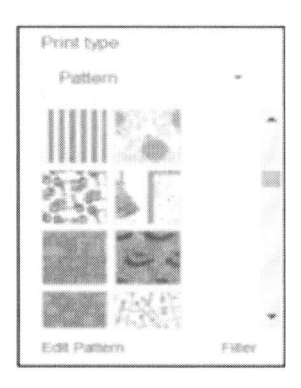

Select All: This tool serves to help you select the entire element in your canvas area. Sometimes it is a hassle to select elements individually, so this tool helps you make multiple selections at a time.

Edit: The Edit icon when clicked on have three tools, the CUT, COPY, and PASTE. With these options, you can copy an element, paste a copied element, or cut off an unwanted element on your canvas.

Once you have made a selection on your canvas, the cut and copy tool gets activated. When you have copied or cut an element, the PASTE option gets activated.

The Align Icon: If you have ever used another design tool, this will be an easy walk around for you. But if you have not, it's easy to get a hang of.

The alignment icon is one you should master as it is very important while working on your project. The alignment tool helps your project stay perfectly organized and in line.

The Align icon has a drop down menu that contains other alignment tools.

Let's take a look at what the functions on the align drop down means.

- Align: This particular tool allows you to align all the elements in your design. It is activated when you select two or more elements on your canvas.

- Align Left: This function takes all the selected elements and align them to the left. Whichever element that is furthest at the left determines the alignment.

- Center Horizontal: Just like every other alignment

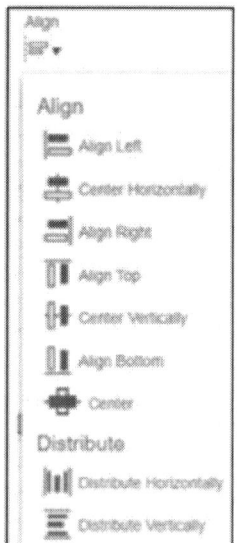

option, this will align all the elements on your project horizontally while the texts and images are centered.

- Alight Right: When you activate this option, all the elements on your project will be aligned to the right. Whichever element that is furthest at the right determines the alignment.

- Alight Top: this options aligns all the elements of your project to the top. Whichever element that is furthest at the top determines the alignment.

- Center Vertically: With this option, all the elements of your project will be aligned to the center. When working with columns and you want them organized and properly aligned, use this option.

- Align Bottom: This alignment option will align the entire selected element on your project to the bottom. Whichever element that is furthest at the bottom determines the alignment.

- Center: When this option is clicked on, it perfectly centers every element on your project; shapes, text, images.

- Distribute: The distribute option gives equal spacing to the entire element on your project. In Cricut design, there is nothing as time consuming as trying to manually allocates equal space between the elements on your project so with this tool; all your problems are solved. For this tool to be activated, two or more elements must be selected on your project.

- Distribute Horizontally: This option will distribute the elements on your project horizontally. The furthest elements left and right on your project will determine the length of the distribution.

- Distribute Vertically: This option will distribute the elements on your project vertically. The furthest elements left and right on your project will determine the length of the distribution.

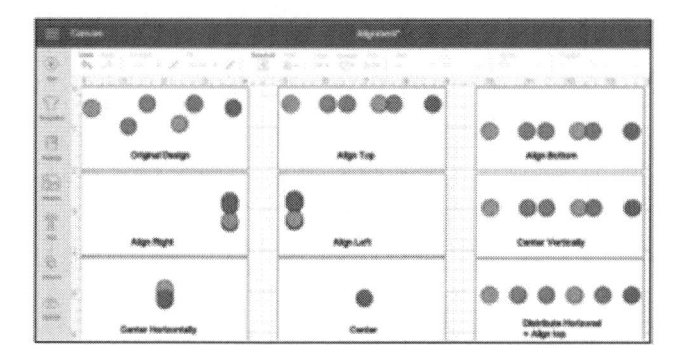

Arrange: The Arrange option helps put the elements on your project the right place. When you are working on a project with multiple texts, images, and deigns, there is every probability that the new elements you add will be placed in front of others, but, in actual sense you want them placed at the back. The arrange option makes it easier to do that.

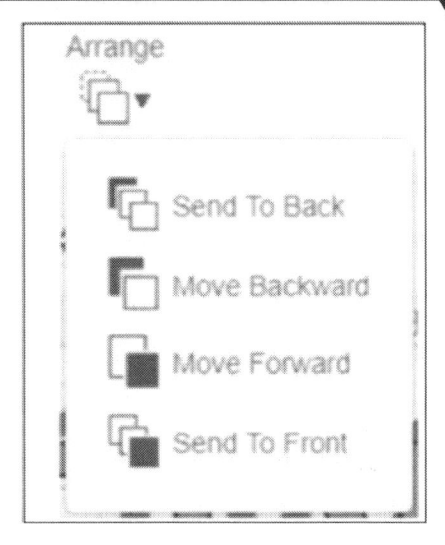

The Arrange option has other sub-options which include:

- Send Back: This action will move all selected element on your project to the back.

- Move Backward: This action will move all selected elements on your project one step back. This simply means that activating this item will just take the element(s) only one step back instead of all the way back behind other elements.

- Move Forward: This action will move selected element(s) a step forward.

- Send to Front: This action will move selected element(s) to the front of every other element on the project.

FLIP: The Flip icon gives you the ability to reflect your designs on your Cricut canvas.

The Flip option has two sub-options:

- Flip Horizontal: This action when activated reflects the images on your design horizontally. When you have a design at the right and want to duplicate same design at the left, Flip horizontally helps you with that.

- Flip Vertical: This action perfectly helps you create a shadow effect on your design by flipping the selected design vertically.

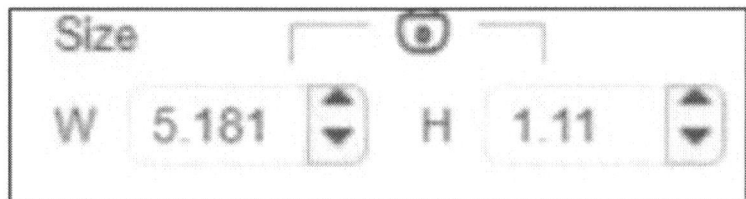

Size: Every element you introduce to your design canvas (text, image, shape) has a size. Sometimes you may not want to alter the size, but, the Size icon gives you the ability to modify elements to any size of your choice.

After modifying the size of an image, it is essential to click the lock icon on the size option. This is telling your Cricut program that you don't want to keep those same dimensions as default.

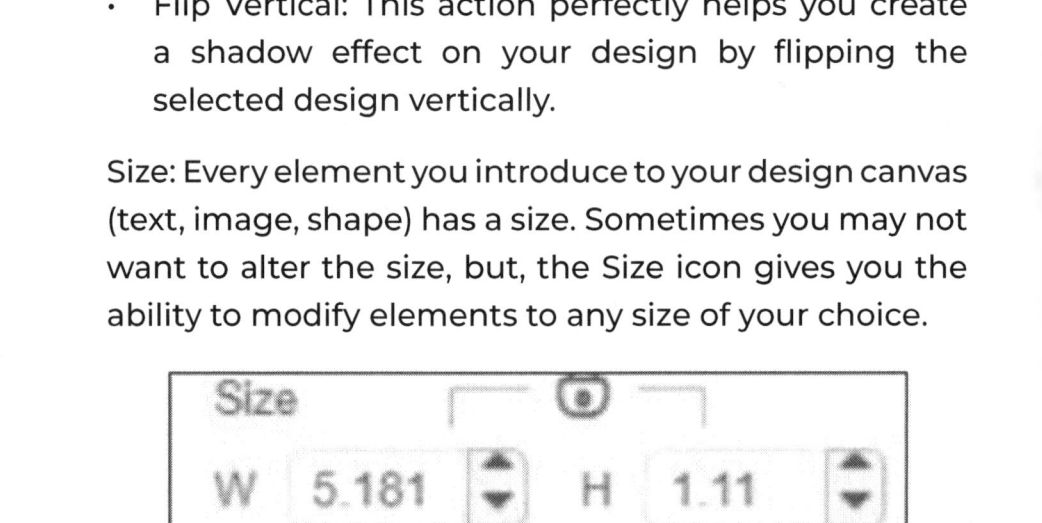

Rotate:

The rotate action helps you rotate an element to your desired angle. It can get tedious trying to get an image on your project to the right angle manually, but with the rotate option, it is very easy.

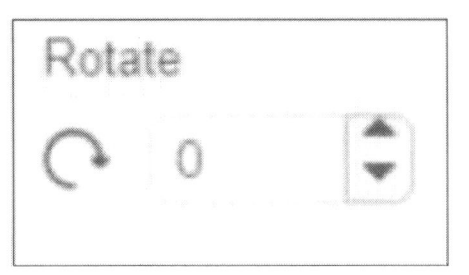

Chapter - 9

How to Upload Image with a Cricut Machine

The capacity to upload your own images into Design Space can be a lifeline, particularly in the event that you can't discover anything remotely like what you're attempting to make. You can upload anything going from a PNG to a multi-layered vector document and Cricut will naturally process it. You will have the option to print, cut, or draw them any way you wish!

After you pick a fundamental image to upload, you will have the option to see the see and select the image to utilize.

Basic images are fundamental and little documents that contrast hues with a strong foundation.

Respectably perplexing images have more detail and shading which you can see by look over them in Design

Space.

Complex Images are definite and mix hues, so it is hard to tell the foundation from the closer view. Fluctuating degrees of concealing and mixing are remembered for this option. You will doubtlessly need to choose this version to do the most nitty-gritty crafting project.

SVG – The Scalable Vector Graphics is the best when utilizing your Cricut machine. They take into consideration more exact cuts than a PNG or JPG record.

In the event that you download an SVG document from the web ensure you extra the SVG record on the off chance that it is downloaded as a ZIP record (.ZIP documents can't be uploaded into Design Space).

BONUS TIP: Google the realistic you are looking for + SVG + allowed to see the entirety of the openly accessible designs that you can bring into Cricut Design Space. Download the SVG record and upload it into Design Space in the event that you can't discover what you're searching for on Cricut's foundation.

Browse the records you have on your PC or distributed storage and discover the image that you might want to upload.

Fundamental Image Upload

Upload the record you might want to import to Cricut Design Space. This will probably be a .JPG or .PNG record type. Next, open the document selector or drag the record into the upload section of Design Space.

You will, at that point, can choose Simple, Moderately mind-boggling, or Complex design types. Select the most pertinent and precise sort at that point; click "Continue."

Identify the cutting lines of the uploaded image. Make certain to utilize the Tools on the left high quality of Canvas, for example, Select, Erase, and Crop. In the event that you see a checkerboard design behind your image that implies the zone has been evacuated successfully.

Click on Preview on to see the cut lines of the uploaded image. On the off chance that you have to change the outcome, click Hide Preview to return to alter (from the past advance). Click Continue once you are prepared to proceed onward.

Name and label your image so you can discover it in your uploaded documents later. Either select "Print Then Cut" or "Cut image" to show what kind of action you might want your Cricut Machine to take. This will decide how the record is spared and ready to be utilized.

Finally, save the image. You will presently have the option to access and utilize your uploaded image.

Vector Image Upload:

1. Select the .SVG document you might want to import to Cricut Design Space. Either intuitive or physically select and import the image from your PC documents.

2. Name the image appropriately so you can think that it's later.

3. The new image document will appear in the Uploaded Images Library at the base of the screen.

4. Vectors will appear on Canvas as an assembled image. You can ungroup them on the correct hand side of the canvas if necessary.

ESSENTIAL IMAGES

Essential images are JPG, BMP, PNG, and GIF records. These are, for the most part, made in programs that work in pixels, similar to Adobe Photoshop.

VECTOR IMAGES

Vector images are SVG and DXF document types. These documents will be naturally isolated into layers subsequent to uploading and sparing. These are, for the most part, made in programs that work in vectors, similar to Adobe Illustrator. Both of these strategies work, yet I regularly discover my Illustrator records are the best on the grounds that the Cricut was designed to cut vector documents, so it peruses them locally. Be that as it may, don't stress; it cuts other pixel-based documents well, as well!

I figured the ideal approach to disclose this is taking a gander at the procedure for cutting a similar image as an essential image and as a vector image. I made this straightforward shirt decal in Adobe Illustrator. I spared it as an SVF and as a JPG. Here's the procedure for uploading each:

UPLOADING A BASIC FILE (JPG) TO THE CRICUT DESIGN SPACE

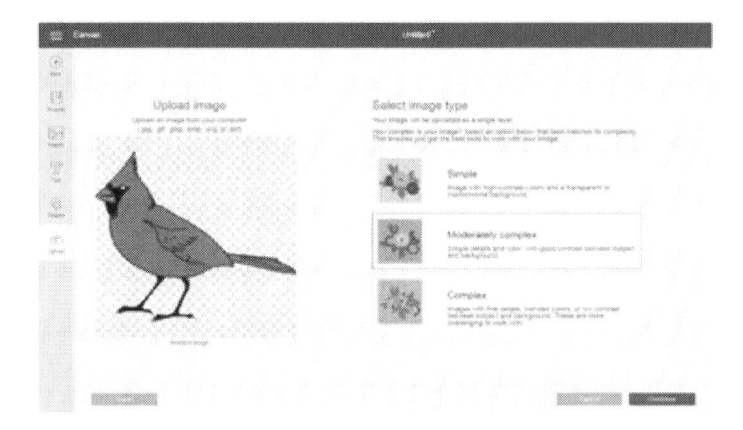

Start by clicking "Upload Image" on the left-hand menu, and explore to the record you need to open. At that point, select it from the rundown of uploaded images and click "Supplement Images."

The Cricut Design Space will at that point solicit you what type from the image you are cutting. I generally select "tolerably complex image" since I think the product works somewhat harder to see the edges than with a straightforward image.

In the following screen, you'll select any piece of the design that is negative space — which means it doesn't get cut. You need to choose any white parts, so they become straightforward (checked). Ensure you zoom in and choose the little regions of your project. Right now, needed to zoom in to click on the little design on the teepee and within parts of the letters.

The last screen has you select whether this is a print-then-cut image or an ordinary cut image. Right now, only a Cut Image — no printing associated with this project.

Once you are done, it will show up on your work screen. The records don't really import at the right size, so you can modify that in the "alter" menu on the left. I zoomed in so you can perceive how the fundamental record is only somewhat unpleasant around the edges. It will, in any case, cut and look incredible. However, a vector document is cleaner. Once you have your document, click GO in the upper right and cut your record!

UPLOADING VECTOR FILE (SVG) TO THE CRICUT DESIGN SPACE

The procedure for uploading a vector record is substantially more straightforward than uploading an essential document. Adhere to indistinguishable instructions from above to import your SVG. Once you find a good pace "Images" button, it will skirt the entirety of the above advances and import your image legitimately into the Cricut Design Space. On the off chance that you designed it at a specific size, those dimensions ought to be held when you import. At that point, click GO in the upper right, and you're high-tailing it!

Chapter - 10

Tips and Tricks to Make Cricut Easier and Efficient

We hope you find the following tips and tricks useful for the many projects you surely will create!

Subscribe to Cricut Access

If you really want to get a full range of use out of both your Cricut Explore machine as well as the Cricut Maker machine, we would recommend you subscribe to Cricut Access right away. There are two options for payment. This works out to be slightly cheaper on a month to month basis. This will give you access to thousands of different predesigned projects as well as Cricut Access exclusive fonts, that you would otherwise have to pay to use. If you are planning to use your Cricut a lot, this will save you a lot of money as opposed to buying every project an image individually. We can all agree it is a lot easier to pay one flat rate instead of having to figure out how much you are actually spending on projects.

De-tack Your Cutting Mat

The Circuit Explore machine will come with a green 12"x12" Standard grip cutting mat. The Cricut Maker machine will come with a blue light grip mat. As you already know, you will place your cutting material onto this mat before inserting it into the machine to cut. As you will come to find out, the green cutting mat is extremely sticky when it is brand new.

Keep Your Cutting Mat Covers

The cutting mats that you purchase for your projects will always come brand new with a plastic protecting sheet over it. You will want to keep this plastic cover as long as you have the mat.

Cleaning the Cricut Cutting Mat

It is very important to keep your cutting mat clean in order for it to remain sticky and be available for use over and over. Ideally, you would want to clean the mat every time after use if not at least every couple uses would suffice. All you will have to do is simply wiping down a clean mat with baby wipes to keep it clean.

Adhere Your Materials to Your Mats with Painter's or Masking Tape

You will find that, as your Cricut mats age, they will slowly lose their grip. Before completely giving up on your mat and throwing it out, considering lining the edges of your project with painter's tape or with masking tape. This will hold your materials in place while they're being cut and will save you the expense of a new mat for some time.

Command Hooks from 3M to Hang Your Cutting Mats When Not in Use

Utilizing your wall space for storage can be invaluable when you're storing something that is delicate and prone to bending, like your Cricut craft mat. Using Command hooks will ensure that your walls won't be damaged by the adhesive and your mats will always be within arm's reach and will never be hidden from you with this method!

Keep the Clear Plastic Sheet That Comes with Your Cricut Mats

When you buy a fresh Cricut mat, you will notice a semi-rigid sheet of plastic that comes stuck to the grip. After you complete each project, re-adhere this sheet to the front of your mat before hanging them up or putting them away! This will keep the grip from getting ruined by dust, hair, rogue glitter, or animal fur in the air!

Take Care of Your Mat

Many mats have met their ends in my care, and there are multiple reasons for this. If the material won't stick to it, the paper, vinyl, and others will all move around while the blade is trying to cut through, and it will end in a disaster.

Don't Be Lazy

Test those projects first! Testing is key to mastering the Cricut even when you feel like you've already gotten the hang of it. It never hurts to assess your projects before doing the final cut or print. Test before you cut. Make it a habit of yours. It should come without a thought. Instead of doing the whole project at once, do a small element of it first. If it doesn't work, you won't need to wait for it to finish before you can fix the settings and cut the new design. It will also save you the pain of losing the material you wanted to use for the project itself.

Try Different Markers

Don't feel limited by the Cricut markers. That's right! When you are using your Cricut machine to write or draw on your project, any marker that will fit will work perfectly. Not only are there cheaper options but the colors and variety of styles are virtually endless. Don't let anyone tell you that you can only use the markers from the Cricut brand. Even though they are of better quality and actually made for the machine, you are not limited to using them. Just make sure your markers fit.

Double-Check the Settings

Just like the testers, this is annoying, but you have to make sure that all of your settings are correct and that you have selected the right material option. If you are not using the Cricut Design Space, this is easy to forget. When you utilize the software, there is a broad selection of tools to choose from. However, when you are only using a cartridge, the materials are limited. Still, regardless of which set-up you wish to handle the design, you should check your settings twice.

Keep Your Blades in a Good Condition

Preferably, get one for every material that you are going to cut. In the list of materials that are available to add to your Cricut purchase, you may see different kinds of blades available. A dull blade is never a good thing, and it will ruin your project as easily as a sharp one will cut it perfectly.

Extend Your Markers' Shelf Life

Keep your markers upside down with the cap-covered tip facing down when you are not using them? Do not leave them in your Cricut when you are not using them. Secure the cap and put them away afterward.

Blades Getting Dull Too Soon? Run Foil Through Your Cricut!

A very popular Cricut trick in use is to stick a clean, fresh piece of foil to your Cricut mat, and run it through with the blade you wish to sharpen. Running the blades through the thin metal helps to revitalize their edges and give them a little extra staying power until it's time to buy replacements.

Cut Slits in the Edges of Your Transfer Tape

If you're transferring a decal onto something that is round, like a cup or mug, you will find it much easier to lay the decal flat if you cut intermittent slits in the transfer tape. You will find these cuts down on its reusability, but you will get more even, less bubbly designs on your products, more reliably.

Reverse Weeding

This is a technique that is best used on designs that have a lot of intricate or delicate letters or lines. The way it is done is, once you've run your vinyl through your Cricut machine, adhere the transfer tape to the front of that vinyl piece. Burnish it with your scraper tool, and then remove the carrier sheet or backing from the vinyl.

Use Baby Powder to Reveal Cut Lines

When using glitter iron-on material, it can be very difficult to see where the cut lines are, thanks to the light refraction off all the glitter pieces. By taking a very small amount of baby powder and brushing it onto the back of your vinyl piece, you can see where those cut lines are more easily, and peel away the excess to reveal your design!

Use a Binder and Page Protectors for Storage

You will find that, as you amass scraps of vinyl, paper, foil, and more, it will be hard to keep your spare materials from getting lost, damaged, curled, or worse. However, this can be completely avoided with this $2 hack! Buy a 3-ring binder and some page protectors. Use those protectors as pockets for similar materials, or organize them by size, or color, and you will find that your scraps are safe and ready to use at all times!

Pegboard Tool Storage

Simply hanging a pegboard over your workspace can keep all your tools readily available. Keeping your tools in a box that gets moved regularly can cause the tools to bump into each other, dulling their points or chipping their handles. Hanging your tools above your workstation ensures you'll be able to find what you need at all times, your tools will stay pristine for longer, and you'll be able to look at your pretty tools at all times!

Degunk Your Blades

If this is the case, remove the housing from your clamp and press the button at the top of the housing. This will extend the blade out of the housing. If you see debris or gunk on your blade, very carefully remove it and return the housing to its place in the clamp. You should find that your cuts are more precise after this!

Leave Your Explore on Custom

On the Explore models of the Cricut, you will find that you need to specify what type of material your machine is cutting. This tells the machine how hard it needs to work to get those precise cuts for you. It is a very common problem among the Cricut community, to leave your machine on the wrong setting, forget to change it, and have a project that doesn't come out exactly as you expected because of it. The solution for this is a simple habit!

Make a Reminder

If you're not a fan of leaving your machine on "Custom," or you can't seem to get that habit down, make a reminder to stick on the side of your machine that will tell you to check your settings for each job! This could be a Cricut project in itself, making a vinyl cling for the side of your machine so you never forget again. Don't forget to cut slits in the edges of your transfer tape for those curved edges!

Remove Your Transfer Tape at an Angle

Removing your transfer tape at an angle can help to eliminate and minimize bubbling under your vinyl designs. The way in which you do this is by peeling up one corner of your transfer tape and pulling diagonally, toward the opposite corner. When using this method, you can also use your XL Scraper to keep your letters down, as described in one of the tips above. This will help keep your letters on even ground when negative pressure is applied while removing the transfer tape!

Don't Remove Your Design from the Mat before Weeding

A common practice among new crafters is to remove the vinyl from the Cricut mat before starting the weeding process. However, weeding on the mat is far easier. With the grip from the mat keeping your project firmly in place, it's like having an extra set of hands when doing the hardest part of your project! Don't underestimate the power of your mat!

Chapter - 11

Beginners Project to Start Using Cricut

By far, the best technique I can teach you, which will help you get closer to pulling off the perfect project, is patience. Take the time to relax, take your time in getting the material to do what you want it to do, and think of creative solutions. Doing so will always yield a higher rate of success with your projects made with the Cricut system? Always go into your projects with a positive attitude that says, "I can do this!" In addition to this, bring a quizzical mindset that asks, "How can I do this differently?" With those and a lot of patience, you will find that your projects roll by quickly and much more smoothly. Plus, you'll have so much more fun when you do it this way!

Let's Get Down to It!

Immediately out of the box, you'll find that your Cricut Explore machine will come with some cardstock, a pen, a blade, and a mat. These tools will get you through the very first of your beginner's projects.

As you get the hang of using the Cricut Design Space application and how the Cricut machine operates, you will find that your skill level with the Cricut system will increase rather rapidly. These beginner projects are all just the right skill level for someone who's starting with their Cricut machine, so pick the one you like and get to work!

Cricut Hello Greeting Card

Take the protective plastic layer off the top of your green Cricut cutting mat and set it aside. Be sure to keep it somewhere it won't become wrinkled or damaged, as this is the layer you'll put back on top of your mats before each time you store them. This will protect its adhesive finish, giving your mats more lasting power throughout your projects.

Line up your cardstock with the upper left-hand corner of the grip on your mat, keeping the textured side of the cardstock facing upward. Smooth down your cardstock with your hands to ensure that no gaps, wrinkles, or folds form in your cardstock.

Once you've lined up your cardstock with the corner of your mat, place the mat under the mat guides in your Cricut machine. Firmly push the mat toward the rollers as you tap the Load/Unload button, which is indicated by the double arrow on the top of your machine.

Open accessory clamp A inside your machine and remove the cap from your metallic Cricut pen, which came with your machine. Place the cap on the back of your pen and slide it snugly into place, so you don't lose it while you're working. Once you've done that, gently push up on the bottom of accessory clamp A while you insert the pen. Push gently but firmly into the clamp until the little arrow on the pen is covered by the clamp, and you hear a click. Close the clamp and remove your finger from underneath it.

Now that your machine is loaded and set up with the right accessories, you will find that you're ready to start your design. If you're having trouble finding the project, or if Cricut Design Space doesn't automatically prompt you to begin with this design, click on the menu and select New Machine Setup. Follow the initial steps once more until the application pulls up the project for you. Alternatively, you can use the project search function with the keyword "Phone." This should pull up the two-layered greeting card design that we're creating here.

Click the "Make It" button to ensure that the design is correctly lined up with the materials on your mat. If this screen is showing you that your design will be cut in a space that isn't covered by your cardstock, unload the mat, adjust your cardstock, then reload it and return to the "Make It" screen, or return to the design space and adjust where the design is laid out. Once everything is plotted out properly, return the mat to the machine, and return to the "Make It" screen.

Set the dial on the outside of your Cricut Explore machine to the "cardstock" setting to ensure that your machine will be applying the appropriate amount of pressure to your blade. This will give you the cleanest, most accurate cuts possible.

Once everything appears to be in order, click the "Go" option. On your Cricut machine, once the Cricut C button begins to blink, give it a press. Your machine will set itself to the task of drawing and cutting your design!

Once that's complete, tap the blinking Load/Unload button and remove your mat from the Cricut machine. Open accessory clamp A, remove your pen, and replace the cap to ensure your pen won't dry out while you're working. Once your pen is capped, put it in the storage compartment in the front of your machine. Now you will always know where it is!

Fold the cardstock in half evenly, and then repeat this step with the blue paper that came with your machine. Once they're both folded evenly, place the paper inside the card, so it shows through the cut spaces in your cardstock.

Congratulations on completing your very first Cricut Design Project! You're doing great.

Happy Birthday Gift Tag

Special materials for this project include three different colors of cardstock to your preference, a roll-on adhesive tape, and a glue pen. If you find that other types of adhesive would work better for you, feel free to use those instead.

Visit the Cricut Design Space web application and select the option to create a new project. Once you're there, click "Images" and search for the word "tag." Select the shape that looks a plain gift tag like this: Once you've selected this image, you should see it populate in the queue at the bottom of your screen.

Now, click the "Categories" option at the top of the screen and select the "Birthday" category, before setting your search filter to "Phrases." Select the Happy Birthday to You image of your choice by clicking on it. We chose the one that looks like it's on a wavy banner.

Once you've made your selection for both images, you can click the green "Insert Images" button in the bottom corner of your screen. This will add the images to your design space so you can manipulate them to fit the design you'd like to create.

Drag the tag image closer to the upper left-hand corner of the Cricut Design Space and use the arrow button on the bottom right of the image so you can resize it to the desired dimensions.

The next thing you'll want to do is use the circular arrow button to rotate the tag 90° so your Happy Birthday image will fit onto the tag with some simple resizing. When you drag the phrase over to your tag however, you may notice that the text disappears beneath the tag image. This is not a problem, as you can simply click "Arrange" at the top of your screen and select the "Move to Front," option. This will put the phrase over the gift tag so it's plainly visible.

Now, let's resize that phrase so it fits properly on the tag with no issues.

Now, let's address the color of your images. While the Cricut machine does not print or affect the color of materials you're using, it does differentiate where to make its cuts based on the color of the materials in its dock. In order to keep your own thinking straight on what cardstock to put where, and to keep your Cricut cutting properly, set your images in Cricut Design Space to fit the color of the cardstock you have on hand.

Simply click on the layer of the image you wish to change; color options will pop up next to the panel. From here, you can simply select the color that most closely fits the cardstock you've chosen for this portion of your project.

If two layers of your project should be the same color, you can make things a little easier in the cutting process by consolidating both of those elements of your design onto the same layer. Simply drag one layer of your design to the one with which you wish to pair it and drop. This will put them both together and will keep them the same color!

Once you've got all the elements of your project to look the way you want, click "Save," give your project a unique name that you'll remember, and click "Save," again. Next, you'll click "Make It," to start the cutting process.

The mat preview screen will show you every step of the cutting process and where on your materials, the cuts will be made. Each of these elements will be separated by color, so you can tell what cuts will be made on your different pieces of cardstock.

If you're interested in making multiple gift tags, simply change the Project Copies quantity to your preferred number, then click "Apply." This will update your view to show you where the cuts will be made on the various colors of cardstock that you've selected.

Images in the preview screen cannot be manipulated in any way, so if you still have changes to make at this stage of the process, simply go back to the Design space. Make your changes there, so the project is laid out to your specifications, and then return to the "Make It" screen to reassess and to start the cutting process.

Once everything looks like it's laid out the way you need it, click the "Continue" button. You will be prompted to take the next steps of your project.

At this stage of the process, you will want to ensure that the material dial outside your Cricut Explore machine is set to "Cardstock," so all the cuts are made as precisely as possible.

Take the first cardstock that is shown on the prompt screen and line it up on your mat. Be sure to line the material up, so it's square with the grid and the grip on the mat. It will line up with the corners of the grid when done properly. Smooth the material down with your hands, making sure no noticeable gaps, wrinkles, or folds form on the material.

Place the mat into the machine by sliding it under the mat guides. Keep the mat pressed firmly to the rollers before tapping the Load/Unload button.

Once your mat is clear, load the next piece of cardstock, as indicated by the screen on Cricut Design Space.

To release your work from the mat, flip it face down on your work surface, so the back of the mat is facing you. Gently curl the corner of your mat back toward you until the cardstock releases from the adhesive surface of your mat. Using your free hand, hold the cardstock down onto your work surface, applying pressure evenly to keep your project from curling as you release it from the mat.

Once you've done this step, you'll find that all that's left on the mat are your design pieces, and some blanks in the lettering. Use your weeding tool to remove the blanks, and the spatula to remove your design pieces from the mat.

Conclusion

To be a professional in any endeavor in life requires dedicated efforts to learn and practice what you have learnt. The Cricut Design Space is, by all standards, what makes the Cricut machine to be best crafting machine in the market.

This guide has been written to help you master the use of the Cricut Design Space which I usually refer to as the backbone of the Cricut machine. With this mastery, you become a champion of champions in the crafting world.

An attempt was made to define what is Cricut Design Space and its general overview including the Design Panel, the Header, the Layers Panel, compatibility, and general requirement for efficient use of the Design Space. I have has shown, once more, my ability to be creative in the tech world with this guide which will help you become a master of the Cricut Design Space. This guide will definitely propel you to start creating beautiful and amazing crafts that beautify our everyday lives. So, what are you waiting for? Get busy, get to work!

Using a Cricut machine should not be a new experience to you by now. However, it would be best if you kept an open mind to new updates. Cricut always give their users a lot of options to choose from, so, try as much as possible to carry out extensive research about their products, materials, and subscriptions. At this stage, we can both agree that Cricut offers a whole lot more than it requires. Do not give up trying to learn how to cut on Cricut machines. Although it might be a little frustrating getting designs right sometimes, keep striving to attain perfection. You'll become professional in no time and probably start teaching other people how to use it. Cricut machines are getting more popular every day. A lot of people have a preference for Cricut machines for many reasons. Some of the reasons are;

User-Friendliness: This is one of the major reasons that people choose Cricut machines to do their cutting job. It's easy to use and also easy to learn if you have the right resources. Almost anyone can set up a Cricut machine because it is not too complicated. All that a new user has to do is to follow the straightforward instructions that come with the box.

Attractiveness: A lot of individuals like having their gadgets come in cool designs and structure. Cricut machines check this box emphatically, coming with very attractive designs and appearance.

Flexibility: Cricut machines are designed to handle multipurpose tasks. A lot of work can be done on it without stress. You can write, score, and cut with the machine. A lot of Cricut users are yet to reach the maximum level usage. With Cricut, people rarely over-utilize, most people only underutilize.

Apart from these three main advantages, you can also gain easy accessibility to Cricut machines and have no need to download software. As you continue to use this platform, you get more attached to it; it's only normal.

Pamela Cutter

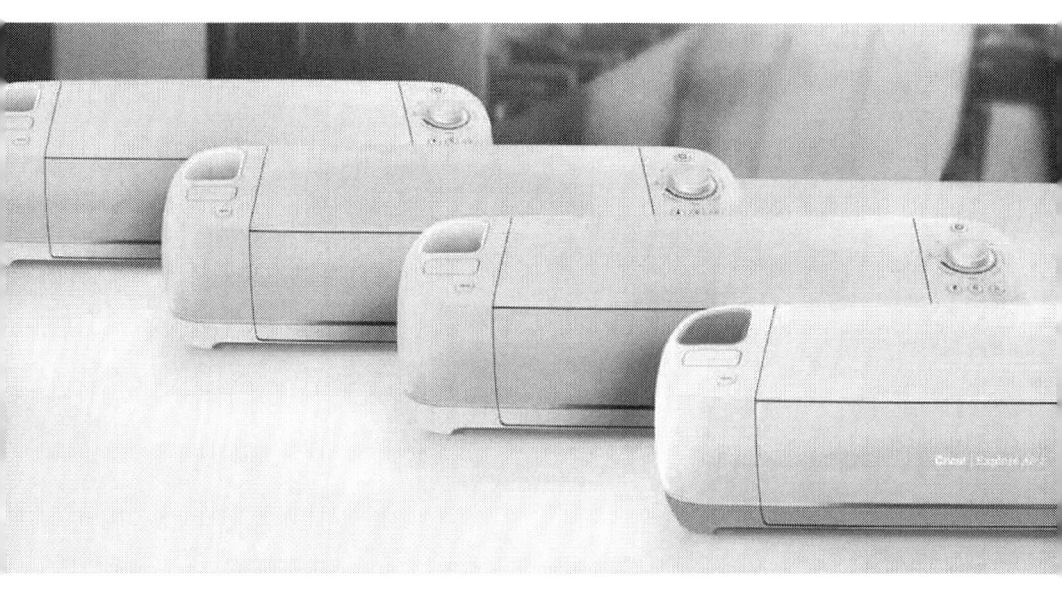

CRICUT PROJECT IDEAS

ILLUSTRATED GUIDE TO CREATE MANY UNIQUE CRICUT PROJECTS WITH TIPS AND TRICKS

Introduction

Cricut is your brand-name of a merchandise array of home die-cutting machines/cutting plotters utilized for scrapbooking and assorted endeavors, created from Provo Craft & Novelty, Inc. of Spanish Fork, Utah. The machines have been used for cutting materials like paper, felt, vinyl, cloth, and other items like fondant. Cricut is one of many digital die cutters utilized by newspaper crafters, card makers, and scrapbookers.

Models

The initial Cricut machine needed cutting coasters of 6in × 12in; the much bigger Cricut explorer simply lets mats of 12in × 12in and 12in × 24in. The biggest machine will create letters by a half inch to 23½ inches. The Cricut, along with Cricut explorer air two, demand mats and blades that may be corrected to cut various varieties of paper, vinyl, and other sheet solutions. The Cricut private paper cutter functions as a paper filler predicated upon cutting edge parameters programmed into the system and looks like a printer. Cricut cake creates stylized edible fondants cut various shapes in fondant sheets, also can be used by chefs at the groundwork and ornamentation of all cakes.

Present Models

These versions are now compatible with the present Cricut design space program.

Cricut research 1

The explore it's a wired die-cutting tool that can cut an assortment of materials from paper to cloth and much more. Be aware: there's a wireless Bluetooth adapter available for sale individually. This machine just had one instrument slot machine compared with other currently supported versions, which have 2.

Cricut research air

The explore air is a wireless die-cutting machine that may cut many different materials from paper to cloth, and much more. This system is the same as its next iteration, aside from the home and slower cutting skills.

Cricut maker

The cricut maker is really a brand-new lineup on august 20, 2017, made to cut heavier materials like some types of wood, non-bonded cloth, leather, and sensed.

The maker is your sole cricut machine which supports the usage of a blade for cutting edge cloth directly, and also a steering wheel with varying pressure to score heavier papers compared to the initial scoring stylus.

Legacy machines

First cricut

The first cricut has a 6" x 12" cutting mat and graphics can be trimmed in a range between 1" into 5 1/2" tall. The first cricut can be used with original cricut cartridges. The first cricut doesn't have the capability to cut many distinct kinds of materials the newer cricut machines may. But, cricut does create a deep cut blade & housing that may allow initial cricut owners to reduce stuff around 1.55mm thick, for example bark, chipboard, and postage materials. The first cricut can also be compatible with all the cricut design craft room.

Cricut expression

The cricut expression® provides several benefits over the former version. To begin with, it permits users to reduce shapes and fonts in a variety between 1/4" into 23 1/2" and has a 12" x 12" cutting edge with flexible slides so users no longer will need to trim down their media to 6" x 12". It cuts a larger assortment of substances, such as vellum, cloth, chipboard, vinyl, and thin foils. Additionally, it offers an lcd display to preview the job, and contains features such amount and auto-fill. Even a "paper saver" style and selection of portrait or landscape orientation also have been included. The fundamental version has two capsules within the buy, planting schoolbook along with accent essentials.

Cricut picture

This system was completely unique because it had an hp 97 ink jet printer built to it that it may either cut or publish pictures. This system had a revamped touch screen interface, also has been extremely big and heavy.

Cricut expression two

The cricut length 2 includes an upgraded exterior from that the cricut expression. It includes a 12" x 12" cutting mat. This system doesn't have the keyboard the first cricut along with also the cricut expression consumed. Rather it sports a brand-new full color lcd touch display. The lcd touch screen shows the computer keyboard on the display and lets you view where your pictures are going to be on the mat before cutting. Additionally, it has the newest characteristic of independent picture sizing and picture turning directly over the lcd display.

Cricut mini

The cricut mini is a tiny private electronic cutting machine. Unlike another cricut machines it simply works using a pc, it cannot cut pictures standing independently. You need to utilize cricut craft room layout computer software. The cricut mini includes over 500 pictures which are automatically unlocked once you join your cricut using all the cricut craft room design applications or your cricut gypsy apparatus. The machine will not have a cartridge jack that's compatible with cricut cartridges except that the cricut picture capsules. The cricut mini also offers a exceptional mat dimensions of 8.5" x 12". The cricut mini may cut pictures in a selection of 1/4" into 11 1/2". Even the cricut mini relied solely on utilizing cricut craft room, computer software which no longer works. Of the legacy cricut machines, the mini is the only person which is outdated and not usable at all. As no recourse has been supplied to the clients who had bought cartridges for that system, Provo-craft has become the focus of several complaints for clients who had been left without a recourse with this sudden pressured 'sun-setting' of this machine.

Cartridges

Designs are produced from components saved on capsules. Each cartridge includes a computer keyboard overlay and education booklet. The plastic computer keyboard overlay suggests key collections for this chance only. Nevertheless, lately Provo craft has published a "universal overlay" which can be used with cartridges released after august 1, 2013. The objective of the universal overlay would be to simplify the practice of clipping by simply needing to learn 1 keyboard overlay rather than being required to find out the overlay for every individual cartridge. Designs could be cut on a pc using all the cricut design studio applications, on a USB attached gypsy device, or could be directly inputted onto the cricut device employing the computer keyboard overlay. There are two forms of cartridges font and shape. Each cartridge has many different creative attributes which could allow for countless distinct cuts from only 1 cartridge. There are over 275 capsules which can be found (separately from the system), including shapes and fonts, together with new ones added each month. The cricut lineup includes a variety of costs, but the capsules are synonymous, but not all choices on a cartridge might be accessible with the more compact machines. A cartridge bought for a stop machine is very likely to turn into useless in the point that the machine is stopped. Cricut reserves the right to stop support for a number of versions of the applications at any moment, which may make some capsules instantly obsolete.

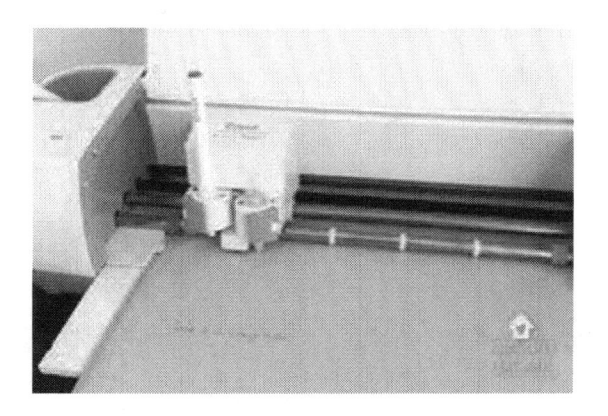

What Can Be a Cricut Machine?

The Cricut Explore Air is really a die-cutting system (aka craft plotter or cutting-edge system). You can consider it such as a printer; you also make an image or layout in your own personal computer and then ship it to your device. Except that Rather than printing your layout, the Cricut machine cuts out of whatever substance you desire! The cricut research air can reduce paper, vinyl, cloth, craft foam, decal paper, faux leather, and longer!

In reality, if you would like to utilize a cricut just like a printer, then it may do this also! There's an attachment slot on your system and you're able to load a mark in there after which possess the cricut "draw" the layout for you. It is ideal for obtaining a stunning handwritten look if your design is not all that good.

The cricut explore air may reduce stuff around 12" broad and includes a little cutting blade mounted within the system. When you are prepared to cut out something, you load the stuff on a sticky mat and then load the mat to your machine. If it finishes, then you unload the mat in the machine, and then peel off your project the mat, and then you are all set to move!

Using a cricut system, the options are infinite! All you want is a cricut system, design space, something to reduce, along with your creativity!

What could I do with a cricut machine?

There are a lot of things you can perform using a cricut device! There is no way that I could list all of the possibilities; however, here are a couple popular kinds of jobs to provide you a good concept about exactly what the machine could perform.

- cut out interesting shapes and letters to get cartoon
- make habit, handmade cards for any specific event (here is an illustration)
- layout a onesie or some t-shirt
- create a leather necklace

- create buntings and other party decorations
- make your own stencils for painting
- create a plastic decal for your vehicle window
- tag material on your cabinet, or in a playroom
- make monogram cushions
- make your own Christmas decorations
- address an envelope
- decorate a mug cup, or tumbler
- etch glass at house
- make your own wall stickers
- create a painted wooden signal
- create your own window
- cut appliqués or quilt squares
- produce stickers to get a rack mixer

...and plenty of different jobs which are too many to list!

Do It Yourself Using a Cricut Cutter

The cricut cutter is not for everybody. It's not right for the man or woman who's just a casual crafter. It doesn't make any difference if you're a beginner or an advanced crafter it's for the man or woman who's seriously interested in paper crafting. It's a sizable investment if you don't want to keep busy in document crafting. You sometimes can come across a cutter produce for about $100 in the event that you appear online. This cost can occasionally create the cricut cutter overly pricey for all. As you think about all of the decals, pre-packaged bling, pre-cut letters, numbers, and shapes many scrapbook fans discover the more dedicated scrappers find it eventually cover it. It's possible to make personalized invitations, gift tags and Christmas cards, and then pack and sell them to recover the cost of this cricut. It's by Provo craft plus they have a good standing in craft, and their products are frequently known to be quite durable, together with replacement components available if desired. With your own cricut cutter it is a lot less difficult to cut through just about any type or feel of paper. You may also create your own paper, so allow it to dry completely, and then media with your iron (no steam). You are able to use your paper to make real one of a kind cards or scrapbooks and among your kind antiques. Things nobody else has or may understand how to replicate regardless of how hard they try. This will permit your layouts to make original scrapbooks employing a number of shades and textures which may not be replicated.

Chapter - 1

Best Materials to Use with your Cricut Machine

Cricut machines have been designed to handle a wide variety of material. Most of the machines can work with a majority of materials, but they do have specialties among them. Read on for more information on the Cricut Explore One, Cricut Explore Air 2, Cricut Maker, and Cricut EasyPress 2 and the materials that work best with each.

Cricut Explore One

This machine only has one carriage, so you might find yourself swapping out tools more often than with the other machines. This machine can cut over 100 different materials. It can also write and score. Here's a sampling of some of the most common materials used with the Explore One machine.

- Vinyl – Vinyl, outdoor vinyl, glitter vinyl, metallic vinyl, matte vinyl, stencil vinyl, dry erase vinyl, chalkboard vinyl, adhesive foils, holographic vinyl, printable vinyl, vinyl transfer tape, iron-on vinyl, glitter iron-on vinyl, foil iron-on, holographic iron-on, printable iron-on for light or dark fabric, flocked iron-on vinyl, and neon iron-on vinyl

- Paper – Cardstock, glitter cardstock, pearl paper, poster board, scrapbook paper, vellum, party foil, cereal boxes, construction paper, copy paper, flat cardboard, flocked cardstock and paper, foil embossed paper, freezer paper, kraft board, kraft paper, metallic cardstock and paper, notebook paper, paper grocery bags, parchment paper, paper board, pearl cardstock and paper, photographs, mat board, rice paper, solid core cardstock, watercolor paper, and wax paper

- Fabric – Burlap, canvas, cotton, denim, duck cloth, faux leather, faux suede, felt, flannel, leather, linen, metallic leather, oilcloth, polyester, printable fabric, silk, and wool felt

- Specialty – Adhesive foil, adhesive wood, aluminum sheets, aluminum foil, balsa wood, birch wood, corkboard, corrugated paper, craft foam, duct tape, emboss able foil, foil acetate, glitter foam, magnet sheets, metallic vellum, paint chips, plastic, sticker paper, shrink plastic, stencil material, tissue paper, temporary tattoo paper, transparency film, washi sheets and tape, window cling, wood veneer, and wrapping paper

Cricut Explore Air 2

The Explore Air 2 can cut the same materials as the Explore One. The difference is that it has two carriages instead of one, so it's easier to swap between tools. It's also a bit faster than the Explore One. The Air machines have wireless and Bluetooth capabilities, so you can use the Cricut Design Space on your phone, tablet, or laptop without connecting directly to the machine.

Cricut Maker

The Cricut Maker has about 10x the cutting power of the Explore machines. It includes a rotary blade and a knife blade, so in addition to all the above materials, it can cut into more robust fabrics and materials. With the sharper blades, it's also better at cutting into more delicate materials without damaging them. Here's a list of some of the additional materials the Maker can cut.

- Acrylic felt
- Bamboo fabric
- Bengaline
- Birch
- Boucle
- Broadcloth
- Burlap
- Velvet
- Calico
- Cambric
- Canvas
- Carbon fiber
- Cashmere
- Challis
- Chambray
- Chantilly lace
- Charmeuse satin
- Chiffon

- Chintz
- Chipboard
- Corduroy
- Crepe paper
- Cutting mat protector
- Dotted Swiss
- Double cloth
- Double knit
- Dupioni silk
- EVA foam
- Eyelet
- Faille
- Fleece
- Foulard
- Gabardine
- Gauze
- Gel sheet
- Georgette
- Gossamer
- Grois point
- Habutai
- Heather
- Heavy watercolor paper
- Homespun fabric
- Interlock knit
- Jacquard
- Jersey
- Jute
- Kevlar
- La Coste
- Lycra
- Mesh
- Metal
- Microfiber
- Moleskin
- Monk's cloth
- Muslin
- Nylon
- Organza
- Handmade paper
- Plush
- Sailcloth

- Satin silk
- Seersucker
- Sequined cloth
- Bonded silk
- Tafetta
- Tulle
- Tweed
- Wool crepe

Cricut EasyPress 2

The Cricut EasyPress 2 is a small, convenient heat press. It works with any type of iron-on material and can adhere them to fabrics, wood, paper, and more. Cricut also offers Infusible inks that are transferred to the material using heat. The EasyPress is a great alternative to iron, as it heats more quickly and more evenly.

Crafting Blanks

The objects you decorate using your Cricut can be referred to as blanks. This can be absolutely any object, and it can be something you stick vinyl to, etch, paint, draw on, write on, or anything else you can think of. They're called blanks because they provide a mostly blank surface to be decorated, though they can also have colors or designs.

Some popular blanks are cups, mugs, wine or champagne glasses, travel mugs, tumblers, and other such drinking vessels. Craft stores will usually sell these, but you can find them at almost any store. They don't need to be considered a "craft" supply for you to use. Most stores have a selection of plain cups and mugs or travel mugs and tumblers with no designs on them. As long as you can imagine a Cricut project with it, it's fair game.

Drink wares aren't the only kitchen or dining-related blanks. Get creative with plates, bowls, and serving utensils. Find blank placemats or coasters at most stores. Decorate mason or other types of jars. Dry goods containers, measuring cups, food storage containers, pitchers, and jugs—anything you can put in your kitchen can serve as a great blank for your projects.

Clothing is another popular choice for Cricut projects. T-shirts are easy to make with iron-on vinyl, and you can find cheap blanks at any store or a larger selection at craft stores. In fact, craft stores will typically have a large selection of clothing blanks, such as t-shirts, long sleeve shirts, ball caps, plain white shoes, plain bags, and so on. Thrift stores or consignment shops can be an unusual option as well. You could find a shirt with an interesting pattern that you'd like to add an iron-on to or something similar.

Glass is fun to work with and has a ton of project options with your Cricut machine. Glass blocks can be found at craft or hardware stores. Many stores that carry kitchenware will have plain glass cutting boards, or you can find them online. Craft stores and home goods stores could sell glass trinkets or décor that you can decorate. You can even buy full panes of glass at your local hardware store and have they cut it to your desired size.

There are plenty of blanks related to electronics, as well. Electronics stores, online stores, and some craft stores offer phone and tablet case blanks. They might be clear, white or black, or colored. Portable battery packs are another option as well. Many times, these blanks are significantly cheaper than already decorated ones, or you can buy them in bulk for a lower price. Get your phone case for a cheaper price and customize it how you like.

Book covers make great blanks, as well. Customize the cover of a sketchbook, notebook, or journal. Repair the cover of an aged book. Or, create a new book cover for a plain one that you have. If you have old books that you aren't going to read, create a new fake cover for them and use them as décor.

Cricut Tools and Accessories

There are several different tools and accessories available for the Cricut machines. This isn't a comprehensive list of the entire collection, but it's a list of the things you should consider getting early on. These are easily available wherever you can buy Cricut products, including craft stores, online, and Cricut's own website. Some of these can also be found in other brands. Just make sure that anything that is a part of the machine is a genuine part to avoid accidental damage.

- Cutting mats – Cricut offers a variety pack that has a 12 x 12 of the Light Grip Mat, Standard Grip Mat, and Strong Grip Mat, which are perfect to get started and complete most of the projects.

- Self-healing mat – Rather than a mat that goes into the machines, this is a mat you can cut on. Cricut has precision cutting bundles that include these mats and a precision blade.

- Blades (Explore machines) – The Cricut Explore machines come with a fine-point blade, which you may need a replacement for after a long time of cutting. Also consider the Deep Point Blade, which is made for cutting magnet sheets, chipboard, rubber, thick cardstock, stiffened felt, foam sheets, and cardboard.

- Blades (Maker machine) – The Cricut Maker comes with a premium fine-point blade and a rotary blade, which you may need replacements for after a long time of cutting. Also consider the Knife Blade, which can cut thicker materials such as balsa wood, basswood, leather, chipboard, matboard, and craft foam.

- Scoring wheel (Maker machine) – If you plan on doing a lot of paper crafting, this is an essential tool.

- Essentials Tool Set – Cricut's essential set contains tweezers, a weeder, scissors, a spatula, a scraper, a scoring stylus, a paper trimmer, a replacement blade for the trimmer, and a scoring blade for the trimmer. This is a great starter set and will get you creating most projects. It even comes in different colors!

- Cricut Pens – Cricut produces specialized pens that fit into the machines. They come in dozens of colors, finishes, and nib sizes.

- Storage – Cricut sells rolling craft totes to carry supplies and accessories and machine totes for the Cricut machines themselves.

- Cricut Bright Pad – This is a light pad that makes it easier to weed your projects. The surface illuminates with a bright but diffused light. You can lay your projects on top of it to see where exactly you need to weed. It can also work well for tracing, paper-piecing quilt patterns, and jewelry making.

Where Do You Find Material

One of the exciting parts of Cricut Design Space is that the materials are not hard to find; they are all around you. There are online stores where you can easily get the materials you want. Although different e-stores have varying prices, the point is to get the ideal quality.

There are four popular online stores where Cricut machine users, both beginners and professionals, get materials for their Cricut projects, and they are; Cricut.com, Amazon, Joann, and Michaels. These stores provide almost every supply and bundles you'll be needing. They have the materials, tools and accessories, and even the Cricut machines needed. Feel free to visit each store and compare their prices before purchasing.

Also, you can look around for stores in your local area where sell the most common types of materials that can be used on Cricut machines, mostly paper products.

At this stage, we have been able to cover most of the basics of Cricut machines, materials, tools and accessories. You should now know their functionalities and purposes to some extent. It's high time we proceeded to the technical and complex part of making use of Cricut for different designs and crafts. From here onward, we will not discuss much about the properties of Cricut machines, materials, tools, or accessories. It will be majorly about how you can set up your Cricut machine and what you can do with it. We're getting to the interesting parts.

If you need to upgrade your Cricut machines, buy any material, tool or accessory, you should make plans for that now. The more resources you have, the more you can explore.

Chapter - 2

What can the Cricut do?

These two functions, however, have over a million uses and can be used on hundreds of materials, making it a truly versatile crafting powerhouse. Breaking it down to these two features seems almost like an injustice to the adaptability and versatility that this machine truly has.

If you like to make ornaments during the holiday season, the Cricut can help you make vinyl decals for that. If you like to make ornate greeting cards for every occasion, the Cricut can cut, emboss, score, and engrave accents for any design you can dream up in the Cricut Design Space. If you like making hats and t-shirts for group and family activities, Cricut has a whole range of iron-on materials that can be used for those!

Personalize everything you can imagine and more with Cricut products that are meant specifically to help you and crafters all over the world express themselves! There will be no project that can't be made better with a stencil, decal, sticker, or accent created or augmented with the Cricut and its host of customization features!

The Cricut Design Space library contains drawings of different colors with which you can use to cut materials or you can decide to input your own image and drawings using Photoshop, your tablet or Illustrator. You can also draw a hand sketch, scan it into your machine to draw and cut for you.

There are more than 50 crafts you can do using your Cricut Machine. Here, I will discuss in simple terms these amazing items:

- Cut fabrics: the rotary blade was designed to cut seamlessly through any fabric including silk, denim, chiffon, and heavy canvass. Coupled with the mat, hundreds of fabrics can be cut without any backing. This is amazing!

- Vinyl Decals and stickers: Is cutting vinyl decals and stickers your hobby, then you need Cricut Maker machine as your companion. Get the design inputted in the Design Space Software and instruct the machine to cut. As easy as that. The delivery will be wonderful. So what are you waiting for? Get to work!

- Greeting Cards: The power and precision of the Cricut Maker makes cutting of paper as well as making greeting cards craft less tedious and saves ample time. You're Christmas cards, birthday cards, success cards and other greeting cards will be delivered with accurate, unique and amazing style.

- Quilts: There are arrays of quilting pattern in the sewing pattern library of the Cricut Maker machine thanks to Cricut teaming up with Riley Blake Designs. With this library, you can cut and join quilt pieces accurately and sew them together using the Cricut Maker machine. The quilt designs are amazing.

- T-shits: Cutting heat transfer vinyl to be transferred on fabrics is a job the Cricut Maker does so well. First design on the Design Space and load into the Cricut Maker. Instruct the Maker to start cutting the heat transfer vinyl. After cutting, you then iron the transfer onto your T-shirt.

- Cuts Balsa Wood: Cutting wood up to this thickness can be done seamlessly using the Knife Blade that comes with the Cricut Maker. This is amazing.

- Sewing patterns: There are hundreds of sewing patterns which you can access once you buy the Cricut maker Machine. Patterns from Riley Blake Designs and Simplicity are included. All you need do is select any of the designs and the Cricut Maker will do the cutting for you.

- Holiday decorations: The rotary blade of the Cricut Maker can cut through fabrics of different types. This is a big plus to crafters assigned with decorations for holiday programmers like the birthday, wedding, anniversary and Christmas celebrations. Let the Cricut Maker do the cutting for you while you do the joining and fixing.

- **Dolls and Toys:** The sewing pattern library still comes to play here. Select the type of design and let the Cricut Maker cut the material for you. Kids love Dolls and toys. Do not deny them this wonderful experience of homemade dolls and toys.

- **Baby Clothes:** You can design those old children's clothes to become new again by being creative or even the ones you just bought from the store.

Cricut subscription

Cricut Access is the software that gives you access to images, fonts, and the like. You will need to purchase this if you plan on using your Cricut machine, period, and if you don't have the software already, I suggest purchasing it.

The monthly option is perfect for beginners and offers over 400 different fonts and 90,000 different images. And it comes with a 10% savings on any additional Cricut purchases you need, as well as a 10% savings on premium images and fonts, such as Disney fonts. You'll also have access to a priority member line.

The next membership option is annual, which is exactly the same as the basic, but you don't have to pay as much – just $7.99 per month, upfront. It's good if you're serious about getting into Cricut.

Finally, you have the premium option, which is the same price as monthly and offers unlimited access to the same fonts and images, savings on both products and licenses, and a 50% extra savings on licensed images and fonts, along with some ready-to-make projects. If you spend over $50 on the Cricut store, you earn free shipping. Personally, I think this is the best option if you plan on spending a lot of money on Cricut items, and you're in it for the long haul. However, if you're just beginning, the monthly membership is probably a better choice, because you can cancel this at any time.

Membership allows you to save a little bit on premium ideas and licensed designs – the more you make with your Cricut machine, the more you save, and you'll realize that you could save a lot really fast. On average, customers say that they make up the subscription costs with the money they save, and the coolest thing is that there is so much to choose from, you can find some beautiful designs. It is definitely great if you want exclusive content.

Craft Stores

If you are someone who enjoys going to a store to purchase items for a project over ordering them online, you too have many options to purchase your materials from. Craft stores have been around for a long time, but they have just recently started providing materials for all the Cricut Machines. You can easily think of a project and run to your nearest craft store and get everything you need to get started on your project that day. This also comes in handy if you are missing something you thought you had, or run out of something you need right away. These stores are always in convenient locations and making material gathering easy for everyone!

Cricut Website

Cricut online provides a great resource for buying materials for your Cricut projects. They keep their products up to date and often offer products that are created by designers. This is a great option for materials that are unlike what is sold in-store and online. Another great perk of buying directly from Cricut is that if you are a Design Space member, you will receive 10% off every purchase you make through them. Cricut takes care of their customers in more ways than one!

Chapter - 3

Cricut Projects

With Cricut, the ideas for projects are so vast; you'll be amazed at how much you can do. So, what are some ideas that could work for you? Here are a few that you can consider and some of the best project ideas for those who are stumped on where to begin!

Easy Projects

Custom Shirts

Custom shirts are incredibly easy. Personally, I like to use the iron-on vinyl, because it's easy to work with. Just take your image and upload it into Design Space. Then, go to the canvas and find the image you want. Once you've selected the image, you click on the whitespace that will be cut – remember to get the insides, too. Make sure that you choose cut image, not print from cut image, and then place it on the canvas to the size of your liking. Put the iron-on vinyl shiny side down, turn it on, and then select iron-on from the menu. Choose to cut, and make sure you mirror the image. Once done, pull off the extra vinyl to remove the vinyl between the letters. There you go! A simple shirt.

Vinyl Decals

Vinyl can also be used to make personalized items, such as water bottle decals. First, design the text – you can pretty much use whatever you want for this. From here, create a second box and make an initial, or whatever design you want. Make sure that you resize this to fit the water bottle, as well.

From here, load your vinyl, and make sure that you use transfer tape on the vinyl itself once you cut it out. Finally, when you adhere the lettering to the bottle, go from the center and then push outwards, smoothing as you go. It takes a bit, but there you have it – simple water bottles that children will love! This is a wonderful, simple project for those of us who aren't really that artistically inclined but want to get used to making Cricut items.

Printable Stickers

Printable stickers are the next project. This is super simple and fun for parents and kids. The Explore Air 2 machine works best.

With this one, you want the print then cut feature, since it makes it much easier. To begin, go to Design Space and download images of ice cream or whatever you want, or upload images of your own. You click on a new project, and on the left side that says images, you can choose the ones you like, and insert more of these on there.

From here, choose the image and flatten it, since this will make it into one piece rather than just a separate file for each. Resize as needed to make sure that they fit where you're putting them.

You can copy/paste each element until you're done. Once ready, press saves, and then chooses this as a print then cut image. Click the big button at the bottom that says make it. Make sure everything is good, then press continues, and from there, you can load the sticker paper into the machine. Make sure to adjust this to the right setting, which for sticker paper is the vinyl set. Put the paper into there and load them in, and when ready, the press goes – it will then cut the stickers as needed.

From there, take them out and decorate. You can use ice cream or whatever sticker image you want!

Personalized Pillows

Personalized pillows are another fun idea and are incredibly easy to make. To begin, you open up Design Space and choose a new project. From here, select the icon at the bottom of the screen itself, choosing your font. Type the words you want, and drag the text as needed to make it bigger.

You can also upload images, too, if you want to create a huge picture on the pillow itself.

From here, you want to press the attach button for each box, so that they work together and both are figured when centered, as well.

You then press make it – and you want to turn to mirror on, since this will, again, be on iron-on vinyl. From here, you load the iron-on vinyl with the shiny side down, the press continues, follow the prompts, and make sure it's not jammed in, either.

Let the machine work its magic with cutting and from there, you can press the weeding tool to get the middle areas out.

Set your temperature on the easy press for the right settings, and then push it onto the material, ironing it on and letting it sit for 10 to 15 seconds. Let it cool, and then take the transfer sheet off.

There you have it! A simple pillow that works wonders for your crafting needs.

Cards!

Finally, cards are a great project idea for Cricut makers. They're simple, and you can do the entire project with cardstock.

To make this, you first want to open up Design Space, and from there, put your design in. If you like images of ice cream then use that. If you want to make Christmas cards, you can do that, too. Basically, you can design whatever you want to on this.

Now, you'll then want to add the text. You can choose the font that you want to use, and from there, write out the message on the card, such as "Merry Christmas." At this point, instead of choosing to cut, you want to choose the right option – the make it option. You don't have to mirror this, but check that your design fits properly on the cardstock itself. When choosing material for writing, make sure you choose the cardstock.

From there, insert your cardstock into the machine, and then, when ready, you can press go and the Cricut machine will design your card. This may take a minute, but once it's done, you'll have a wonderful card in place. It's super easy to use.

Cricut cards are a great personalized way to express yourself, creating a one-of-a-kind, sentimental piece for you to gift to friends and family.

Medium Projects

Cricut Cake Toppers

Cricut cake toppers have a little bit of added difficulty because they require some precise scoring. The Cricut maker is probably the best piece of equipment for the job, and here, we'll tell you how to do it. The scoring tool is your best bet since this will make different shapes even easier, as well. You will want to make sure you have cardstock and the cutting mat, along with a fine-point blade for cutting. The tape is also handy for these.

First, go to Design Space and choose the rosettes you want. From there, the press makes it and follows the prompts. The single wheel will make one crease, and the double wheel will make a parallel wheel that will crease – perfect for specialty items. Plus, the double wheel is thicker, so it's easier to fold.

Once you score everything, you remove it and replace the scoring wheel with the fine-point blade.

From here, you simply fold everything and just follow the line. This should make the rosette, and you can then use contrasting centers and create many of these to form a nice backdrop.

Cricut Gift Bags

Remember to put the foil poster board face-down on the mat itself, to help prevent the material from cracking and showing through to the white backdrop, when you fold them together after you score them.

To make these, you want to implement the template that you'd like to use in Design Space. From here, I do suggest cutting out the initial design first, and then putting it back in to create scoring lines, following the same steps. After that, you can then take your item and fold along the score lines, and then use adhesive or glue to help put it all together. This is a great personalized way to do it but can be a bit complicated to work with at first.

Cricut Fabric Coasters

Fabric coasters with a Cricut maker are great, and they need only a few supplies. These include the maker itself, cotton fabric, fusible fleece, a rotary cutting mat or some scissors, a sewing machine, and an iron.

Cut the fabric to about 12 inches to fit the cutting mat – if it's longer, you can hang it off, just be careful.

From here, go to Design Space, then click shapes and make a heart. You can do this with other shapes, too. Resize it to about 5 inches wide. Press makes it, and you'll want to make sure you create four copies. Press continue, and then choose medium fabrics similar to cotton. You then load the mat and cut, and then you do it again with the fusible fleece on the cutting mat, changing it to 4.75 inches. This time, when choosing the material, go to more, and then select fusible fleece. Cut the fusible fleece, and then attach these to the back of the heart with the iron and repeat with the second.

Clip the curves, turn it inside out, and then fold in the edges and stitch it.

There you go – a fusible fleece heart coaster. It's a little bit more complicated, but it's worth trying out.

Difficult Projects

Giant Vinyl Stencils

Vinyl stencils are a good thing to create, too, but they can be hard. Big vinyl stencils make for an excellent Cricut project, and you can use them in various places, including bedrooms for kids.

You only need the explore Air 2, the vinyl that works for it, a pallet, sander and, of course, paint and brushes.

The first step is preparing the pallet for painting, or whatever surface you plan on using this for.

From here, you create the mermaid tail (or any other large image) in Design Space. Now, you'll learn immediately that big pieces are hard to cut and impossible to do all at once in Design Space.

What you do is section of each design accordingly, and removes any middle pieces. You can add square shapes to the image, slicing it into pieces so that it can be cut on a cutting mat that fits.

At this point, you cut out the design by pressing make it, choosing your material, and working in sections.

From here, you put it on the surface that you're using, piecing this together with each line, and you should have one image after piecing it all together. Then, draw out the line on vinyl and then paint the initial design. For the second set of stencils, you can simply trace the first one and then paint the inside of them. At this point, you should have the design finished. When done, remove it very carefully.

And there you have it! Bigger stencils can be a bit of a project since it involves trying to use multiple designs all at once, but with the right care and the right designs, you'll be able to create whatever it is you need to in Design Space so you can get the results you're looking for.

Chapter - 4

Tips and Techniques

Cricut mats may become dull, messy and lose their adhesiveness over time. how to wipe your cricut mat and make them adhesive again Preferably, these adhesive mats should only be used a few hundred times prior to imperfect, non-sticky materials that could ruin the perfect art, but do not yet throw away! In this segment, we will show you multiple ways to clean and repair your Cricut Mat. In addition, we will present some effective ways to restick and make your mat a new one.

Cricut mats come in multiple variations, but the cleaning method ought to be almost the same. The guide will be useful to you when you have to re-use an aged Cricut, a portrait pad or a cake mat used to bake. You're going to save a nice Cricut pad, a couple of bucks and can be a nice project to boot. So, what are you expecting? Gather old cleaning products and let's start!

Somehow, if the surface becomes defective and cannot make exact cuts, a Cricut mat loses its function. If the materials don't stick as well as they should to, or if the surface is becoming dirty or soft particles come in, you will know when it is time to cleanse the mat. You won't have to use advanced materials to clean the mat. Most of them can actually be noticed in most residences and washing rooms.

Step 1. Light Cleaning

First of all, whip your trustworthy plastic scraper out, which should be bought with the Cricut machine. If not, there will be a similar rigid plastic scraper. Push the substance slowly and methodically along the surface to dispose of small particles. Do it a few times before you take another step.

Step 2. Baby Wipes and Lint Roller

Believe this or not, paper towels are the ideal wiping companions to your Cricut mat because they are soft and moist enough to hold the mat safe. But not all wet wipes are used to clean Cricut mats! Select one that is free of additives and liquor, or risk ever missing the adhesion of the pad. Push the wipe slowly across the surface to cover it all in a single direction. You might be tempted to hit the remover, but it's best to be safe than regret. Baby wipes and lint rollers, and good old-fashioned rubbing alcohol also work wonderfully to make your Cricut mat look repaired and ready to cut. Two roles are performed by lint rollers. Two, sticky rollers can move stickiness to the surface of the mat. The combined effect of wet wipes and lint rollers is sometimes one-two enough just to remove mild build-up.

Step 3. Soap & Water

You'll want to bath your Cricut mat once in a while with a container filled with soap and water. Allow the mat to sit for 10 minutes before removing. If things don't come off, use a scrubby brush and wash with warm water. Make sure you read the directions for the cleaning agent. Oh, and afterwards you'll also have to restick your pad.

Step 4. Air Dry

When you're pleased with how clean it feels, it's time to balance it up. Repeat until the mat is dry before using it again. The use of a towel, tissue or sheet is counter-intuitive because small pieces stick to the surface and reduce overall effectiveness.

Has your Cricut mat lost its adhesion and you can't be as accurate now as you want?

There are many ways to get it secure and usable again. No worries.

A sticky spray, a repositionable adhesive or sticky spray, is required for this. All of these are sold at discount craft department stores retailers and are pretty cheap. Please note that every product might have different usage instructions, so please read them first.

If all the supplies are prepared, let's start.

Use a masking or a painter's tape to protect the sides of your cricut pad. It is necessary not to stick the edges so that the cutting machine does not get damaged.

Step #1

Remove the residue of the adhesive spray to cover the mat uniformly. Apply plain liquor or Goo Gone to the surface, and then use a scrapper over it.

Step #2

Spray or add a sticky spray gradually and evenly cover the Cricut mat board. Many items need you to scrub a few occasions, while others just need touch to work their magic. Also, obey the label directions for the best outcomes.

Step #3

Step 3–Let all the coating rest and bind properly to the mat surface. Extract the tape on the edges after about 20 minutes and check the final product carefully. As fresh and ready to rock your Cricut mat ought to be fine!

It is vital that you clean your cricut mat so that you can apply precision procedures without thinking of dirt, sand or lint. We suggest taking care of the surface of your mat and cleaning it regularly with the above methods.

Moreover, the protection of your crucible mat allows the material to slip uniformly into the cutting machine and holds it intact. Why spend money in the purchase of a new mat when the aged mat is perfectly usable? It only takes a few moments to rejuvenate and make it sticky again and it's not that pricey.

How to quickly weed vinyl

Whether you like to have vinyl or iron-on weeded, I'm sure these strategies will make you weed quicker and less defective! Even the weeding of the most complex vinyl models can be made simpler with these techniques. Let us know if in the comments below you have any other tricks!

Such tips of vinyl weaving refer to all vinyl forms, whether iron-on vinyl or vinyl adhesive. These tips are particularly useful for weaving small numbers and letters or weaving complex mandala designs.

Use the Right Blade

Many vinyl cutting machines have various blades. The variety of Cricut blades includes, for example, the perfect point blade, the deep-sliced blade and the rotating blade. For each material you cut, you want to use the right blade. It is also necessary to check that no pieces of paper or vinyl are attached to the cutter blade and that it is clean.

Blade Setting

When you cut vinyl with the blade put too low, the pattern with the area to be weeded would end up pulling away. So, if you slice too deeply, you will struggle with a carriage board! The modification of the cutting machine to the right depth makes weaving much easier. Make sure the knob is switched to the right material configuration if you are uncertain, do a test if your configurations are correct for the particular vinyl form you use.

For many years I've been using Cricut Explore Air 2, and I don't remember how many times I neglected to set the dial for the right place prior to cutting. I use the Cricut Maker most of these days and before cutting the material configuration is selected on the screen.

Use Quality Vinyl

Now that your cutting settings are flawless, working with great vinyl is important.

A high-quality vinyl with high-quality vinyl sheet would make it much easier to cut a weed for longer without cracking or bleeding.

Siser Easy Weed

Thanks to its fast weeding and pressurized help, you save a great deal of time throughout the weeding phase with this vinyl.

Cricut Iron On & Vinyl

Another quality brand that you can use for your transfer projects is the Weeding tips for cricut vinyl and htv Cricut iron on. It comes in a wide range of colors and different types, which include metal, glitter and lights.

Oracal 651

This is a guaranteed adhesive vinyl, which many consider to be the best craft vinyl adhesive to buy.

Warm Up Weeding Surface

What makes it even easier to weed vinyl is what Siser calls "the trick in the heating press." Heat your low-heat press plates for 2 seconds (set at approximately 300 ° F). Place your HTV on the heated lower plate and the pressure of the backing will release the adhesive. This makes it much easier to remove excess vinyl.

Weed Into Cavities

It's a good idea to first weed out all the inside cavities prior to pulling all your excess vinyl, if you can evidently see what the cut lines are. If you first remove the vinyl excess and then try and get the cavities inside, your hand is stuck to the board. After the cavities inside the letters are removed, your main piece of excess vinyl is removed. There is, however, a right and wrong way to do so!

Once you pull up your vinyl, make sure you do it the other way round. Drag the vinyl back and into the letter cavities effectively. It leads to fewer breaks and accelerates the weeding cycle!

Use Weeding Borders

Another way to encourage weeding is by using weed fronts or boxes.

If you have several different components in one design, you can put a box in your cutting software around each component. Your cutter will cut a box in your design for each part. Then you can weed your entire concept into pieces. You should pull your vinyl into individual strips to make weaving less complicated!

If you cut multiple designs on a vinyl sheet, you can place a box around each design and weed them separately. If you really have small or delicate details, you can put a weeding box around them so you can weave them with extra care.

Reverse Weeding

Reverse weeding is only for vinyl adhesive. It is where you put the whole unweeded decal on a transfer tape and then remove the excess vinyl from the transfer tape instead of from the carrier pad. In theory, weeding for smaller decals is easier than using it regularly! See the extended post for details step by step.

The Cricut Bright Pad

The Cricut Bright Pad is another great way to make it easier to weave vinyl. When you put a cut vinyl template on the Bright Pad (or other weeding vinyl light pad), you can see all the cut lines instantly. The design becomes much more apparent and the region that needs to be removed can easily be identified. The darker the vinyl is, the more the light pad can help.

Good Lighting

If you don't want to spend on the Bright Pad, just make sure that you have direct light on the cut vinyl. Sometimes I use the light of my cell phone. It's super bright and I can see clearly every single cut. Many may prefer a system in which the light shines from below, but I find it easier to put the light above where I work.

Use SVG for Reference

One thing that helps me A Bit with complex designs is that I have a SVG picture in front of my screen. Sometimes it is very difficult to tell what part of the design is and what weeded away is, but it is much easier to get the original image in front of me.

Chapter - 5

Troubleshooting

Material Tearing or Not Cutting Completely Through

This is the biggest problem with most Cricut users. When this happens, the image is ruined, and you've wasted material. More machines have been returned or boxed up and put away due to this problem than any other.

But don't panic, if your paper is not cutting correctly there are several steps you can take to try and correct the problem.

Most important is this: Anytime you work with the blade TURN YOUR MACHINE OFF. I know it's easy to forget this because you're frustrated and you're trying this and that to make it work correctly. But this is an important safety precaution that you should remember.

Make simple adjustments at first. Turn the pressure down one. Did it help? If not, turn the blade down one number. Also, make sure the mat is free of debris so the blade rides smoothly.

Usually the thicker the material, the higher the pressure number should be set to cut through the paper. Don't forget to use the multi cut function if you have that option. It may take a little longer to cut 2, 3 or 4 times, but by then it should cut clean through.

For those of you using the smaller bugs that do not have that option here is how to make your own multi-cut function. After the image has been cut, don't unload the mat just hit load paper, repeat last and cut. You can repeat this sequence 2, 3 or 4 times to ensure your image is completely cut out.

If you are using thinner paper and it is tearing try reducing the pressure and slowing down the speed. When cutting intricate designs, you have to give the blade enough time to maneuver through the design. By slowing it down it will be able to make cleaner cuts.

Clean the edge of the blade to be sure no fuzz, glue or scraps of paper are stuck to it.

Make sure the blade is installed correctly. Take it out and put it back so it's seated firmly. The blade should be steady while it's making cuts. If it makes a shaky movement it's either not installed correctly, or there's a problem with the blade housing.

Be aware that there is a deep cutting blade for thicker material. You'll want to switch to this blade when you're cutting heavy card stock. This will also save wear and tear on your regular blade. Cutting a lot of thick material will obviously wear your blade out quicker than thinner material and cause you to change it more often.

Machine Freezing

When you switch cartridges leaving the machine on it's called "hot swapping" and it can sometimes cause the machine to freeze. This is more of an issue with the older models and doesn't seem to apply to the Expression 2.

You know how quirky electronic gadgets can be, so give your machine a rest for five or ten minutes every hour. If you work for several hours continuously, your machine might overheat and freeze up.

Turn the machine off and take a break. Restart it when you come back and it should be fine. Then remember not to rush programming the machine and give it an occasional rest.

Don't press a long list of commands quickly. If you give it too much information too quickly it will get confused in the same way a computer sometimes does and simply freeze up. Instead of typing in one long phrase try dividing up your words into several cuts.

If you're using special feature keys make sure you press them first before selecting the letters.

Power Problems

If you turn your machine on and nothing happens the power adapter may be at fault. Jiggle the power cord at the outlet and where it connects to the machine to make sure it's firmly connected. Ideally, you want to test the adapter before buying a new one. Swap cords with a friend and see if that fixed the problem. Replacement adapters can be found on eBay by searching for Cricut adapter power supply.

The connection points inside the machine may also pose a problem; here is how to test that. Hold down the plug where it inserts into the back of the machine and turn it on. If the machine powers up but will not cut then try a hard reset.

Here are a few tips especially for Expression 2 users. Have you turned on your machine, you watch it light up and hear it gearing up but when you try to cut nothing happens? Or you're stuck on the welcome screen or the LCD screen is unresponsive.

Well here are two quick fixes to try. First try a hard reset sometimes called the rainbow screen reset to recalibrate your die cutter. If that does not resolve the problem you're going to have to restore the settings.

To help cut down on errors try to keep your machine updated. When an update is available, you should receive a message encouraging you to install the latest version.

For those of you using third party software that is no longer compatible with the Cricut you probably already know that updating your machine may disable that software.

When you cut heavy paper and your Expression 2 shuts down try switching to the normal paper setting and use the multi cut function.

Carriage Will Not Move

If the carriage assembly does not move, check to see if the belt has broken or if the car has fallen off the track. Provo Craft does not sell replacement parts, which is nuts, so try to find a compatible belt at a vacuum repair shop.

If the wheels have fallen off the track, remove the plastic cover and look for a tiny screw by the wheel unscrew it. You now should be able to move the wheel back on track.

Unresponsive Keyboard

If you are sure you are pressing the keys firmly, you have a cartridge inserted correctly and a mat loaded ready to go, but the keypad is still not accepting your selection, the problem may be internal.

You will have to remove the keyboard and check if the display cable is connected to the keypad and to the motherboard. If the connections are secure then you have a circuit board problem and repairs are beyond the scope.

An important reminder, please do not attempt any repairs unless your machine is out of warranty.

Weird LCD Screen

The LCD screen is now showing strange symbols or is blank after doing a firmware update. Try running the update again making sure your selections are correct.

When the image you choose is bigger than the mat or paper size you selected the preview screen will look grayed out instead of showing the image. So increase the paper and mat size or decrease the size of your image.

Also watch out for the gray box effect when using the center point feature. Move the start position down until you see the image appear. The same thing may happen when using the fit to length feature. Try changing to landscape mode and shorten the length size until the image appears.

Occasionally using the undo button will cause the preview screen to turn black; unfortunately the only thing to do is turn the machine off. Your work will be lost and you have to start again.

Cartridge Errors

Sometimes dust or debris accumulates in the cartridge port gently blow out any paper fiber that may have collected in the opening. Make sure the contact points are clean and that nothing is preventing the cartridge from being read properly.

With any electrical machine overheating can be a problem. If you get a cartridge error after using your machine for a while turn it off and let it cool down for about fifteen minutes.

If this is the very first time you're using the cartridge and you get an error I'm sure you know the trick about turning the cartridge around and inserting it in backward.

If you thought you could use your Imagine cartridges with your Expression 2, think again. You will get an error message because you can only use the art cartridges that you can cut with, the colors and patterns cartridge are for printing.

Even brand-new items fresh out of the box can be defective. If you see a cartridge error 1, 2, 3, 4, 5, 6, 9 or 99 call customer service and tell them the name, serial number and error message number and they may replace the cartridge.

Trouble Connecting to Your Computer

All Cricut machines come with a USB cord that lets you connect to your computer and allows you to use the other products like the Cricut Design Studio software, Cricut Craft Room or the Cricut Gypsy with your machines.

Double check your USB connection and try another port.

Check to see if you may have a firewall or antivirus software that is blocking the connection.

See if you're running the latest firmware. You may need to update. Older machines update via firmware (Personal Cutter, Expression, Create and Cake) the newer (Expression 2, Imagine and Gypsy) use the Sync program to update.

When anything else Fails

You don't' want to do anything that might void the warranty on a machine that is truly defective.

Sadly, Prove Craft is known for its long wait times and sometimes less than stellar service. Stick it out and demand that your machine is fixed or replaced.

After a while, you may notice some of your projects coming out in a condition that is less-than-crisp.

Ensure your machine is on stable footing.

This may seem pretty basic but ensuring that your machine is on a level surface will allow it to make more precise cuts every single time. Rocking of the machine or wobbling could cause unstable results in your projects.

Ensure no debris has gotten stuck under the feet of your machine that could cause instability before proceeding to the next troubleshooting step!

Redo all Cable Connections

So, your connections are in the best possible working order, undo all your cable connection, blow into the ports or use canned air, and then securely plug everything back into the right ports. This will help to make sure all the connections are talking to each other where they should be!

Completely Dust and Clean Your Machine

Your little Cricut works hard for you! Return the favor by making sure you're not allowing gunk, dust, grime, or debris to build up in the surfaces and crevices. Adhesive can build up on the machine around the mat input and on the rollers, so be sure to focus on those areas!

Check Your Blade Housing

Sometimes debris and leavings from your materials can build up inside the housings for your blades! Open them up and clear any built-up materials that could be impeding swiveling or motion.

Chapter - 6

Project and Ideas with Vinyl

Project 1 - Perpetual Calendar

Woodblock calendars are a cute addition to any décor. Many teachers use them on their desks, or they fit in anywhere in your home. You can find unfinished block calendars online or at most craft stores. They'll usually have two wooden cubes for the numbers, two longer blocks for the months, and a stand to hold them. Painting the wood will give you the color of your choice, but you could also stain it or look around for calendars made of different types of wood. You can use the Cricut Explore One, Cricut Explore Air 2, or Cricut Maker for this project.

Supplies Needed

- Unfinished woodblock calendar
- Acrylic paint in color(s) of your choosing.
- Vinyl color(s) of your choosing
- Vinyl transfer tape
- Cutting mat
- Weeding tool or pick
- Mod Podge

Directions:

Step #1

Paint the woodblock calendar in the colors you'd like and set aside to dry.

Step #2

Create a square the correct size for the four blocks.

Step #3

Select the "Text" button in the lower left-hand corner.

Step #4

Choose your favorite font, and type the following numbers as well as all of the months: 0, 0, 1, 1, 2, 2, 3, 4, 5, 6, 7, and 8

Step #5

Place your vinyl on the cutting mat.

Step #6

Send the design to your Cricut.

Step #7

Use a weeding tool or pick to remove the excess vinyl from the text.

Step #8

Apply transfer tape to each separate number and the months.

Step #9

1, 2, 3, 4 around the sides of the first block

Step #10

0 and 8 on the top and bottom of the second block

Step #11

1, 2, 6, 7 around the sides of the second block

Step #12

Remove the paper backing from the tape on the months, and apply them to the long blocks, the first six months on one and the second six months on the other.

Step #13

Rub the tape to transfer the vinyl to the wood, making sure there are no bubbles. Carefully peel the tape away.

Step #14

Seal everything with a coat of Mod Podge.

> **Step #15**
>
> Arrange your calendar to display today's date, and enjoy it year after year!

Project 2 - Wooden Gift Tags

Dress up your gifts with special wooden tags! Balsa wood is light and easy to cut. The wood tags with gold names will give all of your gifts a shabby chic charm. Change up the color of the vinyl as you see fit; you can even use different colors for different gift recipients. People will be able to keep these tags and use them for something else, as well. An alternative to balsa wood is chipboard, though it won't have the same look.

Supplies Needed

- Balsa wood
- Gold vinyl
- Vinyl transfer tape
- Cutting mat
- Weeding tool or pick

Directions

Step #1

Secure your small balsa wood pieces to the cutting mat, and then tape the edges with masking tape for additional strength.

Step #2

Select the shape you would like for your tags and set the Cricut to cut wood, and then send the design to the Cricut.

Step #3

Remove your wood tags from the Cricut and remove any excess wood.

Step #4

In Cricut Design Space, select the "Text" button in the lower left-hand corner.

Step #5
Choose your favorite font, and type the names you want to place on your gift tags.

Step #6
Place your vinyl on the cutting mat.

Step #7
Send the design to your Cricut.

Step #8
Use a weeding tool or pick to remove the excess vinyl from the text.

Step #9
Apply transfer tape to the quote.

Step #10
Remove the paper backing from the tape.

Step #11

Place the names on the wood tags.

Step #12

Rub the tape to transfer the vinyl to the wood, making sure there are no bubbles. Carefully peel the tape away.

Step #13

Thread twine or string through the holes, and decorate your gifts!

Project 3 - Pet Mug

Show your love for your pet every morning when you have your coffee! A cute silhouette of a cat or dog with some paw prints is a simple but classy design. You're not limited to those two animals, either. Use a bird with bird footprints, a fish with water drops, or whatever pet you might have! You can add your pet's name or a quote to the design as well. You have the freedom here to arrange the aspects of the design however you'd like. You could put the animal in the center surrounded by the paw prints, scatter the prints all around the mug, place the animal next to its name and paw prints along the top, or whatever else you can imagine. Think of this as a tribute to your favorite pet or dedication to your favorite animal, and decorate accordingly. You can use the Cricut Explore One, Cricut Explore Air 2, or Cricut Maker for this project.

Supplies Needed

- Plain white mug
- Glitter vinyl
- Vinyl transfer tape
- Cutting mat
- Weeding tool or pick

Directions:

Step #1

Select the "Image" button in the lower left-hand corner and search for "cat," "dog," or any other pet of your choice.

Step #2

Choose your favorite image and click "Insert."

Step #3

Search images again for paw prints, and insert into your design.

Step #4

Arrange the pet and paw prints how you'd like them on the mug.

Step #5

Place your vinyl on the cutting mat.

Step #6

Send the design to your Cricut.

Step #7

Use a weeding tool or pick to remove the excess vinyl from the design.

Step #8

Apply transfer tape to the design.

Step #9

Remove the paper backing, and apply the design to the mug.

Step #10

Rub the tape to transfer the vinyl to the mug, making sure there are no bubbles. Carefully peel the tape away.

Enjoy your custom pet mug!

Project 4 - Organized Toy Bins

How much of a mess is your kids' room? We already know the answer to that. Grab some plastic bins and label them with different toy categories, and teach your child to sort! You can use the type of bins that suit your child or their room best. Many people like to use the ones that look like giant buckets with handles on the sides. There are also more simple square ones. You could even use cheaper laundry baskets or plastic totes with or without the lids. You can add images to the designs as well—whatever will make your child like them best! You can use the Cricut Explore One, Cricut Explore Air 2, or Cricut Maker for this project.

Supplies Needed

- Plastic toy bins in colors of your choice
- White vinyl
- Vinyl transfer tape
- Cutting mat

- Weeding tool or pick

Directions:

Step #1

Select the "Text" button in the lower left-hand corner.

Step #2

Choose your favorite font and type the labels for each toy bin. See below for some possibilities.

Legos

Dolls

Cars

Stuffed animals

Outside Toys

Step #3

Place your vinyl on the cutting mat.

Step #4

Send the design to your Cricut.

Step #5

Use a weeding tool or pick to remove the excess vinyl from the text.

Step #6

Apply transfer tape to the words.

Step #7

Remove the paper backing and apply the design to the bin.

Step #8

Rub the tape to transfer the vinyl to the bin, making sure there are no bubbles. Carefully peel the tape away.

Step #9

Organize your kid's toys in your new bins!

Project 5 - Froggy Rain Gear

Kids love to play outside in the rain. Decorate a raincoat and rain boots with a cute froggy design that will have them asking to wear them! A simple raincoat and boots that you can find at any store for a reasonable price become custom pieces with this project. The outdoor vinyl is made to withstand the elements and last for ages. You can use the Cricut Explore One, Cricut Explore Air 2, or Cricut Maker for this project.

Supplies Needed

- Matching green raincoat and rain boots
- White outdoor vinyl
- Vinyl transfer tape
- Cutting mat
- Weeding tool or pick

Directions:

Step #1

Select the "Image" button in the lower left-hand corner and search for "frog."

Step #2

Choose your favorite frog and click "Insert."

Step #3

Copy the frog and resize. You will need three frogs, a larger one for the coat and two smaller ones for each boot.

Step #4

Place your vinyl on the cutting mat.

Step #5

Send the design to your Cricut.

Step #6

Use a weeding tool or pick to remove the excess vinyl from the design.

Step #7

Apply transfer tape to the design.

Step #8

Remove the paper backing and apply the design to the coat or boot.

Step #9

Rub the tape to transfer the vinyl to the rain gear, making sure there are no bubbles. Carefully peel the tape away.

Step #10

Dress your kid up to play in the rain!

Project 6 - Snowy Wreath

Wreaths are a popular decoration year-round. This one is perfect for winter. You can buy premade grapevine wreaths at almost any store, or you can get really crafty and assemble one yourself. The berry stems can be found in the floral sections of craft stores. Silver will fit the snowy theme well, but you could also use red for a holiday-themed look or an entirely different color. You can also change up the whole project to theme it toward your winter holiday of choice. You can use the Cricut Explore One, Cricut Explore Air 2, or Cricut Maker for this project.

Supplies Needed

- Grapevine wreath
- Silver berry stems
- Spray adhesive
- Silver and white glitter
- Piece of wood to fit across the center of the wreath

- Wood stain, if desired
- Drill and a small bit
- Twine
- White vinyl
- Vinyl transfer tape
- Cutting mat
- Weeding tool or pick

Directions:

Step #1

Thread the silver berry stems throughout the grapevine wreath.

Step #2

Use the spray adhesive and glitter to create patches of "snow" on the wreath.

Step #3

Select the "Text" button in the lower left-hand corner.

Step #4

Choose your favorite font and type, "Let it snow."

Step #5

Place your vinyl on the cutting mat.

Step #6

Send the design to your Cricut.

Step #7

Use a weeding tool or pick to remove the excess vinyl from the text.

Step #8

Apply transfer tape to the words.

Step #9

Remove the paper backing and apply the design to the wood piece.

Step #4

Rub the tape to transfer the vinyl to the wood, making sure there are no bubbles. Carefully peel the tape away.

Step #4

Drill two small holes in the corner of the wood and thread the twine through.

Step #4

Hang your wreath and sign for the winter season!

Chapter - 7

Project and Ideas with Paper

Cricut projects.

Cardstock is usually the first choice, as its sturdy and can handle a lot of folding, cutting, and art supplies. There are hundreds of thousands of varieties of paper, though, and you can experiment to see what you like best. The types of paper listed for each project is merely a suggestion. Paper also has the advantage of working well in every Cricut machine.

With paper, in particular, you'll want to make sure your blade is sharp and clean. Anything out of the ordinary will tear the paper. Dull blades are the biggest culprit when you find tears in your paper. Make sure you're using the appropriate blade for the weight of the paper as well. Some thicker papers might just need a second pass rather than a sharper blade. It's good to have some spare paper that you can do test runs with.

If you're using a new cutting mat, you'll need to condition it before you put your paper on it. New mats are very sticky, and you won't be able to get the paper off again without tearing it. Conditioning is quick and easy, though. Simply touch the mat with your hands. The oils on your skin will decrease the stickiness without damaging your mat. Touch repeatedly until mat feels less sticky, and make sure to get all of the edges and corners. Test the mat with some scrap paper before using it for your project. Paper can be found at just about any store. However, some specialty stores and websites will actually give you a cheat sheet on how to cut their different papers with different cutting machines. You might find a list of all of their papers and which blades and settings to use for them. Some will even offer instructions for creating a custom material for specific papers. Check out the help section of specialty paper websites to see if they have this. The Cricut machines don't just cut paper; they can also write and draw. Cricut offers a wide selection of different pens, and there are other brands that will fit in the machine as well. A couple of the following projects take advantage of this feature, but you can incorporate it into the others as well. You can draw or write anything on any of your patterns. With the Cricut Explore One and Cricut Explore Air 2, you'll need to swap out pens if you want to change colors. The Cricut Maker has two tool carriages, so you can do at least two colors at once without swapping.

Paper Bouquet

Flowers are nice, but it doesn't take long for them to wilt. How about some paper ones instead? They'll last you forever! Use this bouquet as décor in your home or for an event. Budget-conscious brides can even carry this down the aisle instead of an expensive floral arrangement! You will find plenty of templates in the Cricut Design Space for different flowers. You can also search online for more, or you can try your hand at making your own. A bouquet can be made up of one type of flower, the same flower in different colors, a variety of flowers, or a variety of flowers, all in the same color. It depends on the look and feel that you are going for, so use whatever method sounds best to you. You can use plain cardstock, patterned cardstock, or use watercolor to create a color gradient you love. For the stems, pipe cleaners are easier to work with and can be covered with tissue paper or something similar. Or, it can be left visible for a crafty look. The floral wire will give a more realistic look, but it's thinner and takes some work. You can use the Cricut Explore One, Cricut Explore Air 2, or Cricut Maker for this project.

Supplies Needed

- Cardstock
- Glue gun
- Lightstick cutting mat
- Weeding tool or pick
- Green pipe cleaners or floral wire

Directions:

Step #1

Select the "Image" button in the lower left-hand corner and search for "paper flowers."

Step #2

Select the image with several flower pieces and click "Insert."

Step #3

Copy the flowers and resize for variety in your bouquet.

Step #4

Place your cardstock on the cutting mat.

Step #5

Send the design to your Cricut.

Step #6

Remove the outer edge of the paper, leaving the flowers on the mat.

Step #7

Use your weeding tool or carefully pick to remove the flowers from the mat.

Step #8

Glue the flower pieces together in the centers, with the largest petals at the bottom.

Step #9

Bend or curl petals as desired to create multiple looks.

Step #10

Gather your flowers together in a vase or wrap them with tissue paper.

Enjoy your beautiful bouquet!

Leafy Garland

Garlands are an easy way to spruce up any space, and there is an infinite variety of them. Create a unique leafy one to give your home a more naturalistic feel! Feel free to change the colors of the leaves to suit you, whether you stick with green or go a little more unnatural. Tweaking the size of the bundles you make and how close you put them together will change the look of the garland. You can use different types of leaves as well. Experiment a little bit to see what you like best. Bending the leaves down the center and curling the edges a little will give you a more realistic look, or you can leave them flat for a handmade look. You can use the Cricut Explore One, Cricut Explore Air 2, or Cricut Maker for this project.

Supplies Needed

- Cardstock – 2 or more colors of green, or white to paint yourself
- Glue gun
- Lightstick cutting mat
- Weeding tool or pick
- Floral wire
- Floral tape

Directions:

Step #1

Select the "Image" button in the lower left-hand corner and search for "leaf collage."

Step #2

Select the image of leaves and click "Insert."

Step #3

Place your cardstock on the cutting mat.

Step #4

Send the design to your Cricut.

Step #5

Remove the outer edge of the paper, leaving the leaves on the mat.

Step #6

Use a pick or scoring tool to score down the center of each leaf lightly.

Step #7

Use your weeding tool or carefully pick to remove the leaves from the mat.

Step #8

Gently bend each leaf at the scoreline.

Step #9

Glue the leaves into bunches of two or three.

Step #10

Cut a length of floral wire to your desired garland size, and wrap the ends with floral tape.

Step #11

Attach the leaf bunches to the wire using the floral tape.

Step #12

Continue attaching leaves until you have a garland of the size you want. Bundle lots of leaves for a really full look, or spread them out to be sparser.

Step #13

Create hooks at the ends of the garland with floral wire.

Step #14

Hang your beautiful leaf garland wherever you'd like!

Easy Envelope Addressing

Christmas cards are wonderful to send out, but they can take forever to address. Address labels just don't look as personal, though. Use the Cricut pen tool in your machine to "hand letter" your envelopes! You can use this for your batch of holiday cards or even for other cards or letters. This takes advantage of the writing function of your Cricut machine. For the most realistic written look, make sure you select a font in the writing style. It will still write other fonts, but it will only create an outline of them, which is a different look you could go for! Cricut offers a variety of Pen Tools, and there are some other pens that will fit as well. For addressing envelopes, stick to black or another color that is easy to read so that the mail makes it to its destination. You can use the Cricut Explore One, Cricut Explore Air 2, or Cricut Maker for this project.

Supplies Needed

- Envelopes to address
- Cricut Pen Tool
- Lightstick cutting mat

Directions:

Step #1

Create a box the appropriate size for your envelopes.

Step #2

Select the "Text" button in the lower left-hand corner.

Step #3

Choose one handwriting font for a uniform look or different fonts for each line to mix it up.

Step #4

Type your return address in the upper left-hand corner of the design.

Step #5

Type the "to" address in the center of the design.

Step #6

Insert your Cricut pen into the auxiliary holder of your Cricut, making sure it is secure.

Step #7

Place your cardstock on the cutting mat.

Step #8

Send the design to your Cricut.

Step #9

Remove your envelope and repeat as needed.

Step #10

Send out your "hand-lettered" envelopes!

Chapter - 8

Project and Ideas with Glass

Vinyl cut with your Cricut machine can help you create beautiful glass projects. There are several different ways you can use it, as well. Any glass object can be a blank for these projects. You might already have some things in your kitchen that you'd like to decorate. These make wonderful gifts, too—no one will believe that you made them yourself and that they're not expensive gifts.

Glass etching cream is an interesting product that lets you easily create etched glass projects. There are several different brands that you can find at craft stores or online. You may be able to find them at hardware stores as well. Read the instructions carefully and follow them exactly, to get your desired results and to be safe. This may vary between brands, but often, stirring the cream around during its setting time will make the etching more pronounced. This will be a permanent effect on the glass.

Besides etching, you can also create beautiful glass projects using vinyl. Outdoor vinyl, which is permanent, is the best choice if you want the design to stay put through use and washing. Removable vinyl will be temporary, and you can peel it off; it won't survive being washed. Window-cling vinyl sticks to glass via static, so they are quite temporary but can easily be changed out and reused.

Etched Monogrammed Glass

Glasses are one of the most-used things in your kitchen, and it's impossible to have too many of them. It's actually quite easy to customize them with etching, and it will look as if a professional did it. Simply use glass etching cream that you can find at any craft store! Be sure to read the instructions and warning labels carefully before you begin. The vinyl will act as a stencil, protecting the parts of the glass that you don't want to etch. Be sure to take your time to get the vinyl smooth against the glass, especially where there are small bits. You don't want any of the cream to get under the edge of the vinyl. You can use the Cricut Explore One, Cricut Explore Air 2, or Cricut Maker for this project.

Supplies Needed

- A glass of your choice – make sure that the spot you want to monogram is smooth
- Vinyl
- Cutting mat

- Weeding tool or pick
- Glass etching cream

Instructions

Step #1

Open Cricut Design Space and create a new project.

Step #2

Select the "Image" button in the Design Panel and search for "monogram."

Step #3

Choose your favorite monogram and click "Insert."

Step #4

Place your vinyl on the cutting mat.

Step #5

Send the design to your Cricut.

Step #6

Use a weeding tool or pick to remove the monogram, leaving the vinyl around it.

Step #7

Remove the vinyl from the mat.

Step #8

Carefully apply the vinyl around your glass, making it as smooth as possible, particularly around the monogram.

Step #9

If you have any letters with holes in your monogram, carefully reposition those cutouts in their proper place.

Step #10

Following the instructions on the etching cream, apply it to your monogram.

Step #11

Remove the cream and then the vinyl.

> **Step #6**

> Give your glass a good wash.

Enjoy drinking out of your etched glass!

Project 27: Live, Love, Laugh Glass Block

Glass blocks are an inexpensive yet surprisingly versatile craft material. You can find them at both craft and hardware stores. They typically have a hole with a lid so that you can fill the blocks with the items of your choice. This project uses tiny fairy lights for a glowing quote block, but you can fill it however you'd like. The frost spray paint adds a bit of elegance to the glass and diffuses the light for a softer glow, hiding the string of the fairy lights. Holographic vinyl will add to the magical look, but you can use whatever colors you'd like. This features a classic quote that's great to have around your house, but you can change it. You can use the Cricut Explore One, Cricut Explore Air 2, or Cricut Maker for this project.

Supplies Needed

- Glass block
- Frost spray paint
- Clear enamel spray
- Holographic vinyl
- Vinyl transfer tape

- Cutting mat
- Weeding tool or pick
- Fairy lights

Instructions

Step #1

Spray the entire glass block with frost spray paint, and let it dry.

Step #2

Spray the glass block with a coat of clear enamel spray, and let it dry.

Step #3

Open Cricut Design Space and create a new project.

Step #4

Select the "Text" button in the Design Panel.

Step #5

Type "Live Love Laugh" in the text box

Step #6

Use the dropdown box to select your favorite font.

Step #7

Arrange the words to sit on top of each other.

Step #8

Place your vinyl on the cutting mat.

Step #9

Send the design to your Cricut.

Step #10

Use a weeding tool or pick to remove the excess vinyl from the design.

Step #11

Apply transfer tape to the design.

Step #12

Remove the paper backing and apply the words to the glass block.

Step 13

Smooth down the design and carefully remove the transfer tape.

Step #14

Place fairy lights in the opening of the block, leaving the battery pack on the outside.

Enjoy your decorative quote!

Project 28: Unicorn Wine Glass

Who doesn't love unicorns? Who doesn't love wine? Bring them together with these glittery wine glasses! The outdoor vinyl will hold up to use and washing, and the Mod Podge will keep the glitter in place for years to come. Customize it even more with your own quote. You could use a different magical creature as well—mermaids go great with glitter too! Customize this to suit your tastes or to create gifts for your friends and family. Consider using these for a party and letting the guests take them home as favors! You can use the Cricut Explore One, Cricut Explore Air 2, or Cricut Maker for this project.

Supplies Needed

- Stemless wine glasses
- Vinyl transfer tape
- Cutting mat
- Weeding tool or pick
- Extra fine glitter in the color of your choice
- Mod Podge

Instructions

Step #1

Open Cricut Design Space and create a new project.

Step #2

Select the "Text" button in the Design Panel.

Step #3

Type "It's not drinking alone if my unicorn is here."

Step #4

Using the dropdown box, select your favorite font.

Step #5

Adjust the positioning of the letters, rotating some to give a whimsical look.

Step #6

Select the "Image" button on the Design Panel and search for "unicorn."

Step #7

Select your favorite unicorn and click "Insert," then arrange your design how you want it on the glass.

Step #8

Place your vinyl on the cutting mat, making sure it is smooth and making full contact.

Step #9

Send the design to your Cricut.

Step #10

Use a weeding tool or pick to remove the excess vinyl from the design. Use the Cricut Bright Pad to help if you have one.

Step #11

Apply transfer tape to the design, pressing firmly and making sure there are no bubbles.

Step #12

Remove the paper backing and apply the words to the glass where you'd like them. Leave at least a couple of inches at the bottom for the glitter.

Step #13

Smooth down the design and carefully remove the transfer tape.

Step #14

Coat the bottom of the glass in Mod Podge, wherever you would like glitter to be. Give the area a wavy edge.

Step #15

Sprinkle glitter over the Mod Podge, working quickly before it dries.

Step #16

Add another layer of Mod Podge and glitter, and set it aside to dry.

Step #17

Cover the glitter in a thick coat of Mod Podge.

Step #18

Allow the glass to cure for at least 48 hours.

Enjoy drinking from your unicorn wine glass!

Chapter - 9

Cricut Projects with Infusible Ink

Cricut launched a brand new system called Infusible Ink to help you achieve professional quality, personalized heat transfers on clothing items, and more at home for the first time.

There are also Infusible Ink Pens and Markers available in the market that will allow you to design your own transfer sheets from scratch. Currently you can use Infusible Inks on T-shirts, tote bags ad coasters referred to as Cricut blanks or Infusible Ink compatible blanks.

Infusible Ink Transfer Process

Step #1

Select desired Cricut Blank for your project along with the Infusible Ink Transfer Sheets and Infusible Ink Pens and Markers.

Step #2

Create a design to show off your creativity. Cut Infusible Ink Transfer Sheets using any Cricut cutting machine or draw the design using Infusible Ink Pens and Markers on laser copy paper.

Step #3

Transfer your design to the Cricut Blank by applying heat. You can use regular household iron that can reach up to 400°F or one of the Cricut EasyPress devices.

Now that you understand the standard process for all Infusible Ink projects, let's make some of our own now.

Personalized T-Shirt

Materials needed – Cricut Explore, standard grip machine mat, Infusible Ink Transfer Sheet (rainbow), Cricut Women's T-shirt Blank, Cricut EasyPress 2, EasyPress mat, lint roller, tweezers, white cardstock, butcher paper, scissors.

Step #1

To create a new project, after you have logged into your Cricut account using your Cricut ID on the Design Space, click on the New Project button on the top right corner of your screen and you will be taken to a blank canvas.

Step #2

Click on the Images icon on the Design Panel and type in xoxo or MC42F3A6 in the search bar to select the image used for this project. Feel free to choose any other image and follow the instructions below. Once you have selected the desired image, click on Insert Images at the bottom of the screen.

Step #3

Your selected images will appear on the Canvas. Look at the Layers Panel on the right of the screen to select the layers that you want to edit. You could resize the grouped image or the individual layers if you would like.

Step #4

Click on the Save button and give the desired name to the project, for example, Infusible Ink T-shirt and click Save again.

Step #4

Simply click on the Make It button on your screen to view the required mats and material on the screen.

Step #5

Click Continue at the bottom right corner of the screen. Connect your Cricut Explore to your computer and turn the smart set dial to Custom, and then select Infusible Ink Transfer Sheet to cut your design.

Note – If images and/or fonts used for your design are not free and available for purchase only, then the Continue button will not appear, and instead, a Purchase button will be visible. Once you have paid for the image or font the Continue button will be available to you.

Step #7

Place the Infusible Ink Transfer Sheet with its liner side down on the cutting mat. Load your mat into your Cricut machine and follow the prompts on the Design Space application to cut the design.

Step #8

Use the cracking method to weed out the Infusible Ink transfer sheets by first peeling the mat away from the cut design, and then slightly bending and rolling the cut paper, which will generate a light cracking sound as the design is separated. Use the tweezers to remove negative pieces of the design then cut the clear liner, so it does not extend beyond the size of the EasyPress 2 heat plate.

Step #9

Place your Cricut Women's T-shirt Blank on top of the Cricut EasyPress Mat. Insert the cardstock sheet in the t-shirt to protect the mat and the project. Using a lint roller get rid of any residual fibers that may be present on the surface of the t-shirt then cover it with butcher paper.

Step #10

First, preheat your EasyPress 2 for 15 seconds then press on your transfer target area for 5 seconds to get rid of any moisture and wrinkles. The recommended temperature for this project is 385 °F. Now remove the butcher paper and let the t-shirt cool completely.

Step #11

Time to put your design face down on the target area with a clear liner on top. Now, cover the design with butcher paper, which should be larger than the size of the heat plate of the EasyPress 2 device.

Step #12

Now heat the area while applying pressure for 40 seconds and slowly lift the press up without disturbing the design and the butcher paper.

Step #13

Wait for about a couple of minutes to let the project cool completely prior to removing the butcher paper and peeling off the liner with the design. And you are all set!

Personalized Tote Bag

Materials needed – Cricut Explore, standard grip machine mat, Infusible Ink Transfer Sheet (Animal Brights), Infusible Ink Tote Bag Blank, Cricut EasyPress 2, EasyPress mat, lint roller, tweezers, white cardstock, butcher paper, scissors.

Step #1

To create a new project, after you have logged into your Cricut account using your Cricut ID on the Design Space, click on the New Project button on the top right corner of your screen and you will be taken to a blank canvas.

Step #2

We will be using an already existing project from the Cricut library and customizing it. So click on the Projects icon on the Design Panel and click on the Infusible drop-down menu to view all existing projects that you can select from.

Step #3

You will able to view all the projects available by clicking on them, and a pop-up window displaying all the details of the project will appear on your screen. The geometric flower tote bag project was selected for this example.

Step #4

Click on Customize so you can edit the project to your preference.

Step #5

The selected design will be displayed on the Canvas. You can see in the Layers Panel that this design has only one layer that can be edited. You can change the color of the layers or fill in a pattern and use the same Infusible Ink Transfer Sheet that matches your selection. Click on the Linetype Swatch to view the color palette and select the desired color for your design.

Step #6

Click on the Save button on your screen and give the desired name to the project, for example, Infusible Ink Tote Bag and click Save again.

Step #7

Simply click on the Make It button on the top of your screen to view the required mats and material on the screen.

Step #8

Click Continue at the bottom right corner of the screen. Connect your Cricut Explore to your computer and turn the smart set dial to Custom, and then select Infusible Ink Transfer Sheet to cut your design.

Note – If images and/or fonts used for your design are not free and available for purchase only, then the Continue button will not appear, and instead, a Purchase button will be visible. Once you have paid for the image or font the Continue button will be available to you.

Step #9

Place the Infusible Ink Transfer Sheet with its liner side down on the cutting mat. Load your mat into your Cricut machine and follow the prompts on the Design Space application to cut the design.

Step #10

Use the cracking method to weed out the Infusible Ink transfer sheets by first peeling the mat away from the cut design, and then slightly bending and rolling the cut paper, which will generate a light cracking sound as the design is separated. Use the tweezers to remove negative pieces of the design then cut the clear liner, so it does not extend beyond the size of the EasyPress 2 heat plate.

Step #11

Place your Infusible Ink Tote Bag Blank on top of the Cricut EasyPress Mat. Insert the cardstock sheet in the tote bag where the design will be transferred to protect the mat and the project. Using a lint roller, get rid of any residual fibers that may be present on the surface of the tote bag, then cover it with butcher paper.

Step #12

First, preheat your EasyPress 2 for 15 seconds then press on your transfer target area for 5 seconds to get rid of any moisture and wrinkles. The recommended temperature for this project is 385 °F. Now remove the butcher paper and let the tote bag cool completely.

Step #13

Time to put your design face down on the target area with a clear liner on top. Now, cover the design with butcher paper, which should be larger than the size of the heat plate of the EasyPress 2 device.

Step #14

Now heat the area while applying pressure for 40 seconds and slowly lift the press up without disturbing the design and the butcher paper.

Step #15

Wait for about a couple of minutes to let the project cool completely prior to removing the butcher paper and peeling off the liner with the design. And you are all set!

Custom Ceramic Coasters

Materials needed – Cricut Explore, standard grip machine mat, Infusible Ink Transfer Sheet Patterns (Rainbow Cheetah), Ceramic Coaster Blanks, Cricut EasyPress 2, EasyPress mat, lint roller, tweezers, white cardstock, butcher paper, scissors.

Step #1

To create a new project, after you have logged into your Cricut account using your Cricut ID on the Design Space, click on the New Project button on the top right corner of your screen and you will be taken to a blank canvas.

Step #2

The best way to explore all available designs for coasters is by searching for the relevant Cricut Cartridges. So click on the Images icon on the Designer's Panel, and then click on Cartridges. Type coaster designs in the search bar to view all the designs that are tagged for coasters.

Step #3

You will able to view all the images that are part of a cartridge by simply clicking in the cartridge that you like. You can always go back and keep searching until you have one or more images for your project.

Step #4

Click on the image that you have chosen for your design and if you want more than one image, than simply click on all those images as well and finally click on the Insert Images button.

Step #5

The selected images will be displayed on the Canvas and can be edited. You can change the color of the layers or fill in a pattern and use the same Infusible Ink Transfer Sheet that matches your selection. Click on the Linetype Swatch to view the color palette and select the desired color for your design.

Step #6

Click on the Save button on your screen and give the desired name to the project, for example, Infusible Ink Coaster, and click Save again.

Step #7

Simply click on the Make It button at the bottom of your screen to view the required mats and material on the screen.

Step #8

Click Continue at the bottom right corner of the screen. Connect your Cricut Explore to your computer and turn the smart set dial to Custom, and then select Infusible Ink Transfer Sheet to cut your design.

Chapter - 10

Understanding Cricut Rewards

Cricut rewards are excellent because they specifically target saying and silhouette cutting machine clients. We love our private artwork cutters and are continuously purchasing several types of equipment like cricut vinyl. Vinyl has become quite popular due to its simplicity of usage, number of colors and quantity of lengths and sizes. As a good deal of us is extremely price conscious, we want the best value when purchasing cricut supplies. Reward software help reduce our overall cost of the supplies while demonstrating our loyalty to customer friendly businesses which produce a consistent efforts to recognize our purchases.

Vinyl cricut rewards are much more specific and valuable. Since vinyl has many applications from the craft marketplace, cricut vinyl sellers are rewarding their customers with innovative discounts depending on the sum of the purchases and their own consistency. Some vinyl cricut suppliers provide affiliate programs that benefit customers for promoting and advertising their particular cricut vinyl provide websites to their partners and friends. Everyone enjoys a fantastic deal and what deal is far better than free vinyl for your cricut. Sharing requires time and effort to get this a wonderful benefit.

Sophisticated cricut vinyl distribution organizations are supplying credits for their clients that are ready to share. Credits are created as cricut users upload and display their own particular cricut files they have made utilizing cricut vinyl. This process is actually a win- win assisting to lower the total price of vinyl supplies and helping to market the cricut plastic supply company as a commendable resource for further cricut users to obtain their vinyl materials. Businesses with eyesight are implementing cricut reward applications and will continue to create long term win-win relationships with their clientele.

Cricut cartridges make scrapbooking fun and straightforward

You have very likely noticed the pleasure with regard to cricut merchandise. Their level of flexibility and popularity are producing the cricut a legend within the scrapbooking and paper crafting world. Cricut is your private cutting system that doesn't have to get a computer.

Its cartridge-based system allows you to cut hundreds of stunning layouts, styles, and phrases in many different styles using only the touch of a button. Cricut typeface and shape cartridges set a number of their best layouts, letters, and phrases created by top scrapbook creative designers at the ends of your fingers.

Assessing out which cricut products you will want and want will be helpful once you begin in working with this incredible product!

Which cricut products will I probably must have?

In the time you purchase your cricut own electronic dispenser, you can expect to get the gear, a shapes cartridge alongside a cutting mat that will assist you begin. Immediately after figuring out ways to use the machine, yet, you're going to undoubtedly be prompted to obtain extra cricut items, probably beginning with additional cricut cartridges.

There are truly a multitude of those cricut cartridges readily available for sale, and they include a range of topics, fonts, and layouts. Your cricut machine employs unique cutting blades and cutting mats which might want to go replaced following numerous applications. Lots of extra optionally available cricut goods are sure to tempt your creativity in addition to that. Cricut supplies exclusive paper, cardstock, along with vinyl sheets, and you could also buy exceptional inks for use while using this machine.

Cricut organizational items such as the storage container, carrying luggage, and messenger bag can help keep your cricut tools organized and easy to transport. These accessories will surely be available wherever cricut products are available for sale, and they can surely be purchased to the cricut.com online website.

The Ideal Way to Purchase Cricut merchandise:

Cricut products are now commonly accessible through many distinct providers. Significant series hobby outlets will be sure to have a substantial assortment of cricut cartridges. Lower cost retail chain retailers also generally give you some cricut cartridges, even though you may have a little bit of trouble looking for each of the cartridges you are considering.

Neighborhood scrapbooking retail outlets an internet scrapbooking provide retailers will also provide cricut cartridges. Online auction sites, such as ebayare a wonderful resource for locating new cricut cartridges at a lowered price!

Registering your very own cricut merchandise:

It is an excellent concept to enroll your cricut products on the cricut site. Cricut goods are meticulously manufactured from the best top quality elements. At case that you have no problem with your cricut merchandise, nevertheless, provo craft includes a limited warranty.

Registering your very own cricut goods will certainly be certain you have implemented the actions required in the function that you may want to make utilization of this warranty. What's more, in the event you will discover in any given instant any kind of recognized problems or issues using cricut products, provo craft may have your current contact info to alert you.

Cricut tips - craft ideas for the cricut cutting machine

Wish a few cricut tips to your cricut cutting machine? Cricut private electrical cutters are revolutionizing hand crafts and individuals throughout the nation are astonished at the quantity of lovely and innovative things they can suddenly make.

The way a cricut works is straightforward: simply load among several available cartridges to the cutter, select what colour card stock you would really like to use for that specific layout and cut away.

Custom greeting cards you name it everything's potential with a cricut.

Perhaps the very endearing cricut craft notion is a calendar. Another page can be made for every month, and each of these different pages can be decorated with several designs. July, for example, will soon be trimmed with the layouts within this freedom day seasonal cartridge while february is the clear choice for the love struck seasonal cartridge. The fun doesn't end there, but alongside the mother's day cartridge is going to be ideal for May while the easter cartridge is a natural for april. December is unique is cricut-land, and cricut customers have a good deal of collections of layouts like the joys of the season cartridge and the snow friends cartridge to select from.

What can life be without scrapbooks to record each and every waking moment of the most prized possessions: our children? Together with the cricut cutting platform, scrapbooks could be personalized to each and every child, and what might be better in comparison to mother and child - or dad and kid - to repay together and select which pictures they'd love to decorate their own graphics with. Small women, on the other hand, would likely turn their flavorful wake up at the robots cartridge but might love the Disney tinker bell and friends cartridge. You'll never be at a loss for cricut scrapbooking ideas.

Your cricut design ideas are not only restricted to pictures, however, and alphabets are also available - such as the sesame street font cartridge in addition to all the Ashlyn's alphabet cartridge - them will come in handy when it is time to customize a present. Ideal presents would include images of critters - or maybe vinyl wall-hangings commemorating a special occasion like that excursion overseas - all, of course, adorned with bright and beautiful cricut cutouts.

Completing a cricut task jointly is also a superb way to find a family to bond, along with the stunning things that are made jointly could be cherished for a lifetime.

With a cricut personal electric cutter just the heavens - and your imagination - are your limit.

What you need to learn about the cricut personal cutter before you purchase

Before purchasing your hard earned cash to some die cutting platform, you must do your own study. There are numerous models available on the industry and after much consideration that this is the one I have selected and why.

The cricut personal cutter device produced by Provo craft is a wonderful edition to your scrapbooking tools. There are a few different cricut personal cutters. The cricut expressions will reduce 12x 24 inch dimension papers. The cricut original cuts 6x12 inch paper. The cricut cutting mat includes a gentle adhesive and retains your paper set up although the cutting is done. Each cricut machine involves a cartridge, the cricut original contains George & basic shapes and it is a fundamental cartridge, which combines capital lettering named George and a choice of shapes. So as soon as you've got unpacked your new cricut personal cutter you will have the ability to start experimenting immediately away. Down the screen you further expand the operation of your cricut system, along with other cricut capsules. Provo craft is publishing new cricut cartridges annually and they have wide assortment of topics, from alphabets, sports, in the garden via to Disney characters.

On the cricut personal cutter you will have the ability to adjust blade depth, cutting and pressure speed. This assists when cutting different materials. Slowing down the cutting edge speed provides a far better result with much more fragile scrapbooking paper, although using medium pressure provides a crisper cut scrapbooking cardstock rather than the softest anxiety setting.

You can cut shapes and letters by adjusting the measurements dial from 1 around 5 1/2 inch. The sizes available are 1, 11/4, 11/2, 2, two 1/2, 3, 31/2, 4, 41/2, 5, 51/2.

The capability to load the scrapbooking paper, then cut a couple of letters, then unload the newspaper and reload to exactly the point you'd been around, saves time and newspaper.

The cricut cartridge George and basic shapes contains six innovative capabilities. Signal, slotted, charm, silhouette, shadow and shadow blackout.

Signal - imagine a picket sign using a lien or silhouette cut out

Slotted - oval ring, a slot cut in the best to thread ribbon or twine

Charm - your correspondence or form cut using a circle attached on top, so you can join the correspondence using a brad to your design

Silhouette - cuts the outline of your correspondence or form. Great for the budget conscious as you are in a place to maintain the negative cut of your letter and use it on a different design.

Shadow - cuts the letters or shapes, somewhat large than normal, these can subsequently be used behind the standard size letter, giving the appearance of a shadow along with a 3d effect for your name. This attribute is on every of these cricut cartridges.

Shadow blackout - like darkness except where there are a cut in the middle of a 0 for instance, shadow blackout simply generates the outdoor shadow with no cutout within the 0

With this a variety of cricut capsules accessible, you wish to appear into the qualities of every one before your purchase, to make certain you will get sufficient use from each investment. Consider if they provide just shapes or shapes and decoration. I've obtained a few shapes capsules and since the contours were so complex, I wasn't particularly bothered that Christmas cheer cricut cartridge did not arrive using an alphabet. The Christmas cheer capsule is just one I would not be without.

Provo craft additionally, it released a stronger cutting blade, which might cut about 1.5 millimeter thickness. This usually means that all the Provo cricut personal cutters, employing this brand new blade, can cut chipboard vinyl, vinyl, cloth and magnetic sheets.

Chapter - 11

Cartridge Techniques

On the off chance that you've been a piece of the general Cricut fever which keeps on clearing the country, at that point you've without a doubt been satisfied that you're never again compelled to pay the first high costs as when Cricut cartridges were at first discharged. The Lite Cupcake Wrappers cartridge isn't a special case to this standard.

The Cupcake Wrappers Cartridge Itself

Maybe you have acknowledged from the name, and this particular cartridge is a piece of the 'Light' collection. The Lite cartridges have immediately ended up being very supported, since their underlying uncovering. Not exclusively do a great deal of them fill in explicit cartridge topic holes inside the full cartridge gathering, however by having unadulterated substance material and significantly less of the generally squandered additional items, they likewise make sense of to be a mess progressively moderate.

The Lite Cupcake Wrappers cartridge was made for each one of those cake (and particularly cupcake) dough punchers around. The round is packaged with 50 one of a kind cupcake holder or wrapper pictures that you're ready to pick and remove to hold your newly prepared cupcake. The arrangement likewise offers a little decision of cupcake topper decorations which are perfect for fixing off your definitive hand crafted a cupcake.

You must love exactly how making every cupcake wrapper is presently so natural and speedy, and the completed visual effect is cute. When you start to utilize this cartridge to adorn the majority of your hand crafted cupcakes, trust me, not simply will an old 'stripped' cake in a flash end up being amazingly uninteresting, yet you will search out chances to heat cakes for any event so as to get every one of the compliments from everyone that sees them.

The Designs and Sizes

Pictures for cupcake wrapper structures vacillate between fragile, for all intents and purposes doily looking examples to increasingly contemporary styles, alongside a few models which incorporate valuable words and expressions, so there is surely a one of a kind format to suit each cupcake occasion.

One of the most incessant inquiries in regards to this particular cartridge is concerning the size. The wrapper structures can be cut in size oblige any size cupcake (sensibly speaking, obviously), yet be admonished that you may need to rehearse on more than one occasion before transforming into a specialist with what measurements your machine should be set to about the particular cupcake boundary. The uplifting news is, you'll without a doubt have the option to get the hang of it in a brief timeframe.

Undertaking Ideas

Normally, in case you're just preparing a lot of cupcakes to expend yourself, you doubtlessly won't have any desire to utilize this cartridge. However, for each other event, it is without a doubt an unquestionable requirement to change over fundamental cupcakes into a touch of something unique. Loads of individuals utilize this specific cartridge to spruce up the standard cupcakes served at kids' parties and for social events, anyway anyplace a cake or two is discovered, the Lite Cupcake Wrapper cartridge can make every one of them simply significantly more exceptional.

Tips on How to Ensure Its Longevity

First of all, ensure that you secure it consistently. When you are finished utilizing it, place a spread over your tangle. Clear plastic can support a major ordeal. On the off chance that you have two mats, at that point you utilize both to cover each other eye to eye. Likewise, clear out any abundance paper that is deserted on the floor covering. You can do this by utilizing child wipes. In any case, if your Cricut mats have just exceeded its normal life regardless of genuine endeavors on your part to look after it, you can utilize a knitting splash to recover its stickiness.

Cartridges are an ongoing discussion among Cricut users for a variety of reasons.

A cartridge is what contains the images and fonts that you'll be cutting. Most cartridges hold 700 or 800 images. Lite cartridges contain about 50 images and have one or two creative features. Despite the limitations you can still be creative and produce hundreds of variations with this less expensive choice.

You usually receive at least one cartridge with the purchase of your machine. Sometimes this is preloaded into your machine as a digital cartridge. You may buy downloadable digital cartridges online for immediate use or you can buy the physical plastic cartridges that you slide into your machine.

When you purchase a cartridge; you can use that physical cartridge in your machine or you also have the option to link that cartridge to the Cricut Craft Room (CCR).

The Craft Room allows you to view your images on your computer screen which makes it easier to see and manipulate your projects.

By linking to CCR, you won't have to bother to switch out your cartridges physically. If you plan ever to sell the cartridges then do NOT link them. Once they are linked you are not legally allowed to sell them. This is understandable. Some people might link them to the Craft Room so they have access to the images and then sell the physical cartridge.

To link your cartridges you'll need to do the following. Load the cartridge you want to add into your machine. Go online to the Craft Room. Under all cartridges select my cartridges. You will see a list of cartridges. Find the cartridge you want to add and click Link and follow the prompts.

Another advantage to adding your cartridges to the Craft Room is that you'll be able to pull images from several cartridges to use at one time. When you're using the physical cartridge you can only use images from one cartridge at a time.

If you buy a used cartridge you need to ask if it's linked. If it is, you will still be able to use the physical cartridge in your machine but you will not be able to link it to the Craft Room. A cartridge can only be linked once. It is possible to use the cartridge in the Craft Room still but you can't link it. You'll have to have the physical cartridge in your machine to cut the images.

It is now possible to purchase cartridges online and download them to your account. This means you don't have to wait for a physical cartridge to arrive in the mail. You have immediate access to the images. These are the digital cartridges that I referred to earlier.

Many people complain that the cartridges are too expensive. Instead of spending $80 on a cartridge with hundreds of images many people would prefer to be able to buy an image they really want for a dollar or two, that's where single images or sets come in to play.

You can buy single digital images or smaller sets for a fraction of the cost of a full cartridge. You can even rent cartridge bundles for 30 days on a monthly subscription on the Cricut home page under the shopping section.

Make sure you take advantage of the free cartridges offered in the Craft Room. The only thing to remember is to finish your projects. Once the cartridge is no longer free, you will not be able to cut your image.

You can save money on cartridges watching for sales and special promotions.

It is possible to share physical cartridges with friends. This is good if they want a few images for a special project but don't plan to use the cartridge enough to justify buying it.

Digital Handbooks for Easy Reference

Did you know you can download the digital handbook of any cartridge and save it as a PDF file on your computer? Just go to Cricut.com click on shop, images, and cartridges. Select any cartridge click on it scrolling down the page till you see the link for the digital handbook, open it and save it to your hard drive for easy reference.

Sharing Cut Files

A cut file is basically a project that someone has already created and laid out on their Cricut. They saved the file and shared it on their blog or in the Craft Room. What this does is it saves you from recreating the wheel so to speak.

If you see a project you like you can save the file onto your computer. Then go to the Craft Room and import that file. You can then make the same cuts without having to figure out how to lay everything out. The images are already sized and laid out for you.

The advantage of this is you can save yourself a lot of time by using layouts that others have already created.

But here's the tricky part, you must already own the cartridges the images are from. You can't make the cuts if you don't own the cartridges the images originated from.

You can also save your own projects and share them in the Craft Room for others to use.

When you see a cute project on Pinterest or on a craft blog, you might want to ask if the cut file is available and if so, what cartridges it uses.

Organization

If you're like most crafters, including me, you'll eventually become overrun with craft "stuff." You'll have paper stacks, vinyl rolls and other material that you're planning to use someday spread all over your craft area.

Your cartridges may be lying around in a pile and you have to spend twenty minutes searching every time you need a specific overlay or booklet.

Eventually, this creates such a feeling of chaos and frustration that you dread going into your craft room or crafting area.

This can all be solved with some organization. You'll no longer feel depressed every time you look at your crafting space.

Craft stores will often have storage containers specially made for certain types of crafts. But you may want to start at your local chain stores. They often have craft and office supply departments where you can find storage units cheaply.

You can find containers where you can sort all your paper into small shelves based on color and type of paper. If you don't like the ones at the craft store then try an office supply store.

Another option is to watch for garage sales that say "craft items." Many people spend hundreds of dollars getting set up for a particular craft and then discover they don't have the time or inclination to spend much time actually doing the craft. This can be a bonanza for other crafters.

Photo boxes can be used to keep your booklets and overlays safe and organized.

Some crafters copy their overlays, laminate them and bind them together on rings where they can easily be added or removed.

There are special carrying cases, binders and totes designed just for cartridges.

Travel Tips

You may occasionally want to travel with your Cricut to crafting events. It's good to have a sturdy case or tote to carry your die cutting machine that prevents it from shaking around too much. You also want to have room to bring a few supplies.

Chapter - 12

How to Make Money with Cricut

Likewise, there are countless things you can make, which are marketable. Independent entrepreneurship is easier than it's ever been thanks to the internet and web platforms that make selling your products a breeze.

You've likely already heard of some of the platforms that make it easy to start a shop of your own.

With the Cricut, making countless items of every type and theme, for any and all occasions, is the name of the game. Doing these projects can be a huge source of joy for the avid crafter, but if you're spending the money on the materials for your projects, it might make sense for you to start generating a return on those, depending on how much you're doing and spending.

We'll cover some of the basics of what it means to go into business for yourself when you're the sole manufacturer of the goods in your store. Without having to provide a brick and mortar space for your shop, overhead can be so much lower that starting a shop or store is viable for people who might not have a lump sum of startup capital ready to hand.

How Do You Know When It's Time to Start a Shop?

If crafting is your passion, if you prefer to spend your time making items with your Cricut than you would going out or any other activity in your downtime, it could be time.

Should I Quit My Day Job and Go All In?

The thing about selling the products you create is that, since there's no brick and mortar location to manage, no store hours to keep to, you can manage your sales and your projects in the spare time that you have. It is best to start your store while you have a stable source of income. This way, as your store grows, you can scale back where it's necessary to do so in your usual work schedule, to allow for more time to spend on your shop.

How Can I Make Sure People Will Buy My Products?

There is a wealth of ways to market a business in today's digital age. Between social media presence, search engine optimization and more, you can put your name everywhere it needs to be to generate interest. However, you might find that when you're starting out, it will be easiest to pick items that are not custom. Make a couple of each type of item, take stunning product photos, upload them to your store, and then sell those as off-the-rack items.

As you start to generate more business, you may find that taking on the occasional custom order or commissioned item will benefit you. By and large, you will find that custom orders will take you more time and cost more to produce, for less of a return. Be watchful of this, and if you find that making 100 of a general design and selling all of those is the best use of your time and resources, stick with that! There's absolutely nothing wrong with going that route.

Do I Need to Make Enough of Each Item in My Shop to Keep and Inventory?

The short answer to this is no. You don't have to make any more of any items than are being ordered at any given time. With the way Etsy works for sellers, you can determine how much time you have before shipping out an order, so you can make the items as they're ordered, so you can be certain you're never wasting product or letting it sit in your craft room for too long.

The only time it would be best to make any sort of inventory would be if you intend to rent a space or booth at a tradeshow or convention. Having a presence at craft fairs, conventions, tradeshows, etc., can generate impulse buys from passing patrons that could be great for your business.

If at all possible, it's best to wait to go to such an event until you're able to narrow down your best sellers. Once you have a smattering of items you can make that are your hottest items, you can make several of each of those, and keep them at your booth or table, ready for immediate purchase!

Do I Need to Create a Shop in Order to Make Money with Cricut?

To be candid, no, you don't need to create a shop if you don't want to. If there is someone else who runs a craft shop, you might ask them to list your items for you in exchange for a share of the profits.

You could create a partnership with a local school, community center, farmer's market, or other establishment to sell your items for you to their patrons.

Making an online store for your Cricut items might be the most direct, hands-on way to generate a stream of income from the items that you make. This does not mean, however, that it's the only way or that it's the best way for you to go about it. Test the waters, see what's available, and pick a path that is most workable for you and the business you're working to create.

How Should I Price My Items?

This, like everything else, is entirely up to you. One method of pricing is to decide on a rate you would like to be paid per hour spent on a project, multiply that rate by how many hours you spent on that project, and add it together with the costs of all the materials you used to make your project.

For instance, I would never take a full-time job that paid me fewer than $15 per hour. We'll use this as our artisan rate to start. You can always adjust your prices as you get better with your craft, as you generate more of a following, and as you get faster at completing each of the projects you sell! So with this $15 hourly rate, we'll put together a little project. Let's say I'm taking a sheet of printable vinyl and printing an image that I own onto it. From there, I'm layering that vinyl onto a cardboard backing. Once that's done, I'm going to run it through my Cricut and make a jigsaw puzzle out of it.

Once I've made my jigsaw puzzle, I'm going to use more cardboard to make a box, which I will then decoupage. The box will be filled with the puzzle pieces, wrapped with a satin ribbon, and sold in my online store. Let's run the tally!

Cricut Printable Vinyl - $9

Cardboard Sheets - $6

Decoupage Glue - $2

Satin Ribbon - $1

1 Hour of Labor - $15.00

Artisan jigsaw puzzle - $33.00

Do not sell yourself short on your labor costs, and do not charge less than you spend on your materials, ever! That's no way to run a business, and it's no way to live. Value your time properly and charge every penny that you're worth. With how beautiful your products are, you will find people will pay your rates, and you will get rave reviews every time!

This question is a little bit loaded and, what it boils down to is which platform is the most convenient, workable, and reliable for you. The business you want to create is going to take up a lot of your time and attention, so it's imperative that you're using a platform that fits all your needs, meets all your expectations, and solves more problems for you than it causes.

We can tend to be forgiving of quirks in new systems when we're learning them. However, take a little extra time to read the experiences and reviews of people who have used that platform for an extended period of time. This will give you a look into what your future could be like with that platform, and it's the only gauge you have to go by when it comes to how that platform will serve you.

You will want to spend a little extra time looking into which platforms are available, what costs are involved (if any), how they treat their sellers, what percentages of your sales are taken, and what the sellers on those platforms think of them.

Here are some of the top platforms you'll want to check into!

- Etsy

- Amazon Handmade

- Facebook Marketplace

- Folksy

- Artfire

- Craftsy

- eBay

- Craigslist

You will mostly find that there are not any items you can make with your Cricut, which will not appeal to someone who would like to buy one. If you sell even one of each item you ever make, you're still coming out way ahead of the game, right? A lot of the items I'm about to list out for you are ones that can be purchased at a low rate from retailers, then customized using your design expertise, Cricut magic, and beautiful vinyl appliques that have sayings, monograms, or appealing designs on them. The choice is yours!

3D Puzzles

3D puzzles are made up of flat pieces that fit together to make a 3D object! Creating patterns for these that can be sold and assembled by your customers is a great way to capture the creatives in your target market!

3D Wall Art

Art that pops off the wall to greet you as you enter a room is a great way to create a dynamic décor that keeps people talking. Marketing art that jumps out at your target market is a great way to make an impression with people who are looking to you to provide a unique focal point for their interior design.

Aprons

Cooking enthusiasts love to have an apron that speaks to who they are as a chef or a baker. Blank canvas aprons are very affordable and, with iron-on vinyl that's available on the market today, from printable vinyl, to glittery iron-on, there is no design you can't create to capture those creative cooks!

Banners

Creating banners for booths, tables, small businesses, product displays, and parties is a great way to break into the custom products market; if that is something you're planning on doing. If you would like to create banners, but aren't looking for the custom angle, you can create banners with basic exclamations like "Sale!" "Happy birthday!" or "Surprise!" These are sure to be a seller for those in the market for party supplies.

Beanies

During the winter months, few things can bring the same warmth and comfort as a knit cap. With adorable designs ironed or emblazoned on them, people can bundle up without obscuring their quirks and personalities from the world! Beanies can be purchased in bulk or on a retail basis, at a fairly reasonable cost, making them a great candidate for your merchandise.

Beer Steins

Occasionally in stores like Target or Dollar Tree, you will find very large, blank beer glasses or steins that are available for sale at a very low price. Adding a decal onto the side of one of these immediately turns it into "Witch's Brew," or a mug with a great design on the side! Get creative with projects like these and you'll find that people will flock to your store for them. They make such great gifts!

Conclusion

I think every enthusiastic crafter should invest in at least one of the Cricut products if you have to add up all the time spent on perfecting lettering and cutting out intricate designs, patterns, and slicing fondant with those pesky blades by hand. While there's nothing that beats homemade products, cards, or personalized coasters, you can still personalize the same things with any of the Cricut machines and have the change to give them a professional and clean finish.

I have done hundreds of projects with my Cricut, and I am still learning every single day. It is like a computer; you will never learn every little trick in one goes. You will have to practice, follow the guide I have given, and add or scratch ideas out until you have your own. Tomorrow I might learn something new, and I will kick myself for not adding that to this guide. Nevertheless, know that I had taught you every trick I know and shared every failure I had encountered in hopes that you can avoid it all and just start crafting like we all so desperately had wanted to do when we first got our Cricuts.

Never stop doing research. Never stop trying new things. Never, ever stop being creative. The Cricut does not make you any less creative; it just makes the process easier and efforts on more important things or personalizing the projects after making the cuts. It takes the tedious work out of your hands and makes everything fun, easy, and fast.

Cricut machines are awesome gadgets to own because they do not only boost creativity and productivity, they can also be used to create crafts for business. With Design Space, crafters can create almost anything, and even customize their products to bear their imprints.

All over the world, people use these machines to make gift items, t-shirts, interior décor, and many other crafts, to beautify their homes, share with friends and family during holidays, and even sell, etc.

There two types of Cricut machines; the Cricut Explore and the Cricut Maker. Both machines are highly efficient in their rights, and experts in the crafting world make use of them to create a plethora of items, either as a hobby or for business. Both machines are similar in many ways i.e. the Cricut Maker and the Explore Air 2, but the Cricut Maker is somewhat of a more advanced machine because it comes with some advanced features, as compared to the Explore Air 2.

One distinct feature about the Maker that sets it apart from the Explore Air is the fact that it can cut thicker materials. With the Maker, the possibilities are limitless and crafters can embark on projects that were never possible with Cricut machines before the release of the Make.

Another feature that puts the Cricut Maker machine ahead of the Explore Air 2 is the 'Adaptive Tool System'. With this tool, the Cricut Maker has been empowered in such a way that it will remain relevant for many years to come because it will be compatible to new blades and other accessories that Cricut will release in the foreseeable future.

Manufactured by Amazon.ca
Bolton, ON